ORIGINS OF THE MONOLOGUE:
THE HIDDEN GOD

The Resurrection of Lazarus, by Gustave Doré

W. DAVID SHAW

Origins of the Monologue:
The Hidden God

UNIVERSITY OF TORONTO PRESS
Toronto Buffalo London

PN
1530
.S45
1999

#4166/922

© University of Toronto Press Incorporated 1999
Toronto Buffalo London
Printed in Canada

ISBN 0-8020-4718-1

Printed on acid-free paper

Canadian Cataloguing in Publication Data

Shaw, W. David (William David)
    Origins of the monologue : the hidden God

    Includes bibliographical references and index.
    ISBN 0-8020-4718-1

    1. Monologue.   2. Dramatic monologues – History and criticism.
    3. English poetry – 19th century – History and criticism.   4. Influence
    (Literary, artistic, etc.).   I. Title.

    PN1530.S52 1999   821'.02   C99-931429-7

University of Toronto Press acknowledges the financial assistance to its
publishing program of the Canada Council for the Arts and the Ontario Arts
Council.

This book has been published with the help of a grant from the Humanities
and Social Sciences Federation of Canada, using funds provided by the
Social Sciences and Humanities Research Council of Canada.

University of Toronto Press acknowledges the financial support for its
publishing activities of the Government of Canada through the Book
Publishing Industry Development Program (BPIDP).

Canada

For my Family and Friends

Contents

Acknowledgments

Northrop Frye once said that 'the human word is neither immortal nor invulnerable, but it is the light which orders our chaos and the power by which we live.' I am grateful for my long association with Victoria College, University of Toronto, Frye's own intellectual home, where I have benefited from the learning of scholars, poets, and literary critics who share Frye's love and cultivation of words. However unfashionable it may now seem, I know I am the product of a particular time and place, bound by affection to a college that has always valued living philology and a fond but exact scrutiny of words.

Origins of the Monologue has been published with the help of a grant from the Canadian Federation for the Humanities, using funds provided by the Social Sciences and Humanities Research Council of Canada. Research was begun with the aid of a Killam Senior Research Fellowship and completed with the help of a three-year Standard Research Grant from the Council.

I am grateful to the Houghton Library of Harvard University for permission to quote manuscripts by Robert Lowell, Randall Jarrell, and T.S. Eliot; and to Mrs Valerie Eliot for allowing me to quote her husband's Harvard lecture notes. I am also indebted to Chris Jennings for bibliographical help and to the Manuscripts Division, Department of Rare Books and Special Collections of the Princeton University Library for permission to quote from letters of D.G. Rossetti and Jane and William Morris. Short excerpts have been taken from the following correspondence: a letter of D.G. Rossetti to Robert Browning in the J.C. Troxwell Collection, MS CO1890, box 8, folder 4; a letter of Jane Morris to Ford Madox Ford, box 27, folder 49; a letter of Jane Morris to D.G. Rossetti, box 27, folder 52; and a letter of William Morris to William Bell, MS xii Acknowledgments

CO1896, box 27, folder 66. Lines from '1915. A Pre-Raphaelite Ending' are reprinted with the permission of Scribner, a division of Simon and Schuster Inc., from *Untitled Subjects* by Richard Howard. Copyright 1969. Lines from Robert Lowell's *The Mills of the Kavanaughs* are reprinted with the permission of Harcourt Brace and Co. For help in defraying permission costs I am grateful to Victoria College, University of Toronto.

I have benefited from the intelligent care of the copyeditor, Dr Judith Williams, and from the sharp accuracy of judgment of three anonymous readers of the manuscript and of four readers consulted by learned journals. I owe thanks as well to the courteous inquiries of audiences who heard parts of chapters 5 and 7 as public lectures. Chapters 3 and 6 contain extensively revised portions of two essays: 'Lyric Displacement in the Victorian Monologue: Naturalizing the Vocative,' *Nineteenth-Century Literature* 52 (December 1997), 302–25, and 'Masks of the Unconscious: Bad Faith and Casuistry in the Dramatic Monologue,' *ELH* 66 (Spring 1999), 439–60. For permission to use and revise this material I am grateful to the editors of the learned journals.

While writing the book I have drawn on the sustenance and love of my wife, Carol. My best model of the monologue's Socratic search for meaning and its contest of opposites is my life with Carol – a marriage of true minds that is also a trust in contraries. Equally bracing is the Socratic give and take of the many conversations I have had on literature and ideas with my friends Andrew Brack, Eleanor Cook, Donald Blais, Elias Polizoes, and Paulo Horta, and with my four daughters and my son.

Just as an older generation once greeted me, so now I welcome the young scholars pressing past me through the door of a profession that will soon close behind me but which I should gladly enter again if I had another life to live. I used to think my only alms for oblivion were the knowledge I had gathered over a lifetime of teaching. Now I think all that slows life's leakage is the truth of the affections and the pursuit of some goal with courage and endurance.

My greatest debt is to my family, friends, and academic colleagues, especially to my brother Don, a professor of physics whose dedication to his profession has been as exemplary as his quiet courage and self-command. From this 'little platoon' has grown my love of a discipline, a college, and even my delayed affection for 'the goodly family of the Sciences, sisterly all,' as J.H. Newman says, 'and sisterly in their mutual dispositions.'

ORIGINS OF THE MONOLOGUE

Tennyson is not only a minor Virgil, he is also with Virgil as Dante saw him, a Virgil among the Shades, the saddest of all English poets, among the Great in Limbo, the most instinctive rebel against the society in which he was the most perfect conformist.

T.S. Eliot, 'In Memoriam'

So just what Dante scorns as unworthy alike of heaven and hell, Botticelli accepts, that middle world in which men take no side in great conflicts, and decide no great causes, and make great refusals. He thus sets for himself the limits within which art, undisturbed by any moral ambition, does its most sincere and surest work. His interest is neither in the untempered goodness of Angelico's saints, nor the untempered evil of Orcagna's *Inferno*; but with men and women, in their mixed and uncertain condition, always attractive, clothed sometimes by passion with a character of loveliness and energy, but saddened perpetually by the shadow upon them of the great things from which they shrink.

Walter Pater, *The Renaissance: Studies in Art and Poetry*

> And Bright and Dark have sworn that I, the child
> Of thee, the great Earth-Mother, thee, the Power
> That lifts her buried life from gloom to bloom,
> Should be for ever and for evermore
> The bride of darkness.

Tennyson, 'Demeter and Persephone'

In every the Wisest Soul lies a whole world of internal Madness, an authentic Demon-Empire; out of which, indeed, his world of Wisdom has been creatively built together, and now rests there, as on its dark foundations does a habitable flowery Earth-rind.

Thomas Carlyle, *Sartor Resartus*

For as I passed along, and observed the objects of your worship, I found also an altar with this inscription, 'To an unknown god.' What therefore you worship as unknown, this I proclaim to you.

Acts of the Apostles, 17:23

For Grote, Socrates' goal was 'to eliminate affirmative, authoritative exposition, which proceeds upon the assumption that truth is already known – and to consider philosophy as a search for unknown truth, carried on by several interlocutors all of them ignorant.'

Eduard Zeller, *Socrates and the Socratic Schools*

A Truth in art is that whose contradictory is also true ... The truths of meta-physics are the truths of masks.

Oscar Wilde, 'The Truth of Masks'

Contentious and self-justifying, Browning's people direct their will at a hidden God. The poet is their advocate, caught in the same condition, and he refuses to give the game away.

Geoffrey Hartman, *Beyond Formalism*

Introduction: The Hidden God

As the sprightly dance music of the masked balls yields to a sterner music in Browning's monologue 'A Toccata of Galuppi's,' a sinister figure steps forth to claim the women as his brides of darkness: 'Death stepped tacitly and took them where they never see the sun' (30). Behind the ubiquitous Death of Browning's monologue it is hard not to discern in Victorian culture at large a masked god more menacing than any reveller at a Venetian carnival. I am referring to the God of nineteenth-century agnostic theology, the Kantian God of Sir William Hamilton, H.L. Mansel, and T.H. Huxley, who hides behind such logically contra-dictory attributes as the Absolute, the Infinite, and a First Cause. The masks of such a God tend to be as protean and unstable as the world disclosed by the new geologies of Charles Lyell and Robert Chambers. Operating as a capricious Prospero, their Heraclitean God turns hills into shadows and 'solid lands' into melting mist (*In Memoriam*, 123.7) until, like an 'insubstantial pageant faded,' even 'the great globe itself' assumes the shape of cloud and disappears (*The Tempest*, 4.1.153, 155). I show how the author of dramatic monologues is created in the image of this protean god, a magician of negative capability described by one Victorian critic, W.J. Fox, as 'a transmigrating Vishnu.'[1] My book is the first to trace the rise of the monologue to the dangerous legacy of agnos-tic theology and the first to link the enigmatic poet behind the masks to nineteenth-century theories of Socrates' *agnostos theos* or unknown God.

All scholars and critics of Victorian monologues have been refreshed by the unjaded thinking of Robert Langbaum, enhanced by the culti-vated taste of Herbert Tucker and Donald Hair, and graced by the luminous learning of Isobel Armstrong and Eric Griffiths. But no scholar has shown how the dramatic monologue, the most spectral genre of the post-Romantic period, is also the most Socratic and agnostic. Ranging from monologues by Chaucer, Donne, and Rochester to masterpieces of the genre by Robert Lowell and Randall Jarrell, this book attributes the ascendancy of the monologue to three neglected causes: to the agnostic thought of Kant, Sir William Hamilton, and H.L. Mansel; to new theories of the unconscious associated with John Keble, Thomas Carlyle, and E.S. Dallas; and to nineteenth-century adaptations of three legacies: the dialogues of Socrates, the conversation poems of Coleridge, and the Keatsian poet's licentious practice of endlessly proliferating his identities through self-created masks. T.S. Eliot claims that Tennyson was 'the most instinctive rebel against the society in which he was the most perfect conformist.'[2] This study traces the origins of the monologue to a subversive tradition within a literature and culture that is too often assumed to endorse mainly conservative values in ethics, politics, and religion. Tennyson, Browning, and Morris are master subverters of the social discourse they borrow: as in Socrates' dialogues, there are few customs – moral, political, or religious – that their best monologues do not interrogate, turn inside out, or blaspheme.

The dramatic monologue fragments rather than consolidates cultural authority: it speaks, not through a spokesman for the status quo, but through a Socratic interrogator of it. Instead of affirming his power as head of state, Tennyson's Ulysses defiantly relinquishes it. We hear the delinquent Fra Lippo, not his censorious religious superior, the Prior. Even when Browning's Bishop Blougram appears to be conducting a conventional apology, he subverts as well as consolidates the authority of the church by arguing as a sceptical empiricist on his opponent's own secular ground.

Challenging the monologue's typical subversion of cultural authority are its many silent auditors. The most obtrusive auditors – Andrea's placidly inert wife, the charity worker who chains the mad Rizpah to her bed, the God who resists Demeter's blackmail by refusing to let Persephone dwell the whole bright year with her mother – are usually the most restrictive. As ghosts of a repressive cultural authority, they have to be exorcised by the apostrophic swerves of voice that allow a speaker to turn aside from coercive auditors to auditors more amenable to prayer or persuasion. Andrea defies containment by appealing from Lucrezia to King Francis and God; Rizpah resists restraint by replacing the prison attendant with the ghost of her dead son; even Tennyson's Demeter strives to supplant God, the brother of Pluto's darkness, with a 'Fate beyond the Fates' who will grant her subversive desire to abolish both the underworld – the land of soul – and winter.

In sponsoring a flight from literary texts, cultural studies are the last refuge of scholars who have lost their confidence in literary values. Cultural histories tend to suppress critical intelligence: their ghostly abstractions are no substitute for the verbal surprises and games with words that critics find delightful. I realize, however, that in many quarters aesthetic criticism is now out of fashion. In what follows I offer no analysis of literary texts that is not required by a study of the monologue's origins in nineteenth-century culture. Though I touch on feminist theories of the genre in the final chapter, a treatment of political and economic reasons for the monologue's ascendancy would have required a book-length essay of the kind already written by Norman Feltes or Lee Erickson: it lies outside the mandate of the present study.

The first two chapters show how dramatic monologues disturb and transform two important genres: the Victorian stage play and the Socratic dialogue. The following pair of chapters examines the legacies of two Romantic poets. I show how the monologue's use of silent auditors naturalizes Coleridge's lyric apostrophes to clouds, groves, and oceans in his odes and conversation poems. And I argue that through projection and empathy the monologue simultaneously controls and gives free rein to the licentious art of the Keatsian artist of negative capability, who operates as a nonmoral chameleon or poetic harlequin. The two concluding chapters examine the disturbing impact of new theories of knowledge. I show how Mansel's agnosticism and the nominalist thought of Walter Pater stand behind the spectral art of William Morris's early monologues. And I demonstrate how the genre's increasing use of speakers who suffer from unconscious deception and casuistry coincides with new theories of unconscious motivation pioneered by Thomas Carlyle, John Keble, and E.S. Dallas.

Arguing that monologues dramatize intimacies of consciousness and two-way meanings that are impossible to develop in a Victorian stage play, I explain in the first chapter why Tennyson and Browning are only moderately successful playwrights yet brilliant writers of dramatic monologues. By creating dramas for both the eye and ear, the 'printed voice' of the dramatic monologue cultivates a taste for two-way meaning that can best be satisfied in a private theatre of the mind. To see life whole is to see it unsteadily, and to see it steadily is to see it too myopically. To oppose the fractional, exclusive quality of what we normally see and hear, dramatic monologues promote the two-way syntax, hesitancies, and double meanings that only silent readings can begin to register.

The second chapter examines the impact of a classical genre, the Socratic dialogue, which becomes increasingly influential after Benjamin

Jowett's revival of Platonic studies at Oxford during the 1850s. As Schleiermacher points out in a book on Plato's dialogues that Browning owned, Socrates' relation to Plato may vary widely. When Browning models his monologues on the Socrates of the *Symposium*, who expounds Diotima's theory of eros out of a profound logic and a powerful heart, he uses the oracular David as his mouthpiece, conferring an authority on his biblical hero that makes his theology of love both magisterial and prophetic. Conversely, like Plato's Euthyphro, who beats a hasty retreat when pressed to define piety, the Prior in 'Fra Lippo Lippi,' at a loss to define 'soul,' becomes a target of Browning's amused Socratic irony. Just as unanswered questions about friendship in *Lysis* or about courage in *Laches* reflect the self-doubts and aporias of Plato as well as Socrates, so Browning seems as bewildered as Gigadibs by a Bishop who says 'true things' but calls 'them by wrong names' ('Bishop Blougram's Apology,' 996). Like Plato, who refuses to expound his deepest thoughts in writing because he feels they will be valueless out of context, Browning pays tribute in 'By the Fire-side' and 'One Word More' to a secret wisdom too personal to qualify as communicable information but too important to dismiss as mere wayward impulse or whim.

Chapter 3 shows how the dramatic monologue's convention of addressing a silent human auditor disturbs and transforms Coleridge's practice of addressing flowers, clouds, and nightingales in his odes and conversation poems. The sudden decline of John Keble's illuminated Book of Hours, his cycle of devotional poems *The Christian Year*, into the fragmentary book of moments recorded in Tennyson's *In Memoriam* creates a crisis of religious faith. Victorian monologues respond to this crisis by humanizing Romantic poetry's obsolete convention of lyrically apostrophizing natural objects. Instead of talking to the dawn, Tennyson's Tithonus addresses a beautiful human auditor, the goddess Aurora. By humanizing the objects addressed, Victorian monologues are better equipped than lyric poems to oppose the dogmas of a secular and scientific age in which an antiquated belief in oracles, prophecies, and knowledge as divination is in rapid and widespread retreat.

Turning from Coleridge to a younger Romantic poet, chapter 4 explores Keats's dangerous legacy of negative capability. W.J. Fox develops and refines Keats's idea of dramatic impersonation when he demonstrates how the young Tennyson, as a kind of Hindu god or 'transmigrating Vishnu,' submits to the indignity of even the lowliest incarnations. Though Keats's artist of negative capability is the quintessential role-player, Fox recognizes that he may degenerate into a moral cipher who gains the whole world yet loses his own soul. It is precisely the incapacity of the Keatsian role-player to bring his scruples of reserve to any decisive conclusion that allows the reader to participate in the fantasies of the many eccentric misfits and 'beautiful losers' in post-Romantic monologues. Because the eminent Victorians are notoriously self-divided, often at war with themselves, they seem to feel a temperamental affinity for the dramatic monologue, a genre that keeps its speakers in touch with their buried lives and that often allows us to trespass on their most intimate reveries and free vagrancies of mind.

Examining the first of two epistemological models, the fifth chapter explores the impact of Victorian agnostic thought on the Arthurian monologues of William Morris. Both Walter Pater and Morris offer reductive definitions of such theological and metaphysical concepts as 'sacredness' and 'being.' In *Plato and Platonism* Pater strips the Greek philosopher of any metaphysical illusions by dismantling Plato's doctrine of being, while retaining in Plato's pleasing aesthetic masks a poetry of 'pure surface over void.' A striking example of this same creative nominalism can be found in the purist art of Morris's monologues in *The Defence of Guenevere, and Other Poems*. Morris's Arthurian monologues have their priest, rite, church, and congregation, but no god. Their art is endotelic, an art of surface masks, which preserves the sacred space of theology as a place apart from the secular world, without any of theology's controversial doctrines or creeds.

The sixth chapter shows how nineteenth-century theories of unconscious knowledge help explain the presence in many monologues of unconscious deception or bad faith. When the studied rhetoric of Donne's metaphysical Don Juan in 'The Ecstasy' is replaced by the unselfconscious or inadvertent disclosures of Browning's seducer *manqué* in 'Two in the Campagna,' unconscious motivations can be used to distinguish the bad faith and involuntary deceptions of Browning's speakers from the carefully calculated rhetoric of their seventeenth-century predecessors.

A synchronic study of the monologue's two-way meanings, silent auditors, and bad faith or casuistry is always useful. But since the differences between the bad faith of Chaucer's Pardoner and the bad faith of Browning's Andrea del Sarto are more instructive than the similarities, a diachronic study of the genre's evolving properties along an axis of change is also necessary. Just as the parallax of space is used to chart the precise location of a star, so the parallax of time can be used to find the exact position of the post-Romantic monologue on a diachronic scale of conscious and unconscious motivations.

Though a hypocrite like Browning's Mr Sludge pretends to be better than he is, and an ironist like Fra Lippo Lippi pretends to be worse, both assume that, because the masked self is known to the speaker who dons the mask, the mask's removal will reveal a fully achieved identity. In marked contrasts are the masks of bad faith or unconscious lying assumed by speakers like St Simeon Stylites and Andrea del Sarto, whose masks hide dark truths and hidden powers of which the speakers themselves are never fully conscious. Only in the course of an unconscious liar's monologue may a repressed self begin to swim into focus for the speaker in a process understood and explored by such Victorian theorists of the unconscious as Carlyle, Keble, Ruskin, and E.S. Dallas. In dramatizing the fragility of both culture and the ego, the widespread nineteenth-century use of masks confirms Carlyle's sense that below our precariously constructed identities 'lies a whole world of internal Madness.' Like a 'habitable flowery Earth-rind,' each mask is poised on the edge of a boiling nether deep, 'an authentic Demon-Empire.'[3]

The Great in Limbo: Rebel Ghosts and the Rise of the Monologue

When Tennyson affirms that 'there lives more faith in honest doubt' than 'half the creeds' (*In Memoriam*, 96.11–12), he is evoking the ghost of Socrates, the most subversive and Utopian of Greek philosophers, the agnostic theist whose 'dreams' he and Hallam used to 'thread' together in *In Memoriam* (89.36). He is simultaneously defending the honour of all sceptics and agnostics, especially the Victorian counterparts of those neutral angels whom Dante meets in the vestibule to hell. Memorably evoked by T.S. Eliot as the inhabitant of a neighbouring region of hell, as 'a Virgil among the Shades, the saddest of all English poets, among the Great in Limbo,'[4] Tennyson is also – and more importantly – identifying in the 'honest doubt' of these rebel ghosts (Socratic and Dantean) and in their release from dogma an important source of the most innovative poetic genre of the nineteenth century.

   The dramatic monologue stands aside from the zeal of commitment. It flourishes in an atmosphere of learned ignorance that is best cultivated in the detached 'middle world' described by Walter Pater: a neutral region where 'men take no sides in great conflicts, and decide no great causes, and make great refusals.'[5] To defend the quiet privilege of this middle world is to uphold the value of sceptical reserve. It is to claim for the monologue's release from certitude and for its cultivation of two-way meanings the same respect that most people of practical capacity confer on unexamined precepts and partisan ideology.

In exploring the subversive demons that in a ghostly rebel like Tennyson's Demeter are inseparable from the spirit of belief in her attack on Zeus, this book also traces the monologue's rise to a venerable Socratic tradition of learned ignorance and self-doubt. After examining the decision of Tennyson and Arnold *not* to decide between such valuable but contradictory alternatives as heroism and repose, faith and self-reliance, in 'Ulysses' and 'Dover Beach,' I explore the Socratic quest of Browning and Tennyson for an unknown God, 'the Nameless of the hundred names' ('The Ancient Sage,' 49, 238–9). I show how Victorian monologues secularize Romantic apostrophes to God by introducing vocatives of direct address to silent human auditors. And I demonstrate how this effort to preserve religious values in a non-theistic age reinforces attempts by Keats, W.J. Fox, and his successors to celebrate in the democracy of a masked God or 'transmigrating Vishnu' the power and danger of negative capability. Reassessing the influence of H.L. Mansel's masked God, I show how the monologue's inversions and reversals of folly are a source of self-knowledge. The search for lost power and hidden gods restores the dignity of those neutral angels in Dante who make the great refusal by scrupulously withholding their assent. It also reaffirms the teaching of Socrates and Nicholas of Cusa that learned ignorance is the greatest wisdom.

The monologue's gravest danger is its tendency to substitute self-deception and play-acting for acts of self-discovery. Speakers like the Duke of Ferrara and Andrea del Sarto lack character. Since all their energy is consumed in role-playing, they abandon themselves to any form of bad faith or dishonesty that allows them to seem real to themselves. But monologues also supply a safeguard against this danger. By providing modern ethics with the missing middle term between what *is* and what *ought* to be, speakers as different as Tennyson's Demeter and Browning's Caliban consider what *might* be the case. As oracles in whom powerful insights take place, Demeter and Caliban perceive injustice in terms of concrete alternatives. They have a dialectical vision that allows them to see more than the gods Setebos and Zeus can see. Instead of hiding the truth, a mask may also reveal it. Precisely because Tennyson seems preoccupied with something else in his classical monologue 'Demeter and Persephone,' the daughter's descent to hell as a bride of darkness can deeply and frighteningly implicate him in the thought of his son's death, which 'tears' him 'to pieces,' so full of promise was the boy and so young. Paradoxically, by allowing us to trespass on a grievous reticence, the mask's apparent safety makes the poet vulnerable.

Brides of Darkness: The Monologue's Ghostly Origins

In raising the ghost of Pluto's bride of darkness in 'The Mills of the Kavanaughs' or the ghosts of such precursor poets as Hopkins and Tennyson in 'Mother Marie Therese,' Robert Lowell, like every writer of dramatic monologues, perfects Browning's art of functioning as the medium at a historical seance. Browning concedes that 'to raise a ghost' by 'commission[ing] forth' half the poet's soul may seem at first satanic. We think of his zombie-like Lazarus, well suited after his resuscitation (perhaps by mesmerism) for a Victorian Chamber of Horrors. Resuscitating a corpse, however, need not be a form of Faust's black magic. It may be a benign act, a miracle of resurrection.

> '... then write my name with Faust's!'
> Oh, Faust, why Faust? Was not Elisha once? –
> Who bade them lay his staff on a corpse-face.
> *The Ring and the Book,*   1.52–4

Adam Roberts convincingly identifies Browning's magician with the alchemist Cornelius Agrippa, whose *De incertitudine* and *De scientiis* the poet owned and annotated.[6] As a black magician, the alchemist is a Victorian Faust. Indeed, as Roberts notes, a mid-Victorian *Dictionary of Universal Biography* compares Agrippa to Faust, a sorcerer who consistently abuses his powers.

As a Victorian Prospero, however, Agrippa's alchemist has two commendable duties to perform. The alchemist may speak authoritatively through historical ghosts as God speaks through his prophets. And as an odd combination of the biblical Elisha and the Austrian physician Mesmer, the alchemist may resuscitate historical corpses. Both a conjurer and a healer, the benign magician has power to reverse Keats's haunting phrase about his living hand, now warm and capable, but soon to be touched by the coldness of death.[7]

Hillis Miller contends that the invocation of a personified subject is 'the inaugural trope of narration.'[8] It gives a voice and a face to what is otherwise silent and imageless, a phantom from the past. Far from giving off a whiff of the hoax or the charnel house, the communication of Lowell's nun with the ghost of the drowned Mother Therese or the communion of his New England Persephone with the ghost of her dead Pluto may be tongued with fire beyond the language of the living. In conducting a seance where readers may eavesdrop on the one-sided conversations of ghostly rebels like Bathsheba and Marie de Medici, or of poetic precursors like Hopkins and T.S. Eliot, Lowell even becomes the channel of communication between the living and the dead. The lines of his monologues are lines of a ghostly lineage: no one can come to the spirit world except through him.

Victorian mesmerists think that the divine spark may be a magnetic field or an electric current. But Browning knows that the only hypnosis or entrancement that matters is an imaginative art, not a science of inducing physical states. For Browning, Shelley is the Promethean Sun-treader whose legacy is the gift of fire. Victorian positivism is the new Prometheus, and its gift is the inductive method. Despite George Grote's attempt to remake Socrates in the image of Jeremy Bentham and James Mill, the so-called Socratic method is not a method at all. Whereas methods strive to put doubt at rest, Socratic questions are never a quest for certainty. And as an art of irony and metaphor, they differ from a science like engineering or a technique like computer programming in that they cannot be taught. There is no rule for writing good dramatic monologues or Socratic dialogues.

In nineteenth-century culture, fools and ironists are too often casualties of natural selection. But they enjoy a temporary revival in the monologue's promotion of the truth of opposites. In challenging the barbarism of the positivist, who can achieve only single understanding of an object, the ironist and fool show how knowledge of the self depends upon a reversal of follies and illusions. The ghost of the aporetic Socrates enjoys a vigorous posthumous life in the dramatic monologue, a genre that uses the shadowed wall in Plato's cave as a mirror in which images can be shown passing back and forth between opposite forms of understanding. The inversion of the ordinary is the art of both the ironist and the fool. Tennyson's Rizpah is a female Lear, and Browning's Fra Lippo a kind of holy clown. Rizpah convinces us of the essential sanity of her madness; Fra Lippo forces us to see through the Gnostic Prior's mindless advocacy of the spirit to an equally plausible praise of the body that is Gnosticism's reverse image. Whereas positivism always promotes a one-sided view of the world, the humanism promoted by the dramatic monologue also explores the mirror images of things. Caliban's inverted mudbound view is an underworld image of dark doubles and shadow selves. Only speculative thought can finish what the ironist or the fool initiates. But without the fool or the ironist the truth of opposites could never be affirmed.

One of the mask's abiding paradoxes is that the harder a monologue tries to penetrate the mystery of its hidden gods, the more it discovers that anything worth unmasking cannot be unmasked. Historians and critics of the monologue also confront the related paradox of having to honour and preserve the inversions and two-way meanings of a genre that their own necessarily stable discourse tries to banish. To be faithful to the Socratic spirit of the best dramatic monologues, they must acknowledge that any theory about the genre is only an unguarded partial truth. It is not enough for literary historians and critics to unmask the disguised ideology of the monologue in agnostic theology or a theory of the unconscious. They must also show how the monologue's deception, bad faith, and irony challenge a culture's idols. Ideally, the genre's inversion of favoured fictions and its reversal of light and shadow should renew self-knowledge and restore in its hidden gods and brides of darkness, in its Plutos and Persephones, the wisdom of a whole and examined life.

The Subversive Turn: Modern Criticism of the Monologue

A dramatic monologue has three defining features. As a species of talking verse, it is a poem of one-sided conversation in which a speaker, not to be confused with the poet, addresses a silent auditor. Secondly, as M.H. Abrams recognizes, a monologue's unconscious self-revelations are usually more important than the meanings its speaker is conscious of expressing. A third feature of the genre is the speaker's unpredictable apostrophes or swerves of voice. These swerves have the important function of allowing the speaker to address a double audience by deflecting attention from the ostensible auditor to a more important hidden one.

Without some theory of a monologue's defining features, it would be impossible to trace the genre's history. We should have difficulty studying its origins or understanding how it is disturbed or transformed by the shock of cultural change. Unfortunately, generic criticism is also a traditional enemy of literary texts. Ralph Rader,[9] for example, one of the monologue's most ingenious critics, tries to differentiate a dramatic monologue like 'My Last Duchess' from a dramatic lyric like 'Dover Beach,' a mask lyric like 'Ulysses,' and an expressive lyric like 'Tintern Abbey.' Though 'Dover Beach' and 'Tintern Abbey' impose justifiable boundaries on the genre, Rader's taxonomy of the intermediate territory is unproductive. A definition of the monologue that includes 'My Last

Duchess' but excludes such masterpieces as 'Andrea del Sarto' and 'Ulysses' tells us more about the rigidity of Rader's categories than about the immensely protean and impish genius of the genre he is trying to analyse. Since we cannot expect the monologue to lie down in the tidy bed that Procrustean critics have built for it, I prefer to work with more flexible categories. Attention to 'apostrophic swerves' and 'bad faith,' to 'double audiences' and 'hidden gods,' invites a reader to find the *least* distorting misfit between a theory of the monologue and Browning's idiosyncratic conduct of a given poem. At a certain stage it may even be useful to treat each monologue *sui generis*. Drawing attention to family resemblances between Donne's 'The Ecstasy' and Browning's 'Two in the Campagna,' for example, or between Tennyson's *Maud* and T.S. Eliot's 'The Love Song of J. Alfred Prufrock,' is a species of wit-criticism. In blunting the equally important differences between these monologues and monodramas, such criticism may ignore the qualities that make each poem unique.

Many influential modern critics have identified and analysed diverse features of the monologue. In his pioneer study of the genre, Robert Langbaum posits a disequilibrium between the sympathy a monologue elicits for its speaker and the moral judgment that it manages to hold in abeyance – or at least to neutralize as our least appropriate response. Eric Griffiths believes that a monologue explores the conflicts of a self-divided mind, and that these conflicts can be explored most subtly and inclusively in a silent reading of the poem. For Isobel Armstrong the monologue is a genre in which a female counter-tradition in Victorian poetics can successfully oppose the aggressive male projections of an impersonator like Browning, who tends to objectify women.

T.S. Eliot interprets the genre more rhetorically: in a monologue he hears neither the first voice of the lyric poet nor the third voice of the playwright, but the second or rhetorical voice of the poet speaking to an audience through a mask. Interpreting the genre more ironically, Adena Rosmarin maintains that in a dramatic monologue the speaker's meaning can always be distinguished from the poem's meaning. Alan Sinfield discerns a slightly different irony: the monologue, he claims, tilts seductively in the direction of lyric poetry, because it uses the first-person pronoun. This lyric tilt turns out to be a mere 'feint,' however, because unlike a lyric poem the monologue adopts a third-person or dramatic view of its world. Distinguishing between Romantic idealism and Victorian attempts to repair a fragmented culture, Loy Martin lends support to Browning's theory that dramatic monologues resuscitate historical corpses. The archives of history and legend are a valley of dry bones: the monologue's task is to revive these bones and restore to muted witnesses the gift of living speech.

Ekbert Faas traces the influence on Victorian monologues of early psychiatry and nineteenth-century psychological theories of poetry. His appendix of dramatic monologues written by minor Victorian poets may be usefully combined with Elisabeth A. Howe's chronological listing of monologues, which includes Polish and French as well as English examples. Given the innovations of Eugenio Montale and the resourceful experiments of Fernando Pessoa with masks and heteronyms, scholars may wish to debate Howe's claim that the modern monologue plays a dominant role only in English-speaking cultures.

In a recent article on Amy Levy, Cynthia Scheinberg revises Robert Langbaum's theory of poetic sympathy by observing that the auditor in a dramatic monologue is often 'unable to identify with the speaker, and so often misses the larger point that the speaker attempts to make.'[10] Her theoretical move is anticipated by John Maynard, whose article on 'Reading the Reader in Robert Browning's Dramatic Monologues' demonstrates the importance of a critic's own sensibilities in determining meaning.[11] Like Maynard, Dorothy Mermin believes that 'poems with auditors' reflect 'the ambivalence with which Tennyson, Browning, and Arnold regarded their prospective readers.'[12]

Whereas Maynard and Mermin are less interested in silent auditors than in the response of attentive readers, other Browning scholars have reversed their emphasis. In *Browning the Revisionary* John Woolford analyses the silent auditor's function in eliciting intelligent sympathy for the speaker. Both Browning and Tennyson are poets of deep silence and reserve: in many of their monologues the feeling of being alone is intensified by the presence of aggressively silent auditors. In her essay 'The Pragmatics of Silence' Jennifer Wagner-Lawlor shows how silence is 'not mere absence of speech, but is itself heavy with communicative value.'[13]

Like the short story or the novel, the dramatic monologue is a frisky and elusive genre: at different times it exhibits all the features I have touched on. Because unconscious motives are stronger than conscious ones, speakers in monologues also tend to exhibit bad faith or unconscious deception rather than outright lies that they are conscious of perpetrating. When we sense the presence of Eliot's poet addressing an audience through a mask, we can usually identify a norm that allows us to measure any deviations from that norm. Such is not the case, however, in other less magisterial, more searching monologues, where double irony replaces single irony, and where not even the poet himself may know the answers to the questions he has asked.

Having offered my own definition of the monologue at the beginning of this section, I must briefly explain what I mean by the monologue's third and least understood feature: its use of unpredictable apostrophes or swerves. Apostrophe or *aversio* is not merely a figure of address but a trope of deviation. Instead of addressing his immediate auditor, the envoy, Browning's Duke in 'My Last Duchess' turns aside to marvel at the portrait of his late wife. As Douglas Kneale has shown, it is difficult for discourse to assimilate apostrophe because, as a trope of deviation, it never renders 'voice as such': it renders instead a switch or loss of voice. In boldly apostrophizing a dead musician, a portrait of a murdered wife painted on a wall, or a tomb that resembles a baroque conceit in stone, dramatic monologues as diverse as 'A Toccata of Galuppi's,' 'My Last Duchess,' and 'The Bishop Orders His Tomb' turn dangerously aside from life itself. The genre assimilates what Kneale calls 'the passing of voice, its want or lack, even its sudden removal.'[14]

A proper study of apostrophe also invites us to distinguish the direct address of Dante's Ulysses to the pilgrim in *The Divine Comedy* from the genuine deviation or turning aside of the speaker's address to his mariners in Tennyson's monologue 'Ulysses.' As the speaker in the monologue moves freely from Dante to Shakespeare, he berates the Ithacans in words that Hamlet uses to denounce his own sluggish behaviour: 'What is a man,/ If his chief good and market of his time / Be but to sleep and feed?' (*Hamlet*, 4.4.33–5).

> I mete and dole
> Unequal laws unto a savage race,
>
> That hoard, and sleep, and feed, and know not me.
>
> 'Ulysses,' 3–5

Resolving a moment later to 'shine in use' instead of 'rust unburnished' (23), Ulysses deflects his voice into a second Shakespearean play by brilliantly reversing Othello's injunction: 'Keep up your bright swords, for the dew will rust them' (*Othello*, 1.2.59).

> How dull it is to pause, to make an end,
> To rust unburnished, not to shine in use!
>
> 'Ulysses,' 22–3

The resilient quality of a well-tempered blade returns at the end of the monologue in the shining metaphor of the mariners' 'One equal temper of heroic hearts' (68). The figurative turning away from weapons that are literally dewed with blood represents a final movement of voice: a translation or carrying over of address from exhortation to celebration and self-praise. Instead of justifying his decision to leave Ithaca or exhorting his comrades, Ulysses now glories in the mariners' whole physical endowment of heart, lungs, and muscle, keen as a well-tempered sword as they strain in unison to the 'delight of battle ... / Far on the ringing plains of windy Troy' (16–17).

Wavering between heroic adventure and elegiac repose, Tennyson's monologue uses apostrophe or the trope of deviation to fluctuate between different audiences and tones of voice. After deflecting attention from the savage Ithacans to the prudent Telemachus, Ulysses redirects his voice a second time by turning to his beloved comrades, his third and most important audience. His mind is flashing and scythelike, full of great swoops and curves dangerous to lesser minds standing in its way, but with a cutting edge capable of turning on itself, wounding Ulysses and his fellow mariners as well as the Ithacans.

Like many monologues, 'Ulysses' is a poem in search of an audience. So wayward is its drift of voices that the words we hear seem at times to blow through the windy spaces of an old man's head. Since Homer's Ulysses is the sole survivor of the Trojan war, his most bracing vocatives may be a mere pep talk to ghosts, a momentary drift into focus of an old man's reveries (despite Dante's heroic fiction to the contrary). Is it possible that Ulysses, seemingly the most vigorous of speakers, should be a Greek Gerontion, a shade with neither 'youth nor age / But as it were an after dinner sleep / Dreaming of both' ('Gerontion,' epigraph)?

In identifying the pivotal turning points in most dramatic monologues, Ulysses' swerves of voice provide a historical scheme of apostrophe that differs from the customary picture of the trope. As Douglas Kneale has shown, a new and proper understanding of apostrophe must distinguish *aversio* from two quite different figures, prosopopoeia and *exclamatio*, to which the swerves of voice and mood in a monologue are too often assimilated. An example of what Isobel Armstrong calls the 'double poem,' most monologues also subvert language in a second way. They reconstruct their culture by their Socratic testing of convention and by their humane appeal from morality or custom to a sense of how life might be lived more fully and self-critically.

Dramatic monologues address a double audience: Andrea del Sarto's immediate audience is Lucrezia, the present object of his conscious or applied persuasion. His ideal audience is alternately God, King Francis, and his parents: the absent subjects of his unconscious, disinterested persuasion. The subversive apostrophes or turns of voice in a monologue occur whenever a speaker switches audiences by redirecting his words to a hidden god. Their introduction of a new audience and rhetoric can be just as arresting as the entrance of a new character in a play. For each swerve or turn the reader is invited to invent a motive: the pressure exerted on the reader's creative invention is an important source of the monologue's power.

The masked or hidden audience, whose silence is primary and inviolable, explains a paradox to which D.G. Rossetti draws attention in a letter to Browning. 'The surprises' of *The Ring and the Book* 'are infinite,' he marvels, despite the fact that, 'by its plan, surprise seems almost excluded.' Since the end of a monologue is implicit in its beginning, there are no conversions. And yet expectations are continually being betrayed by the use of endings that are the opposite of obvious. Only the existence of a masked auditor or hidden god makes Rossetti's paradox intelligible. As Guido in his second monologue swerves violently aside from his immediate auditors, the judges, he rises through an octave of wild apostrophes to potential saviours before identifying his true deliverer at the top of the scale.

> I am yours,
> I am the Granduke's – no, I am the Pope's!
> Abate, – Cardinal, – Christ, – Maria, – God, ...
> Pompilia, will you let them murder me?
>
> *The Ring and the Book*, 11. 2416–19

In this 'terror-stricken flash of truth,' as the wretch 'winds up his shriek to the saving powers with the name of his wife,' Rossetti shrewdly equates Guido's frantic swerves of voice with the genius of the monologue form. 'When you wrote that line,' Rossetti says admiringly to Browning, 'you must have felt you owed your Muse a votive wreath; as the world, reading it, awards one to you.'[15] The apostrophic swerves from visible to hidden auditors achieve the kind of shock effect that all dramatic monologues – from the Pardoner's Epilogue to Robert Lowell's 'Colloquy in Black Rock' – exist to express.

1

Disturbing and Subverting the Stage Play: Spoken versus Printed Voices

Eric Griffiths, building on the work of Christopher Ricks, is the first major critic to insist that, because dramatic monologues (unlike stage plays) are the preferred medium of self-divided minds, the words in a monologue often look two ways at once. Since the printed voice of Victorian poetry appeals to both the eye and ear, Griffiths is able to show that in the silence of a private reading the monologue's drama for the eye may subtly qualify the drama for the ear, allowing fractional values and ampler sympathies to be felt. To do full justice to a monologue's two-way meanings, we may have to read the monologues silently, refusing to opt for one meaning rather than another, as we would have to do in an oral recitation.

Strong Speech Meets Strong Silence: A Theory of the Monologue

Though portions of 'My Last Duchess' can be treated as an actor's script, I want to argue that there are important differences between a speech in a stage play and a dramatic monologue. Even in supplicating a voice from the printed page, Browning's best dramatic monologues are often unvoiceable. Whereas a soliloquy from *Hamlet* is meant to be spoken aloud, not even the most experienced actor can hope to reproduce the complex tones conveyed in a silent reading of 'My Last Duchess' or 'Andrea del Sarto.'

According to Eric Griffiths, a defining feature of dramatic monologues is what Browning in *The Ring and the Book* calls 'the printed voice.' 'The absence of clearly indicated sound from the silence of the written word creates,' Griffiths says, 'a double nature in printed poetry, making it both itself and something other.'[1] Included in the half of this 'double nature' that aligns a monologue like 'My Last Duchess' with an actor's script are its many 'hints at voicing.' Using the text as his script, a reader who is as skilled an actor as the Duke will pick up several tricks of voice. He will register the way Browning's Duke keeps flouting expectations about correct conversational procedures by repeatedly echoing earlier remarks – 'I said,' 'I repeat,' 'as I avowed / At starting' (5, 48, 52–3) – and by sticking on words like 'I' and 'glance' (8, 12). Speaking a fraction too expansively about 'Her husband's presence' or 'The Count your master's known munificence' (14, 49), the Duke veers at other moments to the opposite extreme, contracting language almost to the vanishing point. As strong speech imposes strong silence, meaning hinges on zero values of disjunction and elision: 'This grew; I gave commands; / Then all smiles stopped together' (45–6). Alternating between a leisurely appositional style and an edgy asyndetic one, a good reader, like a good actor, would be expected to master as subtle yet ineffaceable tricks of voice the speaker's habit of saying at once too little and too much.

Unlike the actors in a stage play, however, readers of 'My Last Duchess' often feel the impossibility of adjusting their voice to the rapid changes in tone and to the difficulty of representing in any single reading the several intonations they imagine as equally appropriate and necessary. Most simply, when we 'talk upon paper,' as Elizabeth Barrett Browning says, our words can be given different patterns of stress, which we may want to linger over and ponder.

One of the pleasures of reading a dramatic monologue is the opportunity it affords for the simultaneity of different imagined (as opposed to actually heard or spoken) intonations. What contours of voice are we to elicit from the words 'She had / A heart – how shall I say? – too soon made glad, / Too easily impressed' (21–3)? If we stress the adverb 'how,' the emphasis falls on the speaker's artful pause for emphasis, on the mere style or manner of his disclosure. But if we give even more stress to the natural iambic accent on 'say' – 'how shall I *say*?' – then we can hear the words pausing tremulously on the brink of the line's second dash. A natural reticence or incomprehension has brought the speaker to the edge of speech; only with reluctance can he then cross the two framing dashes and the line-break to find a voice for what he has to say. Both alternatives must be imagined rather than heard, however, since no actor can voice the questions '*how* shall I say?' and 'how shall I *say*?' simultaneously. Nor can he simultaneously say 'That's my last *Duchess*' and 'That's my *last* Duchess painted on the wall' (the last of many). Even in an elegiac monologue by Hardy, 'Without Ceremony,' only a silent reading can register the two meanings: 'So, now that you *disappear* / *For ever* – in that swift style' and 'So, now that you disappear – / *For ever in that swift style*' (11–12). The first reading dramatizes the finality of the going; the second, the mere habitual manner.

How could an actor, in a dramatic reading of 'My Last Duchess,' ever hope to vocalize the quotation marks that set spoken words apart from indirect discourse, even when these words are part of a non-conversation, an exchange that never takes place?

> ... and say, 'Just this
> Or that in you disgusts me; here you miss,
> Or there exceed the mark'
>
> 'My Last Duchess,' 37–9

The moral calculus of these unheard words, which are part of the Duke's mincing geometry, transforms the Duchess into an impudent schoolgirl, 'plainly' setting 'Her wits to [his],' as though chopping logic with her master. Under the circumstances, the Duke could have done only one thing more repulsive, and that is the course he has in fact pursued: he has said nothing at all. The quotation marks of the printed voice break against their hard edges the even harsher precision of words – disdainful in themselves – that have been made even more disdainful by being scornfully withheld. It is difficult in a soliloquy or a play to distinguish between words that are merely thought or imagined and words that are meant to be heard. By contrast, a monologue we are invited to read and ponder in silence is particularly adept at evoking the silences of Browning's unheard words, including the conversations in his poetry that never take place. By disclosing forms of nonpresence, 'My Last Duchess,' a poem supposedly spoken but actually written, reveals an important law of its own genre.

A monologue also provides more opportunity than an actor's script for a poet to speak with two minds upon a subject. To the eye, a parenthesis framed by dashes can attach itself grammatically to either of the two elements it straddles.

> Even had you skill
> In speech – (which I have not) – to make your will
> Quite clear
>
> 'My Last Duchess,' 35–7

A silent reading allows the interpolated phrase, 'which I have not,' to look two ways at once. It can be construed as a self-deprecating demurrer, a *paralipsis*, a denial of rhetorical skill in the very act of exercising it. But if the phrase is allowed to attach itself, not to 'skill in speech,' but to 'skill' in the exercise of one's tyrannical will, then the words are a painful admission, spoken without any benefit of irony. An actor who is merely using the monologue as a script would have difficulty registering both meanings simultaneously. To pause more over the alliterating syllables, 'skill in speech,' would emphasize the rhetorical irony at the expense of the damaging personal disclosure. And to pause more over the exercise of volition, over the infinitive phrase 'to make your will / Quite clear,' would emphasize the admission of impotence at the expense of the irony. Only in the privacy of a silent reading does it seem feasible to register both possibilities at once.

As words break against the line-endings, the printed page even allows us to anticipate outcomes that do not occur. After boasting how 'all smiles stopped together,' the Duke says 'there she stands' (46). The slight pause at the end of the line invites us to imagine a syntactical completion for this alarming news. It sounds at first as if the Duchess's ghost is standing there. Has she returned from the grave to judge the Duke? We know that when tossed into a ditch like Shakespeare's Banquo, the dead may come back to haunt the living. But our alarm, in this case, is groundless. For as we round the corner of the next line, we discover that the Duke, unlike Macbeth, lacks even the imagination of guilt. Far from being tormented by a ghost, the Duke has moved the Duchess back into her picture space, where she can be safely immured. In taking us back to the poem's opening lines, 'That's my last Duchess painted on the wall, / Looking as if she were alive,' the phrase 'As if alive' (47) reminds us that the only permanence the Duchess enjoys after death is, not as a Banquo-like wraith, as we may fleetingly imagine, but as paint on a canvas. Displayed on a wall, the 'faint / Half-flush that dies along her throat' (18–19) is as much a pun on the painter's dyes as a comment on the tragic precariousness of her beauty. With the flicker of a pun the Duke revives the origin of 'infection' in 'inficere' or 'dye.' He diagnoses in a dying glow that stains his wife's throat an infection of her heart. Such is the latency of words on the printed page, and the loss incurred in any voicing of these words, which in a monologue often look two ways at once, creating a chance for a polyphony that no speaking voice can hope to catch.

Sticking on phrases like 'how shall I say?,' 'I know not how,' and odd migrations of the verb 'to stoop' (22, 32, 34, 42–3), the Duke is identified in a reader's imagination with repeated tricks of voice. But often the most meaningful of these repetitions, echoing each other across long spans of verse, will register only on readers who can read the text in silence, attuned to features of syntax and rhythm that they might pass over in an oral recitation. Like the muted rhymes, the subtler, more concealed these repetitions are, the more ironic the disparities they can then disclose between the way the speaker hears the words and the quite different way the poet and the reader hear them.

> she liked whate'er
> She looked on, and her looks went everywhere.
>
> 'My Last Duchess,' 23–4

The paratactic syntax, with its lordly echo of lines 3–4: 'Fra Pandolf's hands / Worked busily a day, and there she stands,' allows the two expansive gestures to call to each other across twenty intervening lines of verse. Though audible only to attentive readers, who are invited to share private jokes with the ironist behind the speaker's back in a silent reading of the poem, these syntactical echoes of God's creative fiat in Genesis ('God said, Let there be light: and there was light') resound subliminally, and alert us to the presence of other allusions, unheard by the speaker, but picked up by Browning and his readers, to create further ironies at the Duke's expense.

In choosing 'Never to stoop' (43), for example, the Duke unwittingly parodies the condescending God of Browning's St John, who 'stoops ... to rise ... Such ever was love's way' in 'A Death in the Desert' (134). Unlike Christ, whose 'stoop of the soul ... in bending upraises it too' ('Saul,' 252), the Duke pretends to 'stoop,' not out of love (for his melodramatic pretensions exclude the imagination of love), but only out of a selfish desire to dramatize his own importance. In aligning the reader with the envoy as secret allies of the poet, who keeps censuring the Duchess's censor behind his back, such repetitions and echoes establish a powerful single irony. We are reminded that, like the Pauline conception of *kenosis*, the emptying out of the divine nature, the duchess's stooping to acknowledge the courtesies of Fra Pandolf or even the attentions of the 'officious fool' who offers her the 'bough of cherries' (27) is an act of generous, unjudgmental giving that the Duke himself is at a loss to understand or describe.

In advising his master the Count of Tyrol to 'take / the old reprobate,' the Duke of Ferrara, 'at his unspeakable word' (200–2), the envoy in Richard Howard's sequel to 'My Last Duchess' uses the adjective 'unspeakable' in a double sense. Casting round for a euphemism that will hint at a crime too monstrous to name, the envoy hits on the term 'severe protocol':

> his poor Duchess, *put away* (I take it so)
>   for smiling – at whom?
>   Brother Pandolf? or
> some visitor to court during the sitting?
> – too generally, if I construe
>   the Duke's clue rightly,
>   to survive the terms
> of his ... severe protocol.

'Nikolaus Mardruz to His Master Ferdinand,
Count of Tyrol, 1565,' 179–86

But how precisely is the chilly phrase 'severe protocol' to be spoken? Does the envoy edge his words with the irony of the unspeakable or with the wonder of the inexpressible? Since only a silent reading of the 'unspeakable word' allows its double force to register, I take it that the Duke's most important meanings are never spoken. It is also difficult to decide whether the Duke's crime is too unspeakably evil to put into words or whether its motive is too ineffable.

It would be foolish to propose a theory of the monologue on the basis of a single poem, even a representative and justly famous one. As long as we remember, however, that 'My Last Duchess' is less complex than many of Browning's later monologues, it seems possible to sketch the first outline of a theory. One might suggest that, unlike soliloquies or other speeches in a stage play, dramatic monologues are not to be treated as actors' scripts or as poems intended for public recitation.

I am not denying that a gifted actor can bring to life the script of a Browning stage play. And I have no desire to depreciate the achievement of Kenneth Branagh or Peter Ustinov when they bring a new Hamlet or Lear into the world. I am merely suggesting that in reading dramatic monologues each of us becomes our *own* director. An *ideal* silent reading, which is a condition of our performing a dramatic monologue but not a stage play, allows greater unresolved complexity of meaning than is possible in any single recitation. As Emily Dickinson says in a letter of 1876, 'a Pen has so many inflections and a Voice but one.'[2]

The hazards of trying to voice all the subtleties and two-way meanings of a monologue's printed words allow Browning to dramatize and explore the precarious status of oral habits in an age of print. In a dramatic monologue, as in a closet drama like Browning's *Paracelsus*, the script, or text of the character's speech, is intended to be read silently. The real action takes place in the private theatre of our minds.

'Talking upon Paper': Browning's Love Letters and Monologues

In his love letters to Elizabeth Barrett, Robert Browning experiments with tricks of voice and written gestures that help distinguish the printed voice of a dramatic monologue from the spoken voice of a stage play. On hearing of their elopement, Wordsworth said, 'So Robert Browning and Miss Barrett have gone off together. I hope they understand each other – nobody else would.'[3] The obscurity Wordsworth objects to is partly a result of their 'talking upon paper,'[4] which is the felicitous phrase Elizabeth uses in her third letter to Robert. The letters are difficult to read because they try to transmit the spontaneity and rush of oral conversation to the stabler medium of script. After blurting out his love for Elizabeth's poems, Robert's first letter to her, postmarked 10 January 1845, delays for a full twenty lines the long-awaited declaration: 'I do, as I say, love these books with all my heart – and I love you too.'[5] Just as his promised meeting with Elizabeth had been postponed for years when Mr Kenyon announced that Miss Barrett was too ill to receive him, so Robert's declaration of his loving the poet as well as her poems is postponed in this letter by a tangle of exclamations, dashes, and digressions in which he takes elaborate pains to tell his correspondent what his letter is not intended to communicate before he blurts out what his full heart impels him to say.

– and this is no off-hand complimentary letter that I shall write, – whatever else, no prompt matter-of-course recognition of your genius, and there a graceful and natural end of the thing:[6]

Because the silences that would punctuate a conversation must be filled up in a letter with digressions and asides, there is as much speculation on the art of letter-writing as printed conversation in Browning's correspondence.

The diffused eroticism of many letters is largely a result of transcribing gestures and tactile sensations to the written page.

And now, my love – I am round you ... my whole life is wound up and down and over you ... I feel you stir everywhere.[7]

Using a cycle of open vowels to rotate the two lovers in a round-and-round hypnotic movement, Browning achieves an emotional intimacy few love letters can equal. Like the savage's use of deictics to count off the thunder rolls in 'Caliban upon Setebos,' the letter writer's 'There – and there!' are the grammatical equivalent of a touch or a caress. They even allow Browning to seal his love letter with two kisses: 'And now I will dare... yes, dearest, kiss you back to my heart again; my own. There – and there!'[8] Apart from the intimacies of the human voice itself, the beloved's handwritten letter, hallowed by the kiss of the sender, is the most personal form of communication.

Robert Frost says it is 'touch and go' with all metaphors, and until one has stretched a metaphor to the limit there is no knowing how far one can take it.[9] Browning makes the same point about letter-writing. Extravagances are permissible in monologues and letters that would be intolerable in real-life conversations.[10] Though one can take language to the limit in a letter, it is critical to stop before the conceit breaks down. In the letter of 11 February 1846, for instance, the inspired perversity of finding good omens in the parts of speech of an Italian grammar book allows Robert to joke about his deepest feelings and to express his wildest jokes in a noncommittal tone. He hopes that Elizabeth will be found in the dative case, and that he will not be left suspended in the ablative absolute case, without any grammatical tie to connect them.

Letter-writing sanctions a seductive play of *double entendres* and sexual innuendoes that would be inconceivable in face-to-face conversation. The omen-seeker dreads the prospect of stumbling over 'conditional moods,' 'imperfect tenses,' and 'singular numbers.' But he is also heartened by the promise held out by such parts of speech as 'conjunction' and 'possessive pronoun.' The high joking about discerning truth in a set of 'Promiscuous Exercises' is inseparable from the inner seriousness of the italicized words Browning transcribes from the Italian grammar book: 'If we love in the other world as we do in this, I shall love thee to eternity.'[11] The swift jumps and turns of phrase are as affecting as they are surprising, and the intimacy usually goes quite deep.

Instead of finishing a sentence fragment, Browning will often leave it suspended, as in casual conversation. More important than the precise meaning is the speaker's baffled tone:

But never, if you would not ... what you will not do I know, never revert to that frightful wish – 'Disappoint me?' – 'I speak what I know and testify what I have seen' – you shall 'mystery' again and again – I do not dispute that, but do not you dispute, neither, that mysteries are.[12]

Elizabeth's frightful wish about not disappointing is too absurdly whimsical to repeat. But having done so, Robert immediately counters it with a biblical quotation from John 3:11 and a reinvention of the word 'mystery,' which he uses as a verb. It is as much in the beloved's nature 'to mystery' as it is in a lark's nature to sing or a believer's nature to worship. Elizabeth can 'disappoint' her friend only if she admits an impediment to the marriage of true minds. She must not profane a love that originates in mystery and ends in acts of courage and trust.

As a double genre, both oral and written, the dramatic monologue resembles one of Robert's letters to Elizabeth: it uses the silence of written language to inscribe a radically oral form of discourse. Every monologue assumes the existence of both the 'I' and the elided 'you' of a one-sided conversation. But because the speaker of a monologue never merely describes something, his utterances are always partly self-referential and therefore partly dense or opaque. Transparent descriptions use signs that tend to fade away and be forgotten as signs in the process of describing something. In a Browning monologue, by contrast, the obliteration of the speaker as a sign is never complete, not even when David becomes the oracle through whom God speaks in 'Saul,' or when Caliban (at the opposite extreme) becomes a mere sensory antenna or a receptacle of unmediated impressions. Many monologues are partially opaque because they refer reflexively to their own utterances. The phrase 'by design' in 'My Last Duchess,' for example, is as much an allusion to the carefully disguised artifice of the Duke's heroic couplets as it is to his manipulation of the envoy.

Monologues favour first and second-person pronouns, and banish the third person, which becomes tantamount to a nonperson. As Alan Sinfield perceives, however, the abolition of the third person is also a 'feint,' a mere deceptive tilt in the direction of a lyric 'I.' For though the first-person voice usually signifies the poet's voice, the 'I' of the dramatic monologue is always a third-person voice in disguise, a voice which is 'teasingly at odds with'[13] the poet's voice even when the poet seems to be using it as his mouthpiece.

Linguistically, the so-called deictic terms ('this,' 'here,' 'now') are separated from proper nouns and definite descriptions and made to cluster round the 'I,' the first and foremost of the indicators. The third-person pronoun can be banished because 'I' and 'you' are sufficient to map out a conversation or a dialogue. On those rare occasions when a speaker in a monologue refers to himself in the third person, it is a mark of his anonymity and lack of selfhood. An 'I' who talks of himself in the third-person like Browning's Caliban is an oxymoron, a contradiction in terms, because he reduces a person to a nonperson by denying his selfhood. Though Caliban's grammar sounds strange, it dramatizes something that is even stranger: the mystery that necessarily attaches to an 'I' whenever it is compared to things that are capable, not of being uttered, but only of being referred to or described.

At the heart of the monologue's interlocution is neither an utterance nor a vocative but a speaking subject – and yet a speaker whose idiosyncratic experience of the world is written down on paper. Part of the monologue's meaning is its status as a double genre, its status as both a spoken utterance and a written document, like one of Browning's love letters or the scroll recording the last testament of Browning's St John.

As an event produced in the world and surviving on the printed page, the monologue is a speech act that has been preserved as a written record or transcript. As a fact among other facts, it belongs to the same world as the objects that are referred to in assertive statements. But as a transcript of spoken words, the monologue also combines utterances purporting to be facts with reflexive speech acts. To the extent that the monologue is the utterance of a speaking subject it is an example of 'doing-by-saying.' To the extent that the monologue is a written transcript of a speech act, it survives the impasses of private experience and takes its place in the public domain as something that can be cited referentially.

An actor's script is not itself a literary genre, but a means toward a further artistic end: the performance of a stage play. A dramatic monologue, by contrast, is the transcript of a speech that is not intended to be translated again into oral speech by being read aloud. The utterance of a monologue's dramatic speaker is a speech act in flesh and blood. But it is also a written transcript that defeats the act of a definitive oral reading almost successfully.

Though the meaning of every monologue is necessarily occasional, the genre's resistance to oral recitation (a fact enshrined in its written transcript of idiosyncratic speech acts) also ensures that the 'token' of any single reading will never be mistaken for the 'type' of an ideal reading.

Such a recitation would preserve all the intimacies of consciousness or all the free vagrancies of mind that a text's two-way syntax may authorize in a select group of interpreters. As a voice committed to paper, whose gestures and phonics share the fate of all written signs and material bodies, a monologue is a body among other bodies. And yet as the breath of a speaking subject, the monologue's voice is *sui generis*, a speech act that, because it is reflexive – a reference to its own utterance – is also irreplaceable and unique.

Intimacies of Consciousness: Stage Plays versus Dramatic Monologues

Richard Wollheim makes an important distinction between 'acting' a dramatic part that can be challenged or tested and 'acting out' a fantasy.[14] To 'act' the role of a martyr in a stage play like Tennyson's *Becket* is to be challenged and 'heckled.' It is to be asked if the desire to become a martyr is not incompatible with the attainment of that state. The satisfactions of a play are never wholly internal: performances can never be totally rehearsed or invulnerable to another actor's challenge. By contrast, to 'act out' a fantasy of martyrdom in a dramatic monologue like 'St Simeon Stylites' is to substitute for an open-ended action the closed enactment of an *idée fixe* or obsession. It is to forfeit the chance of being proved righteous by avoiding the risk of being proved a sham.

'Acting out' a fantasy is to a speaker's performance in a dramatic monologue what the 'acting' of a dramatic part is to a character's performance in a stage play. Preserved from testing or being challenged, the fantasies of the aspiring martyr, Becket, and the fanatical Queen Mary seem to have wandered into their separate stage plays from a different genre. Such obsessions are more congenial to a monologue or monodrama, where the defects of play-acting, fantasy-creation, and the loss of self-identity through verbal trickery can be more readily dramatized and exposed for what they are.

A character in a play should be responsive to people whose resistance to his fantasies might set up a counter-action. But as early as the first scene, Tennyson's Becket says he is 'martyr in [himself] already' (1.1; vol. 9, p. 38).[15] Though Becket's most important motives are the most elusive and obscure, in seeking martyrdom he seems to be inventing a role for himself that can pit him against Henry, his unfaithful soul-mate and brother. He is more resolved to cross Henry's will than make love to Henry's substitute, 'Our holy mother Canterbury,' a woman 'who sits / With tatter'd robes,' destitute and despised (1.1; vol. 9, p. 29).

When Walter Map attacks Becket for acting out a melodrama of rehearsed opposition to the king's conciliatory overtures, Becket cries out:

The State will die, the Church can never die.
...
But I must die for that which never dies.
It will be so – my visions in the Lord:
... And there, there, there, not here I shall rejoice
To find my stray sheep back within the fold.

Becket, 3.3; vol. 9, p. 146

In a sense, Becket is more in love with the idea of dying than with the cause for which he dies. He is resolved to sacrifice political complexities to the clinching force of an antithesis. His agitation and confusion are nowhere more evident than in his frantic use of ostensive definition: 'And there, there, there, not here I shall rejoice.' Closer to the hysteria of Browning's delinquent Caliban, cowering in fear as he counts off another thunder roll, than to the confident faith of Milton's swain, glorying in the promise of paradise at the climax of 'Lycidas,' Becket's fantasies of martyrdom seem anxious to conceal an unnamed affliction.

Acting out a fantasy of martyrdom, a monologue like 'St. Simeon Stylites' is unimpeded by any counter-action: it lacks the antiphonal voice of a 'heckler.' Though such voices can be heard in Tennyson's play *Queen Mary*, the queen's fantasies would be better suited to a monologue because the voices that oppose her have no effect on Mary's resolve to wed Philip and secure the succession of a Catholic heir. Gardiner's honest censure of Philip's ugly portrait and its dishonest praise by the French ambassador and later by Simon Renard set up their own resistance to and compliance in Mary's unshakeable fantasy of falling in love, not with a flesh-and-blood prince, but with an icon. Like the picture of George Osborne which becomes part of Amelia's portable household shrine in *Vanity Fair*, Philip's portrait is one of Mary's palace idols. It is also a metaphor for the distorting fantasy she is determined to act out in defiance of all counsel to the contrary.

Fantasies that may be challenged in a stage play can be indulged with greater impunity in a dramatic monologue or monodrama. Acting out a fantasy of martyrdom allows Tennyson's St Simeon Stylites to remake his life in ways that his Becket and Queen Mary are never wholly free to do. The event-fantasy of the saint's dying gloriously – or ingloriously – on his pillar is imposed on the world as a scenario the speaker would like to rehearse or 'act out' in Wollheim's sense. In the absence of any explicit criticism of the speaker, readers themselves are left to test his fantasy. They are meant to see how Simeon debases the scriptural prophecy that the last shall be first by acting out, at the very summit of a pillar, his fiction of being lowly and least. Taking the biblical text too literally, he falsifies its truth. Simeon's contempt for the body is also a form of worshipping the body. By enslaving himself to his ulcerous sores and loathsome physical decay, he cultivates a perverse inversion of the pleasure principle he claims to scorn. Everything he does and says thinly masks contradictions of humility and arrogance, of asceticism and sensuality, of satisfactions achieved in an intensely private theatre of his mind and satisfactions flaunted publicly on a stage.

By acting out a fantasy the speaker preserves it, and in preserving the fantasy he preserves the contradictory desires it contains. St Simeon acts out his fantasy of expiring slowly on his pillar because it preserves his desire both to loathe and take pleasure in the pains of the flesh. The lover in *Maud* acts out his fantasy of avenging his father's suicide because it preserves his desire both to hate and love Maud's cold and luminous beauty. As a Victorian Hamlet, the lover can conceal the competing desires of his fantasy by playing the role of his father's avenger: he loves the girl but hates her family. In killing Maud's brother and causing Maud's own death, the lover can misrepresent his masochistic desire to destroy and hate what he loves as a natural correction of his earlier idolatry of Maud, whom he celebrates in the sacramental language of the Song of Songs and in some of the most ostentatious love poetry in the English language.

If Simeon did not routinely ascend his pillar day after day, and if Maud's lover did not maintain a protective fiction of hating Maud long after he has fallen in love with her, these speakers might begin to test their fantasies. To become their internal observers is to adopt the view of critical readers, who may find what they see bizarre, grotesque, deranged, or untrue. But as Wollheim explains, every time a fantasy is acted out it will seem more normal to the speaker. This is why the lover's belief that he hates what he loves and loves what he hates becomes a little more secure against the threat of criticism each time he rails against Maud's brother or father, or each time the ghastly glimmer of Maud's ghost appears to him like lightning under the stars.

When Simeon acts out his fantasy of being ascetic, he remains self-ignorant of the hedonism that allows him to derive a perverse physical pleasure from his pain. In his self-ignorance he is not aware of his desire to be glorified by being humiliated, or of striving to be exalted by pretending to be low and abased. In his self-error he also attributes to himself a desire to be a theological model, a pattern or example to the religious community.

> But thou, O Lord,
> Aid all this foolish people; let them take
> Example, pattern: lead them to thy light.
>
> 'St. Simeon Stylites,' 218–20

As a self-centred masochist, Simeon cannot experience the pure selfless-ness of a true martyr. But stories of martyrdom allow him to conceal his real motives. And because they are rich in fantasy, they appeal to both Simeon's and Tennyson's theatrical sense. Richard Wollheim goes fur-ther by ingeniously attributing the 'self-error' of such an actor to his 'loan' from the martyr's rich repertoire of dramatic parts.[16]

One reason why Tennyson writes better monologues than plays should now be clear: the rich fantasy life of a would-be saint or martyr is better explored in 'St. Simeon Stylites' than in *Becket* or *Queen Mary*. No histori-cal drama can be composed entirely of moments of psychological break-through in which the playwright conscripts a character to convey information that is not fully accessible to the character himself. But this kind of self-characterizing speech, in which Tennyson's King Henry is only subliminally aware of what he is characterizing, is a defining fea-ture of dramatic monologues, where disclosures are often inadvertent or involuntary. Because St Simeon Stylites' most important revelations are unconscious, we can hear him telling one story about himself while Tennyson is telling an ironically different story.

Though the politics of state requires Tennyson's Henry to be a stern censor of a friend turned enemy, this is not what his language of inti-macy reveals him to be.

> Co-mates we were, and had our sport together,
> Co-kings we were, and made the laws together.
>
> *Becket*, 2.2; vol. 9, p. 105

Parities of syntax bind the verses, as they bind the friends, with words that recur without variation at the head and end of successive lines. The repeating elements are as constant as the two friends. They reveal Henry instantly as a soul-mate, someone whose sport with Becket has its own marvellous freedoms.

The intimacy of the two male friends is something the monk-king, Louis, tries in vain to fathom. But there is also a wariness in friendship's celebrant, something almost furtive, that makes Henry's glimpse into his past only a glimpse, a truth he is half resolved to hide. We are surprised he should say as much as he does, and so is Henry, especially since his auditor, Louis, is 'too cold to know the fashion' of love's freedoms.

Tennyson's historical stage plays are often most successful when they begin to transgress their genre, aspiring to the condition of a dramatic monologue. When Henry discloses his former hope that he and Becket could have been 'Two sisters gliding in an equal dance, / Two rivers gently flowing side by side' (1.3; vol. 9, p. 60), it is hard not to find in this astonishing switch a drama of repressed affection and sexual reversal, held in an excitable state of tension. In the 'Prologue' Becket had claimed that Henry befriended him, 'not as a statesman,' but as a 'true lover' ('Prologue,' vol. 9, p. 5). Here, as in a choral soliloquy, Henry reveals a whole new dimension to the action: his capacity to love and hate Becket simultaneously.

We are closest to Tennyson's speakers when they relax their will and momentarily allow the free vagrancy of their consciousness to suspend their role-playing. As in a lyrical monologue, Becket may find himself momentarily outside the dramatic action, in a different world – the world that might have been.

> Better have been
> A fisherman at Bosham, my good Herbert,
> Thy birthplace – the sea-creek – the petty rill
> That falls into it – the green field – the gray church –
> The simple lobster-basket, and the mesh –
> The more or less of daily labour done –
> The pretty gaping bills in the home-nest
> Piping for bread – the daily want supplied –
> The daily pleasure to supply it.
>
> *Becket*, 2.2; vol. 9, p. 111

As the imagination wanders, so does the syntax. Its loose inventory of workaday maritime impressions seems as innocent of contrivance as the early-age wonder of marvels and commonplaces it freshly evokes. However unexpected, there is a pause here, as Becket and the audience stop to enjoy a moment of effortless pleasure. Such idyllic asides are like intermissions in a play: the role-player who acts out his fantasies of martyrdom momentarily imagines an alternative play in which he might perform a different role. Or he may briefly contemplate the pleasures of renouncing play-acting altogether.

As the climax of his tragedy approaches, Becket has nothing better to do than discuss the discovery of a fowl's nest or the death from leprosy of a fair-haired Norman maid, the world's lily, who once lived in his mother's house:

> I once was out with Henry in the days
> When Henry loved me, and we came upon
> A wild-fowl sitting on her nest, so still
> I reach'd my hand and touch'd; she did not stir;
> The snow had frozen round her, and she sat
> Stone-dead upon a heap of ice-cold eggs.
> Look! how this love, this mother, runs through all
> The world God made – even the beast – the bird!
>
> *Becket*, 5.2; vol. 9, p. 185

These digressions, with their flickers of gratuitous beauty and pathos, are the recollections of someone who seems to have forgotten what the play is about. The disturbing imperatives of impending martyrdom are never totally ignored, but they are also subtly resisted, as if there were something ill about the martyr's heart. The stone-dead bird, frozen upon her heap of ice-cold eggs, like the death by leprosy of the little lily, is oddly consoling to the martyr whose own role seems thrust upon him from outside, as one of the necessities of a tragic outcome.

We are most intimate with Tennyson's speakers when the reflexive understanding they display is too subtle or multilevelled for a stage play to dramatize. Nothing in *Becket* and *Queen Mary*, for example, is quite so touching or dramatic as the unactable moment in his idyll 'Lancelot and Elaine' when Lancelot realizes that Elaine is looking at him, and Elaine is conscious that he knows.

> Then, when she heard his horse upon the stones,
> Unclasping flung the casement back, and look'd
> Down on his helm, from which her sleeve had gone.
> And Lancelot knew the little clinking sound;

And she by tact of love was well aware
That Lancelot knew that she was looking at him.

'Lancelot and Elaine,' 973–8

A stage play offers little opportunity for one-sided looking. Like the silent auditor in a monologue, however, Lancelot is not allowed to see or speak. When Elaine looks at him, she reduces him to the quintessential object. Ashamed to return her look, he cannot disarm her unstated censure by making her an object of his own gaze. The best comment on the passage comes from Christopher Ricks: 'The tact, the tenderness, the unmentioned bruises: to me the lines are unforgettable.'[17] As in Tennyson's monologue 'Tithonus,' however, where the speaker looks forward to a time when he can withhold his look from the goddess who must still look down on his grave –

Thou seëst all things, thou wilt see my grave;
Thou wilt renew thy beauty morn by morn,
I earth in earth forget these empty courts,
And thee returning on thy silver wheels

'Tithonus,' 73–6

– the true poignancies of this drama are too multiple and reflexive to be transferred to the stage.

There is a final important difference between stage plays and dramatic monologues. Because each speech in a closet drama is treated as a set piece in relative isolation from all the other speeches, sustained impersonation of the speakers is seldom really possible. The language of *Paracelsus* comes to life, not in the external interaction of one speech with another (as in a stage play) and not in the interior interplay of a speaker, a silent auditor, and a dramatic occasion (as in a monologue). Browning builds his closet drama out of declamations or orations, the equivalent of arias in an opera. Accordingly, while the silent performance of a dramatic monologue points the genre in the direction of a closet drama, its genius for impersonation preserves an even stronger link between an actor's public performance in a stage play and the reader's private staging of a monologue. As one commentator says, Browning's monologues 'are profoundly untheatrical just because they make the reader himself a theatre, and so dispense with the externalized elements of theatrical performance.'[18] Since the monologue's subtlest dramatic effects are often unvoiceable by any physical voice we could actually hear on a stage, the strong speech of a Duke of Ferrara should ideally confront the equally strong silence of the reader. Replicating in a private theatre of the mind the active silence of the monologue's critically vigilant auditor, this reader is often a muted heckler or adversary in disguise.

'On the earth the broken arcs,' says Browning's Abt Vogler, 'in the heaven, a perfect round' ('Abt Vogler,' 72). As earth's 'broken arcs' displace the 'perfect round' of heaven, even the tendency of monologues to close upon themselves may be endlessly deferred, since as free artists of their own identities speakers in monologues are constantly trying to revise the stories they tell about themselves. Too little attention has been paid to 'scenarios of closure' in Victorian literature. J.H. Newman's strong awareness of teleology imparts an almost Aristotelian sense of closure to each chapter of his spiritual autobiography *Apologia Pro Vita Sua*. By contrast, George Borrow's open-ended experiments with self-making and role-playing in *Lavengro* and *The Romany Rye* defy closure: they stop rather than conclude. Many Victorian monologues veer toward Newman's sense of some informing teleology or final cause. But then, like an experiment in role-playing that is necessarily incomplete, they conclude by means of an optional stop rule. In substituting for a stage play's externalized performance a private theatre of readerly meditation, most monologues remain alive precisely because they are unsettled, open to endless reversals and revisions. There is no limit to the winds of change that keep blowing through the openings created by the genre's endless resistance to closure.

The State of Being in Two Minds: A Culture in Crisis

In trying to purge from his own poetry, partly for political reasons, all traces of influence from the so-called Spasmodic school of Byronic and Shelleyan imitators, Matthew Arnold in the Preface to his *Poems of 1853* professes to despise his own achievement in *Empedocles on Etna*. In exploring the two-way pull of a self-divided mind, Empedocles' monologue does nothing to animate men: the critic rejects as 'morbid' and 'monotonous' his poem's 'continuous state of mental distress, ... unrelieved by incident, hope, or resistance, in which there is everything to be endured, nothing to be done.' Arnold's conservative classical aesthetic, in which the 'action itself, its selection and construction,' are 'all-important,'[19] must be seen as his response to the political radicalism of the Spasmodic poets and, like his essays on the Romantic poets, to his own complex and changing reactions to the cockney Keats.

But in advocating a neoclassical aesthetic that covertly attacks his rival, the Spasmodic poet Alexander Smith, Arnold is also disparaging as a critic the source of his astonishingly acute reflections in poems like 'Resignation' and 'Dover Beach.' In Arnold and Browning alike the substitution of 'Action in Character for Character in Action,' which Browning boldly endorses in his Preface to *Strafford* in a striking reversal of Aristotle's priorities, invites that self-critical mental play and that delight in divided loyalties which are the crowning achievement of the best dramatic monologues. Whereas Arnold tries to revise a classical aesthetic and John Keble tries to usurp Aristotle's mantle by equating classical theories of imitation with his own antithetical doctrines of Romantic expression, Browning openly acknowledges his break with classicism by reversing Aristotle's own privileging of action over character.

The desire to honour two-way meanings is part of a larger Victorian desire to see inclusively. In his sonnet 'To a Friend,' Arnold praises Sophocles for seeing life 'steadily' and seeing it 'whole' (12). In a similar vein, J.S. Mill's *Essay on Liberty* affirms that, unless even heretical views are expressed and then vigorously opposed, truth itself will lack eloquent defenders. Though inclusive vision is one of Arnold's and Mill's most cherished ideals, it is also an ideal that is constantly being compromised in practice. As George Eliot recognizes in her parable of the pierglass in *Middlemarch*, steady vision is the result of too exclusive an optical selection. Only the candle of an observer's egotism can impose upon the scratches of the glass a 'flattering illusion of concentric arrangment.'[20] To see life whole is to see it unsteadily, and to see it steadily is to see it myopically. In such monologues as 'Dover Beach' and Tennyson's 'Ulysses' the open nerve of this dilemma, though raw with hurt, is also soothed by language fraught with two-meanings and nuances, to which only the Empsonian attentiveness of a private reading can do justice.

Poised between the playful levity of 'Geist's Grave,' an elegy for the family dachshund, and the high seriousness of a classical tragedy, 'Dover Beach' introduces just enough frisky indirection to trigger the high jinks of Anthony Hecht's spirited parody, 'The Dover Bitch: A Criticism of Life.'

So there stood Matthew Arnold and this girl
With the cliffs of England crumbling away behind them,
And he said to her, 'Try to be true to me,

And I'll do the same for you, for things are bad
All over, etc., etc.'
Well now, I knew this girl. It's true she had read
Sophocles in a fairly good translation
And caught that bitter allusion to the sea,
But all the time he was talking she had in mind
The notion of what his whiskers would feel like
On the back of her neck ...
...
                                  To have been brought
All the way down from London, and then be addressed
As a sort of mournful cosmic last resort
Is really tough on a girl, and she was pretty.
                'The Dover Bitch: A Criticism of Life,' 1–11, 16–19

Anthony Hecht's playful subversions are encouraged by the double, sometimes opposite, kinds of meaning that abound in 'Dover Beach.' As an example one might cite the world that 'lies' before Arnold's bridegroom 'like a land of dreams' (31). Does it repose in beauty or deceive through illusion? Because only a silent reading can register a monologue's nuances, the silence of the genre's vigilant and often aggressive auditors may find its most appropriate echo in the reader's own private voicings. Syntax must be explored as part of print space, even as the primacy of its printed word is being challenged by efforts to imagine the poem as a heard event.

In 'Dover Beach' Arnold tries to reinvent the values of his culture by experimenting with heroic, sceptical, and reductive theories of knowledge. The more Arnold and Newman try to justify their cultural or religious beliefs, the more these beliefs tend to diverge from the grounds they have for holding them. Without trying to close the gap, a sceptic like Browning's Caliban simply acknowledges the divide that separates a God of absolute caprice and power from his bewildered creation: 'here are we, / And there is He, and nowhere help at all' ('Caliban upon Setebos,' 248–9). By contrast, a reductionist like Pater in *Plato and Platonism* tries to scale down Plato's doctrine of Ideas to make it fit the antimetaphysical ground of his own beliefs. A religious apologist like Newman opts for a third, more heroic alternative. In the fifth chapter of his *Apologia* Newman courageously leaps over the abyss separating 'the promise' from 'the condition' of man's being by affirming that even in being betrayed by his children God has left behind tokens of his presence.[21] Deploying a mixture of all three methods, Arnold's speaker in 'Dover Beach' is alternately a disillusioned sceptic, a reductive secularist, and a heroic affirmer of joys whose grounds are true.

If we heed content alone, the speaker's despair and dispossession seem irreversible. In a powerful echo of Newman's Oxford sermon on 'Faith and Reason' (1839),[22] which ends with Thucydides' account of the 'night battle, where each fights for himself, and friend and foe stand together,' Arnold reverses the import of the lover's plea to his bride by summoning up his poem's true subject – the trauma of pointless conflict, in which each disputant fails to understand what his adversary means. For a panic moment, in which the earlier appeal to love seems swallowed up in nightmare, obliterating everything of value, the speaker breaks out into bereavement. From nostalgia for his grand illusion, to an odd, reverberating, reproachful kind of lament, to the full surge of terror, all the steps of repressed fear, forcing its way to consciousness, are embodied in Arnold's rhymes, grammar, line-breaks, and metre.

Because Arnold wrote 'Dover Beach' on his return from a delayed honeymoon, it is possible to read the monologue as a thinly veiled confession – or as what Ralph Rader prefers to call a 'dramatic lyric.'[23] If neither religion nor culture can save him, perhaps the speaker's love for his bride can be a new locus of faith. But 'faith' is a complex word, and in Victorian culture the descriptive and emotive meanings of 'faith' are in constant flux. Browning's Bishop Blougram, for example, has to redefine 'faith' in order to accommodate the Bishop's joke that Gigadibs, like his wine, is 'cool i' faith' (2), or the novel fact that 'faith means perpetual unbelief' (666). Like Bishop Blougram, Ernest Pontifex in *The Way of All Flesh* retains the favourable emotive meaning of 'faith,' while altering its descriptive meaning to identify the concept with its use. 'The just shall live by faith, that is to say that sensible people will get through life by rule of thumb.'[24] For Butler's Ernest, as for Browning's Bishop, what works is made the measure of what ought to be. What ought to be is not appealed to as the sanction of what works.

In 'Dover Beach' there is nothing to indicate, of course, that the speaker has recently married – or is even married at all. Anthony Hecht's parody exploits this ambiguity by turning the so-called bride into an amused prostitute or testy mistress. But by making his speaker a scholar who can quote Newman as well as Dr Thomas Arnold's translation of Thucydides, Matthew Arnold has boldly decreased the distance between poet and persona. The substitution of faith in his bride for faith in God initially exalts and ennobles the speaker. Because he retains the favourable emotive meaning of faith while radically altering its descriptive meaning, he cannot, however, allay his fears for long. After the auxiliary verb of illusion, 'seems, 'the infinitive 'To lie' (31) evokes a double sense of lying 'before us' in a gesture of repose and of lying in the sense of concealing truth.

> Ah, love, let us be true
> To one another! for the world, which seems
> To lie before us like a land of dreams,
> So various, so beautiful, so new,
> Hath really neither joy, nor love, nor light,
> Nor certitude, nor peace, nor help for pain;
> And we are here as on a darkling plain
> Swept with confused alarms of struggle and flight,
> Where ignorant armies clash by night.
>
> 'Dover Beach,' 29–37

Even after the sea of faith has ebbed away like the tide, God may not have died: he may merely have entombed himself in a dead descriptive language. If this is so, God may come to life again in the lover's appeal to the woman. But if we read the poem autobiographically, what assurance has the speaker that he can be any truer to her than to his lost Marguerite? Perhaps Arnold on his honeymoon is deceiving his bride about his love affair with Marguerite, whom the glimmering lights off the French coast seem to recall in the opening lines of the monologue. Instead of exposing everything in an act of faith, Arnold and his bride may be concealing something through deceit and falsehood. The dream of variety, beauty, and novelty is then no longer a mere semblance or illusion: it becomes an outright deception or lie.

At the same time, in rescuing faith from a mummified mythology, Arnold's speaker finds that a heroic alternative to sceptical and reductive options is still available to him in the bracing rather than defeatist tone of the concluding lines. The melancholy, long, withdrawing roar of the penultimate stanza, which establishes an enchanting vowel music to lull the mind into oblivion like one of Frost's snow poems, is countered in the last stanza by an equally slow-wheeling but obdurate resistance to death, as if Arnold were responding to a stirring call to arms. Since the sound of the closing lines is slightly at odds with their sense, however, the poem continues to look two ways at once: a reader who listens attentively will hear no dull stamp of stoic fortitude, but the incremental energy of subtly interlacing syntactic units and a triad of heroically defiant rhymes.

No one knows better than Arnold, the author of *Merope* and the neo-classical Preface to the *Poems of 1853*, that monologues may indulge more easily than stage plays in fantasies of self-gratification and solipsism. But if his speaker in 'Dover Beach' is too transparent a mask for Arnold himself, the poet's delicacy of touch prevents his disturbed and disturbing thoughts from disintegrating altogether into personal nightmare. Balance and sanity survive in the monologue's appeal to Sophocles, in medieval therapies for the agony and strife of human hearts, and in a memorable allusion to Wordsworth's power both to hear and subdue 'the still sad music of humanity.'

The monologue is the genre best suited to express the pull and counter-pull of self-division,[25] the state of being 'in two-some twiminds,' as Joyce calls it. In Tennyson's monologue 'Ulysses,' for example, the flicker of incongruous pictures is so speeded up as to seem almost instantaneous. The disparate frames that Ulysses mounts in his spacious line 'Far on the ringing plains of windy Troy' (17) are more like the montage in a cinema than a sequence of reinvented portraits. Ulysses' quick re-vision of Troy in a kind of 'double take' combines subliminal impressions of 'ringing plains,' alive with the clamour of war, and empty windswept ruins. By presenting separate pictures of battle on the darkling plain and of Troy as the bare ruined choir of wasting winds, Ulysses collapses the space filled by years of conflict into a direct confrontation of pride and ruin. Though 'Ulysses' is a short monologue, we may feel at its end that we have just finished reading a long epic poem. Tennyson vindicates Homer's inspired use of 'windy' as an epithet for Troy by allowing vast winds of sadness to sweep through his poem. Conflicting impressions of glory and ruin are so inseparable that readers are allowed to defer recognition of the painful truth that some great goods like heroic enterprise and cultural stability – the conflicting values of Ulysses and Galahad, on the one hand, and Telemachus and Arthur, on the other – cannot exist together.

Browning achieves similar results by different means. In 'Abt Vogler' he uses Germanic word order to delay a sentence's principal verb and to create a state of felt uncertainty, a condition of being in two minds (as intimated by the German word for 'doubt,' 'Zweifel'). Even in an oral reading of 'My Last Duchess' a gifted reader must often decide between exclusive variants, A and not-A. But because in a silent reading we can also 'choose not to choose,' as Sharon Cameron says,[26] a monologue may permit us to forget momentarily that we are all doomed to choose in the end, and that every choice between equality and restraint, for example, or between the goods of the moral and intellectual life, is likely to entail some irreparable loss. Though experiencing such losses is one of the events that make us human, many readers find it difficult to admit that values worthy of being pursued as ends in themselves – values such as Hebraism and Hellenism, justice and mercy, liberty and equality – may actually exist in inverse proportion. If more strictness of conscience entails less spontaneity of consciousness and vice versa, then how can Jerusalem be reconciled with Athens? How can Christ and Plato be united in some larger whole? While nineteenth-century culture is confronting its crises of choice, its dramatic monologues are giving fractional values their due. In the interest of seeing life steadily and seeing it whole, monologues may momentarily allow the Victorians to be both John Knox and Alcibiades, while recognizing with John Stuart Mill that it is better to be Socrates than either.

2

Socrates' Subversive Legacy: Irony and the Monologue

For proof of Socrates' important but neglected influence on the nineteenth-century dramatic monologue, we have only to turn to Browning, who exhibits in many of his monologues' one-sided conversations the overflow of intellectual high spirits to be found in the best Socratic dialogues. After 1863 Browning became a close friend of Benjamin Jowett, the most influential Victorian scholar of Socrates. Though Jowett's personal influence on Browning came too late to be formative, Jowett's use of Plato's *Republic* as a blueprint for Oxford education after 1855, when he became Regius Professor of Greek, made the influence of Socrates on mid-Victorian culture decisive. Of more practical interest is Browning's ownership of an 1836 translation of the monograph in which Friedrich Schleiermacher distinguishes between Socrates' magisterial dialogues and his dialogues of search. Unlike Jowett's edition of Plato's *Dialogues*, which he presented to Browning as a gift in 1871, Schleiermacher's work came early enough to influence the composition of even Browning's first dramatic monologues.

Like the Socrates of the magisterial dialogues, Browning's Bishop Blougram is a single ironist in firm possession of the truth: Gigadibs's deviation from it is a deserved target of his censure. But as a double ironist who resembles the Socrates of the dialogues of search, Browning shows in 'A Toccata of Galuppi's' that there is truth on both sides of an issue: his speaker's moral censure of the life-loving Venetians is itself a target of the poet's censure. When the dead musician refuses to answer the speaker's battery of rhetorical and heuristic questions, he refuses like Socrates to consolidate the mental level on which these questions are asked. Galuppi's ghost encourages the speaker to subvert his own cultural assumptions of privilege and pride by posing new, more searching questions.

For proof of Browning's early familiarity with Socrates we have only to turn to his love letters to Elizabeth Barrett. Responding to Robert's own Socratic insight that 'the simplest, plainest word or deed' can be changed to mean 'its opposite,' Elizabeth wittily identifies herself with Socrates in a letter written to Robert on 6 March 1846: 'Always *you*, is it, who torments me? – always you?' she teases. 'Well! – I agree to bear the torments as Socrates his persecution by the potters: – & by the way he liked those potters, as Plato shows, & was fain to go to them for his illustrations.' The potters' portrayal of Socrates on their flasks, which Daniello Bartoli construes as an indignity or insult, Browning interprets more charitably as a deed of 'affectionate admiration.'[1] In such contradictory interpretations of Socrates, as in the Socratic dialogues themselves, Browning clearly identifies the subversive potential of the many double ironies that pervade his best dramatic monologues and that make his debt to Socrates explicit.

A crisis in nineteenth-century thought occurs when Plato, the most spiritual and idealistic of Greek philosophers, is appropriated as a radical reformer and sceptic by the Utilitarian historian George Grote. Whereas William Sewell, John Stuart Blackie, Brook Foss Westcott, and Jowett all champion a prophetic Plato who upholds vestiges of Christian doctrine in the wake of Utilitarian ethics, George Grote, J.S. Mill, and later Walter Pater all celebrate in Plato a resourceful sceptic and agnostic. In the words of one intellectual historian, 'Grote argued that Plato had no other purpose in his dialogues of search, which usually concluded in skepticism, new questions, or the simple admission of ignorance, than to illustrate the ameliorative, liberating power of the negative dialectic. Plato's message was his very method. The movement of testing, exercising, refuting, but not finding or providing constituted the primary weapons for ending the rule of King Nomos, or inherited customs, ideas, and prejudices.'[2] The post-Romantic monologue displays the same sceptical temper as Grote, who follows Hegel and Mill in portraying Socrates as a radical questioner, as an ethical immoralist and creative agnostic, rather than as the defender of established moral and religious values.

As an important example of Isobel Armstrong's 'double poem,' the monologue is a genre of self-testing, analysing, refuting, which, in George Grote's words, 'gives free play and ... prominence to the negative arm' in his incisive Hegelian account of Plato's 'dialogues of search' in *Plato, and the Other Companions of Sokrates* (1865).[3] But such a genre is not merely agnostic and sceptical. It both subverts and reconstructs its culture by its Socratic testing of convention and by its humane appeal from morality or custom (what Hegel calls *Sittlichkeit*) to a more informed sense of how a truly ethical life should be lived. The free play of this subversive Socratic spirit in the post-Romantic monologue challenges its culture's ascendant values, not with a view to dismantling them, but with a view to rebuilding culture on a firmer foundation of truth.

As well as owning copies of Jowett's edition of Plato's *Republic*, John Stuart Blackie's *Greek and English Dialogues for Uses in Schools and Colleges*, and his wife's translation of the dialogue between Criton and Socrates, Browning owned Schleiermacher's *Introduction to the Dialogues of Plato*, where an important distinction is drawn between Plato's aporetic and magisterial dialogues. Treatises like *The Republic* that set forth Plato's own ideas are magisterial or 'constructive,' to use Schleiermacher's phrase. He assigns these 'constructive' dialogues a later date than the 'preparatory' dialogues that are merely experimenting with the 'dialogistic method'[4] or that are trying to work out answers to questions that puzzle Socrates as well as his auditors. *Lysis*, *Charmides*, and *Laches*, for example, pose critical questions about friendship, temperance, and courage, respectively, but none of these questions is finally answered. In the constructive dialogues, by contrast, the double ironies and doubts of the aporetic dialogues are finally resolved. As Schleiermacher says, 'Socrates no longer comes forward with questions in the character of a man who is ignorant, and only looking for greater ignorance in the service of the god.' Instead, 'as one who has already found what he seeks, he advances onwards, bearing along with him in strict connection the insights he has acquired.'[5] George Grote makes a similar distinction between Plato's dialogues of 'search' and 'exposition.' Like Browning, he favours such dialogues of 'search' as the *Hippias*, the *Protagoras*, the *Gorgias*, and the *Laches*, where some heckler is always ready to challenge the speaker's dogmatism by playing a subversive and sceptical Socrates to Socrates himself.

Like Socrates, many Victorians send one message to the custodians of their culture's established values and another to their own attentive coterie of followers and friends. Because they speak with a forked tongue, their truest beliefs are often hidden and their most cherished values masked. In *In Memoriam*, for example, Charles Lyell's new science of universal flux forces Tennyson to come to terms with the apparent lack of cosmic support for what he loves and cares about. To address this problem Tennyson first perfects the art of speaking as a conservative sage or seer on behalf of his culture's official belief in 'the great world's altar-stairs / That slope through darkness up to God' (55.15–16). Having won respect in high places for his conformity, the poet laureate then introduces furtively rebellious doctrines about God's wild poetry and the unsettling thought that, compared with the dinosaurs, man is a cosmic misfit and tragic accident, ill suited for life and love in a world 'red in tooth and claw' that refuses to share the poet's dream of cosmic harmony (34.7, 56.15, 21–4).

Since the Victorians' goals may be as elusive as Newman's 'illative sense' or Arnold's 'imaginative reason,' the official scaffolding of Victorian culture is often held in place by values that are wayward, fugitive, and hard to formulate. I am thinking of the instinctive satisfaction that Newman and Arnold each find in the free play of an educated mind unaffected by any desire for practical results, or of the subtle delight that Browning and George Eliot each take in tracing the geometry of new and complicated moral labyrinths.

The dramatic monologues serve the same function in Victorian culture as Socrates' dialogues did in his: without seeming to do so, they subvert official values by transferring allegiance from visible to hidden gods. By combining sympathy with playful distance, Socratic irony also allows the poet to preserve intact secrets about the dangers, limits, and fragility of human knowledge. The values that the Socratic ironist is forbidden to promote publicly are often fragile but disciplined responses to life, too personal to qualify as official arguments, but too tenacious to dismiss as mere proclivities or whims.

The Aporetic Socrates: Subversion and the Monologue

By the aporetic Socrates I mean the probing, inquiring Socrates: not the magisterial architect of *The Republic* but the Socrates of the *Protagoras*, who doubts at the beginning if virtue is 'teachable' but who learns from his adversary and is even converted to his adversary's point of view by the end of the debate. Playfully ironic, Socrates displays genuine regard for Protagoras: as Benjamin Jowett observes in his edition of *The Dialogues of Plato*, 'Protagoras has the best of the argument and represents the better mind of man.' Plato reveals the truth 'by lights and shadows, and far-off and opposing points of view, ... not by dogmatic statements or definite results.'[6] The bracing uncertainties and buoyant scepticism of such a dialogue anticipate the intellectual high spirits of Clough's Claude in his epistolary monodrama *Amours de Voyage* and of Tennyson's subversive atheist in his monologue 'Lucretius,' who as a kind of Roman Socrates does not the know the answers to many of the questions that he asks.

As the champion of a new intellectual culture, the Socrates of Grote and Hegel is the critic of traditional moral and religious norms. Like Arthur Hugh Clough and Matthew Arnold, he is a metaphysically displaced person, wandering between two worlds, 'one dead, the other powerless to be born' ('Stanzas from the Grande Chartreuse,' 85–6). Though Socrates' genius is subversive, his goal is not subversion for its own sake but a genuine Arnoldian search for joy whose grounds are true.

We feel close to agents of subversion like Clough's Claude in *Amours de Voyage* because the intimacies of his consciousness and the free vagrancies of his mind make him ineffective as a man of practical capacity or action, just as they incapacitate Hamlet. Meaning, Claude muses, is an accident of context. Like his interest in Mary, it is a mere quirk of placement: 'it is only juxtaposition, – / Juxtaposition, in short; and what is juxtaposition?' (1.11.225–6). Among other things, juxtaposition neatly imitates the decline of lofty abstraction into casuistry, special pleading, or evasion. Aspiring 'evermore to the Absolute only' (5.4.59), Claude is prevented from bringing his love affair to any satisfactory conclusion. Clough uses juxtaposition to write eloquently about the heartbreaking waste of Claude's imaginative gifts. The decline of Hope, the second of Paul's three Christian virtues, into hope: 'As for hope, – to-morrow I hope to be starting for Naples' (5.10.203) dramatizes the decline of the man without 'Hope,' who is subject to mere velleities and whims.

When Claude expands the end of a railway journey into the end of time and the intrusion upon him of some eternal tie (3.6.111–12), we sense the peculiar force with which a half-dreaded, half-desired knowledge thrusts itself upon his mind. Like Browning's Karshish, Claude keeps running away from what he seems running toward. He even tries to run away from his knowledge that he is running away. An obsessive curiosity about what lies behind the masks is always matched by a fear of knowing too much. The expansive, circling hexameters of Clough's epistolary monologues roll over and over each other like huge ocean waves, but without actually seeming to advance. They dramatize the panic of the great refusal, the anxiety of someone who is conscious of more than he can allow himself to know. The conflict is not between truth and deception, but between the comfort of masks and the desolation of trying to confront more reality than human kind can bear.

For comparable self-doubt and refusal in Browning's monologues we must turn to his Victorian Prufrock, the censorious aesthete in a 'A Toccata of Galuppi's,' who feels old beyond his years. Browning's aesthete is riddled with doubts. Though he responds to the genius of the toccata's lesser Mozart, 'good alike at grave and gay' (26), he betrays deep misgivings about a life devoted to the gratification of the senses. The two-way pull allows the speaker to experience a panic-stricken sense of the transience and hence the seriousness of beauty. Just when we assume that the double irony (or simultaneous endorsement of contradictory codes) is collapsing into single irony and the poet is fully endorsing his speaker's crusade against sinful levity, the monologue restores the two-way pull of its double ironies by unceremoniously toppling the censor from his perch of privilege.

> 'Dust and ashes!' So you creak it, and I want the heart to scold.
> Dear dead women, with such hair, too – what's become of all the gold
> Used to hang and brush their bosoms? I feel chilly and grown old.
>
> 'A Toccata of Galuppi's,' 43–5

Carefully repressed in the first half of the monologue, the word 'Death' grows like a cancer in the last six tercets. The replication of death in the 'cold music,' the 'ghostly cricket,' the twice repeated 'Dust and ashes,' and the 'Dear dead women' is unnervingly repetitive. The shock is greater because of the toccata's lethal ravishments, which displace 'cold' in 'old' and delay the final wrenching transfer of attributes from the music to the speaker: 'I feel chilly and grown old.'

If we have wrongly assumed that the silent poet behind the mask is more sympathetic to his speaker than he is to the censured Baldassaro or the 'dear dead women,' the sudden collapse of the speaker's vaunted superiority in the last chilling line decisively corrects that comforting but dangerous illusion. In 'A Toccata of Galuppi's,' as in Socrates' aporetic dialogues, the 'mastered moment in discourse' is only temporary: it must give way in the end to the 'infinite negativity' that, as Kierkegaard explains, 'finally swept away even Socrates himself.'[7]

In 'Two in the Campagna' the would-be seducer is a Socratic ironist in disguise. Why should the lover's aggressive sexual appropriation of the body of nature – of its 'small orange cup' and 'primal naked forms of flowers' (16, 28) – be all erotic foreplay, without the expected consummation? Why, having touched the woman close, must he stand away, like Joyce's Gabriel Conroy in 'The Dead,' as if he were about to touch a ghost?

Though Browning's ironist wants nothing less than 'Infinite passion' (58) in a single moment, the endless repetition that exalts the celebrant of

'Infinite passion' spells boredom for the Don Juan who wants a single pleasure, sex, an infinite number of times. Bondage to a routine that merely bores and exhausts is precisely the kind of repetitive torture to which Browning's ironist (like the lover *manqué* in 'Dîs Aliter Visum' or in Kierkegaard's book *Repetition: An Essay in Experimental Psychology*) refuses to submit. No monologue better exhibits the irony analysed by Kierkegaard in Socrates' aporetic monologues: an irony which 'in all its divine infinity ... allows nothing to endure.' As a Socratic Samson, the disillusioned lover 'seizes the columns bearing the edifice of knowledge and plunges everything down into the nothingness of ignorance.'[8]

In Browning's monologue 'Dîs Aliter Visum,' the woman who conducts her private inquisition of the modern Byron is a female Socrates who puts into jeopardy whole areas of institutionalized life by placing happy adultery or joyful fornication above a loveless marriage. In her reconstruction of unspoken thoughts, which spares no intimacies of consciousness, the lover she desires is made to muse that any profession of love he would have to 'blurt out' (47) would profane a mystery he can better honour in silence. Ironically, the female inquisitor whom the modern Byron seems to despise means everything to him. Indeed the idea of loving her stirs his imagination and makes him a poet. '"My friend makes verse,"' she observes, '"and gets renown"' (76). But by meaning so much to him, the woman also signs her own death warrant. Because her admirer worships her as an ennobling Muse rather than as a flesh and blood mistress, he refuses to submit their love to the test and challenge of an actual affair.

In dramatizing the terrors that estrange the familiar and domesticate the strange, the woman's mental vagrancy subjects every impulse of her heart to the cold discipline a long-deferred autopsy. For his part, by remaining silent when he should have spoken, the modern Byron seems to have betrayed a hidden god. Such at least is the bearing of the poem's title: 'the gods' thought was or seemed otherwise' (*Aeneid*, 2.428). The source of all joy, the love of repetition, is replaced by despairing recollection, as if the modern lover were at the end of his life while still only at its beginning. In Kierkegaard's words, 'before he begins he has taken such a terrible stride that he has leapt over the whole of life.'[9] What greater elision could there be? He is old before he is young. Before the ironist can propose that the woman become his mistress, he has become an old man, bored by the entire affair.

And yet in sustaining the double irony that keeps alive the subversive spirit of a Socratic dialogue of search, Browning reminds us that there is always another way of interpreting the poem. Instead of saying that the frustrated male lover is deluded, we might say that in his generous response to the embittered female speaker he has been betrayed by his materials. As a tricky exercise in double irony the monologue points two ways at once. It may be intimating that the dreamer who offers exalting beatifications of people is out of touch with the real world. But it seems also to be saying that people ought to live up to the lover's enhancing imagination of them. Just as Kant uses paralogisms and antinomies to mark the limits of conceptual understanding in his *Critique of Pure Reason*, so Jowett believes that Socrates in the *Parmenides* is showing that 'a contradiction in terms is sometimes the best expression of a truth higher than either.' In Jowett's view, Parmenides and Socrates are two 'Gottbetrunkene Menschen' who still believe in 'the idea of "being" or "good," which [cannot] be conceived, defined, uttered, but [cannot] be got rid of.'[10] In this monologue of double ironies and contradictions Browning is also exploring a Socratic truth about hidden gods. He is dramatizing the irreducible mystery and elusiveness of people we admire and are closest to, whom we love and ought to know.

To an ironist like Socrates or Kierkegaard, who pretends to be more ignorant than he is, the dramatic mask is also the instrument of an irony that is the opposite of hypocritical: the Danish philosopher who hides behind a smokescreen of masks, including his infamous *Seducer's Diary*, pretends to be worse, not better, than the real-life Kierkegaard, who is a religious apologist in hiding. Browning's Fra Lippo Lippi is just such an ironist. To show how a religious man hides behind a sensualist's mask, like Kierkegaard in his *Seducer's Diary*, Browning creates the impression of an everyday voice cutting across the worshipful tones and soaring song of a seer who mounts to a plateau of vision where God can be seen creating paradise and Eve. The untroubled conjoining of 'garden and God' (266), whose alliteration half disguises the near syllepsis of seeing God with the same sharp clarity as one sees trees and streams, turns naturally into a more intimate and sensual tone when the monk confesses: 'I'm a beast, I know' (270). The tone of these lyrical lines, half-taunting in their mockery of 'un-learning' what has just been learned, masks the monk's seriousness, just as his seriousness saves the tone from being merely teasing or coy.

Elsewhere the blending of outer humour and inner seriousness that characterizes the Socratic ironist is less assured.

> Signing himself with the other because of Christ
> (Whose sad face on the cross sees only this
> After the passion of a thousand years)
>
> 'Fra Lippo Lippi,' 155–7

There is an uneasy transition from the exalted tragedy of 'Christ's sad face' to the black humour of the murderer's crossing himself in the sanctuary while shaking a fist at his victim's father. Because such bracketed passages seem more in character for Browning than Fra Lippo, they create little holes in the mask. More successful are the passages that balance the claims of colloquial speech and visionary song.

> there's pretty sure to come
> A turn, some warm eve finds me at my saints –
> A laugh, a cry, the business of the world –
> (*Flower o' the peach,*
> *Death for us all, and his own life for each!*)
> And my whole soul revolves, the cup runs over,
> The world and life's too big to pass for a dream ...
>
> 'Fra Lippo Lippi,' 245–51

With the intoxicating lilt and revel of high spirits produced by the strong caesural breaks ('A laugh, a cry, the business of the world'), we become aware of the movement toward prophecy and vision. The lyric design asserts itself, less by the appearance of end-rhymes in 'peach' and 'each' than by the internal resonance of 'whole' and 'soul' and by the overflow of syllables in the hypermetric sixth line, which delicately mimes the overflow of wine in the psalmist's cup.

Like Socrates' wisely ignorant ironist, Fra Lippo Lippi embodies a paradox: as a sensuous cleric, he would seem to be a living contradiction. But he justifies the contradiction by being theologically more orthodox than his Gnostic opponents. Though the friar sounds like the Plato of the magisterial dialogues in his desire to push the sophists from his 'pulpit-place,' his ideas are radically un-Platonic. Like the earlier Platonic school of Augustine and even Anselm, Fra Lippo's chief adversary, the Prior, believes that the only subject worthy of a painter's veneration is the soul, a 'vapour done up like a new-born babe' (185) and wrapped for a time in a negligible envelope called the body. More Platonic than Fra Lippo, the Prior is also less orthodox. For in saving us from the dreadful doom of spirituality, the sensuous friar is also reaffirming the staggering mystery of the Gospel's God-man, a God who ratifies for all time the sanctity attaching to matter and the senses.

Without the disruptive rhythm of the talking voice, there would be no check on the friar's sententiousness: his monologue would deviate into sermon or visionary song. But without the lyric voice to steady the rhythm, the ironist might overshadow the poet behind the mask and eclipse his authority altogether. Instead, at the climaxes of such monologues, Browning allows the tempo and feeling to increase as the rhythm of the speaking voice, riding with surprising force over line-breaks and caesural pauses, brings talking poetry and lyric, speech and song, into a single harmony, where each can support and balance the other.

The most subversive of the classical Victorian monologues, Tennyson's 'Lucretius,' imitates the Socrates of George Grote and Hegel by using Bentham's analytic method of dividing complex wholes into simple components that can be easily grasped. Just as Socrates is careful in the *Apology* to differentiate between his belief in demigods and daemons and his disbelief in the godhead of the sun or moon, so Lucretius makes clear that he is worshipping Venus, not as a sensual appetite, but as a metaphysical principle: 'Ay, but I meant not thee; I meant not her' (85), he says. In search of an ideal auditor or hidden god, Lucretius turns aside from his wife Lucilia to address Venus as two different deities. Like the 'flaring atom-streams' of a universe in dissolution, 'Ruining along the illimitable inane' (38, 40), his swerves of voice trace in the agitated mental state of a Roman Heathcliff the typical trajectory of a Socratic dialogue of search.

Since the sun 'knows' not 'what he sees' (132), Lucretius reaches Socrates' conclusion that the fable of Apollo is absurd as scientific fact. But even as Lucretius tries to salvage from religion an understanding of the gods that will satisfy his imagination without insulting his intelligence, the Roman materialist turns out to be more subversive than Socrates. Whereas Socrates believes there are grounds for moral obligation, Lucretius denies that duty has any meaning in a universe of random atoms: 'Thy duty? What is duty,' he asks the illogically remorseful Lucilia.

Ironically, Tennyson's poetic materialist tries to destroy the imagination in the act of using it. In solemnly presenting the imaginative scheme of science as a true picture of the world, Lucretius's materialism radically distorts imagination by allowing it to strip the world of everything the heart found delightful. Just as Plato's expulsion of the poets from his ideal republic is an act of self-banishment, so Lucretius's atomic philosophy is an effort of the imagination to commit suicide in imitation of the poet-philosopher who expounds a cosmology that leaves no room for his own inventions.

Nowhere is Lucretius more Socratic than in his prayer to Venus, which validates Matthew Arnold's distinction between a pagan religion of the understanding and a medieval religion of the heart. His invocation to the 'myriad universe' (39) is a kind of litany; and in celebrating the ascendancy and omnipotence of 'holy Venus' (67), Lucretius uses the language of prayer. But this is prayer with a difference, for we are participating in a symposium that challenges the adequacy of religion, as does Socrates' *Apology*. Lucretius replaces the worshipper's conventional profession of unworthiness with a blasphemous prediction. He boasts that his own epic, *De Rerum Natura*, will outlast the deity, then he immediately corrects his blasphemy: 'My tongue / Trips, or I speak profanely' (73–4). Afraid that Venus may be angered by his boast, Lucretius ponders whether the gods are capable of anger and speculates about their incapacity for pity even as he appeals to them to pity him. As a stirring example of what Arnold calls religion of the mind, his prayer resembles the subversive Euripides' magnificent invocation in *The Troades*: 'O Zeus, whether thou be intelligence of mankind or compulsion of nature, to thee I prayed.' Lucretius's invocations replace the conventional epithets of praise with searching speculations about the divine nature, and like Socrates and Euripides he tries to work out a definition of the gods in the very act of praying to them.

The Magisterial Socrates and Socrates the Mythmaker

Unlike the aporetic Socrates, who is always a sceptical explorer, the Socrates of the *Phaedo* and *The Republic* is an architect of overarching theories and doctrines. His teaching that justice is the harmony of three parts of the soul in each individual and the harmony of three classes of citizens in the state furnishes Matthew Arnold with his master analogy between four powers in the human person and three classes in society in *Culture and Anarchy*. Plato's doctrine that the world is a pale reflection of true reality also shapes the argument of Joseph Butler's *Analogy of Religion* (1736), which exercises a profound influence on Keble's and Newman's early-Victorian efforts to revive typological readings of secular literature and scripture.

In typological monologues corresponding to the magisterial or 'constructive' dialogues of Plato, Browning and his speaker talk in unison.

The quotation from St Paul that serves as the subtitle to 'Cleon' alerts us to those latent affinities between Greek and Christian thought that allow the words of Browning and his Greek philosopher momentarily to converge. The adjective 'strange,' which tends to be buried in the long, unwieldy title of Karshish's monologue, alerts us to the odd, deeply subterranean affinities between the strange experience of the Arab physician and the Christian apologist behind the mask, who is related to the Christ of history as the resurrected Christ himself is related to the risen Lazarus. When the concerns of Browning and his speaker converge completely in the first half of 'Abt Vogler' or at the climax of 'Saul,' the voice we hear is so authoritative and oracular that the dramatic form is shattered and the monologue turns momentarily into a visionary poem. As a prayerful rhetoric of disinterested attention leads the speaker to substitute God for an absent human auditor, disinterested persuasion begins to replace applied persuasion: at such moments an ideal auditor breaks through the monologue from the far side of silence, disclosing at the centre of each life and at the centre of history itself a superintending pattern or design.

David's first parenthesis in section 17 of 'Saul' is a kind of theological stage direction: '(With that stoop of the soul which in bending upraises it too)' (252); and the second, '('I laugh as I think')' (258) supports Kierkegaard's claim that religion is to ethics what humour or comedy is to irony. The third parenthesis, '(as my warm tears attest)' (275), is a testament to the fact that love transforms 'scientia' or knowledge into the kind of wisdom that is less an abstract concept than a concrete entity of mind and feeling, a person. The stoop that exalts not only prefigures the Incarnation but also traces the curve of David's own exalted feeling of depending on another. When 'God is seen God' (249), it is not because he is naturally immanent in creation, as Paley argues in his *Evidences of Christianity*, but because, as in Schleiermacher's theology, each imperfection or feeling of dependence implies its perfecting counterpart in a God of power and love. Ironically, just after mocking his own impotent volitions ('I will? – the mere atoms despise me!') (292), the self-critical and reluctant prophet changes masks. Switching the auxiliaries of a simple future tense into bold auxiliaries of volition and decree: ('So wouldst thou – so wilt thou!') (300), David launches into his most audacious and convincing prophecy of the Logos, a wisdom that has grown into revelation and vision.

Since it is mad to seek direct contact with God, the way Lazarus does, Browning prefers to encounter God obliquely, as an Other who has abdicated in favour of such mediators of his glory as the biblical David, who can approach God only through his love and moral compassion for Saul. Since sorrow and self-denial are the mark of such love and obligation, Browning reads a story of tremendous rivalry into the Crucifixion. If the Creator had not been crucified, he would have been a lesser being than thousands of such rivals as the suffering David.

The face of a silent auditor always bears a trace of the Other. And the faintness of this trace cannot obscure the fact that in 'Saul' a 'Face like my face' (310) can also be an epiphany, a manifestation of the Other. Because the creative initiative belongs to the Other alone, monologues like 'Saul' and 'Abt Vogler' dramatize an utter dissymmetry. As Paul Ricoeur says, the philosopher 'has to admit that one does not know and cannot say whether this Other, the source of the injunction, is another person whom I can look in the face or who can stare at me, or my ancestors for whom there is no representation.'[11] Though Browning is always trying to replace the lonely God of Power with the loving God of Relationship, he recognizes that the 'Face like my face' in 'Saul' (310) is an elevation – the Face of the Other – and that it summons the self from on high like the voice that speaks to Job through the whirlwind or to Karshish through the thunder.

According to John Keble, great poetry exists only as a fallout from religion. The monologue's vocatives of direct address to a naturalized spirit or daemon are the expressive evidence of divine power. As applied persuasion is replaced by disinterested persuasion, this Other may become as imposing and magisterial as the Voice that speaks to Moses on Sinai. The authority of the unnameable Other restores a dimension of soul-power and mystery to the monologue, as does the Unknown God of Socrates, who is 'past finding out' (*Timaeus*, 28E). Many of the questers in religious monologues are homeless believers, speaking as the alone to the Alone. Against the dark background of natural annihilation, all intensities of consciousness seem merely to terminate in a grave. Cleon's monologue recreates the terror with which the pagan philosopher argues speciously against the nothingness of human matters and tries to avert the consequences of what Browning believes to be the metaphysical and religious dilemma confronting every human being. It is for this reason that a monologue often affirms no doctrine or creed but seeks instead to show what a solitary speaker like Browning's Karshish or Cleon does with his aloneness. When applied rhetoric becomes disinterested and the auditor turns into the silent Other, the speaker's attentiveness becomes an attentiveness without a nameable object: it becomes prayer in its purest form.

Vividly imagining the posthumous tortures of wicked souls in Tartarus and the progressive refinement of more virtuous souls in higher regions of consciousness, Socrates in the *Phaedo* reaffirms as a mythmaker the venerable Greek tradition of evolutionary theology. Just as Aeschylus's Zeus develops a conscience at Athena's insistence in the *Oresteia*, so Setebos, the cruel god of Browning's Caliban, may someday evolve into a moral god, the Quiet, who (like Socrates' ethical hero in the *Gorgias*) would prefer to suffer evil passively than commit it. The analogical daring of Browning's Caliban, who expounds his theology from a swamp, reads as a gloss upon Benjamin Jowett's own comment on Plato's *Parmenides*: 'in the meanest operations of nature as well as in the noblest, in mud and filth as well as in the sun and stars, great truths are contained.'[12]

A monologue of search like 'Dîs Aliter Visum; or, Le Byron de Nos Jours' swerves back and forth unpredictably among several time frames. One hallmark of the magisterial monologue is its use of chiasmus to stabilize these swerves. Instead of merely opposing earth to heaven in an antithetical construction – 'On the earth the broken arcs; in the heaven, a perfect round' ('Abt Vogler,' 72) – a magisterial monologue will often make syntax bend back on itself in a chiastic bow-shape or curve.

> And the emulous heaven yearned down, made effort to reach the earth,
> As the earth had done her best, in my passion, to scale the sky:
> 'Abt Vogler,' 27–8

Thrusting out with the fling of a great cantilever or arc, Abt Vogler's lines offer the most magisterial chiasmus in all of Browning. The firmness of the rhymes secures the juncture, making it as sure a point of contact as God's touching of Adam's finger in the Sistine Chapel painting: 'but here is the finger of God, a flash of the will that can' ('Abt Vogler,' 49).

To create the illusion that he has been careful to evaluate and judge life, even Andrea del Sarto uses the rhetoric of the magisterial Abt Vogler when speaking chiastically: 'so much less! / Well, less is more, Lucrezia,' 'Yet the will's somewhat – somewhat, too, the power' (77–8, 139). At times Andrea talks like a mere parody of a seer, pulling himself up from defeat or decline by formulating some high-sounding but spurious maxim of reversal that forces the syntax to round back on itself instead of opening up spontaneously: 'In this world, who can do a thing, will not; / And who would do it, cannot, I perceive' (137–8). Though such turns on hinge words are inconceivable when Andrea is tracing temporal decline – 'days decrease, / And autumn grows, autumn in everything' (44–5) – Browning often imposes on the linear pathos of such passages the chiastic paradoxes of a sage who has leisure to look back on life and analyse it.

The Apologetic Socrates: Acting versus Acting Out

Socrates' dialogue the *Apology* bears the same relation to most of his earlier dialogues as apologetic monologues like Tennyson's 'St. Simeon Stylites' and Browning's 'Bishop Blougram's Apology' bear to the portrayal of religion or the psychology of martyrdom in stage plays like Tennyson's *Becket* and *Queen Mary*. In the *Apology* Socrates systematically defends himself against the crimes he is charged with. But his accusers Meletus, Antyus, and Lycon are not allowed to speak for themselves. In reformulating Meletus's charge of atheism, for example, Socrates presents it as a playful 'contradiction.' Since Socrates has been charged with simultaneously not believing in the gods and yet believing in them, he concludes that his accuser must be 'reckless and impudent.' Meletus's self-contradiction exhibits 'a spirit of mere wantonness and youthful bravado.'[13]

When compared to a genuine dialogue or a stage play, where speakers may be interrupted or heckled, an apologetic monologue may sound as rehearsed and prescripted as a defence attorney's summation to a jury. 'Bishop Blougram's Apology' contrasts a mere stage-tragedy death with real death, which is unrehearsed and unscripted (66–74). An actor is usually just as suprised or caught off guard by the heckling of a dissatisfied audience as is the actor who played death on stage only to be touched by 'Death himself' (74) when he retires to the dressing room. An off-stage death touches us upon the sleeve familiarly, and it takes place just when we think the play is over, after the curtain falls and no one can see what is happening.

Real death is to its stage-tragedy version what the open-ended action of a play or a dialogue is to Bishop Blougram's own acting out of his apology: a carefully rehearsed defence of a pragmatic theory of faith. Whenever Gigadibs, the sceptical auditor, is allowed to voice an objection, it is because the Bishop has thought of a way of converting his adversary's charge to his own rhetorical advantage, just as Socrates in his dialogue the *Apology* deftly deflects Meletus's charge by showing it is only a 'facetious contradiction.'[14]

Throughout his apology Blougram keeps voicing his adversary's unspoken criticism, 'So, you despise me, Mr. Gigadibs' (13, 143, 970): it is an important part of the apologist's strategy to implant in his adversary's mind the subversive thought that the adversary secretly admires him. Like Socrates, Blougram realizes that he either must not argue with his empirical adversary at all, or must argue with him on empirical grounds. In doing so he is giving Gigadibs not just a theology lesson but preliminary training in dialectic and controversy. Instead, however, of trying to prove logically that Gigadibs as an empiricist cannot consistently dislike a more rigorous empiricist, Blougram acts out this contradiction in his conversation and gestures: 'No more wine?'; 'try the cooler jug – / Put back the other, but don't jog the ice!' (132–3). By using these material comforts as stage props in the closed theatre of his monologue, the Bishop hopes to break down the sceptic's illogical resistance to the benefits of a more consistently applied pragmatism.

Carefully orchestrating his apology, Blougram repeats Gigadibs's objections only when he thinks of ways of cleverly deflecting them. Gigadibs's false disjunction – 'all' or 'nothing' – for example, is easily ridiculed by picturing it as the absurd destitution of the traveller who peeps up 'from ... utterly naked boards' (130) after jettisoning his possessions. Blougram can also allow Gigadibs to make the charge that no dogmas 'nail' (154) the Bishop's faith because the sceptic's grammar is active and the double sense of 'nail' does more to exonerate the Bishop than indict him.

Blougram uses his adversary as his stooge. Instead of catching the Bishop off guard, Gigadibs, the less consistent and subtle sceptic, plays directly into his more intelligent adversary's hands. Blougram wants to show that because being a believer means living the contradiction of good and evil, it also means not being a believer. Gigadibs is allowed to oppose faith to unbelief only because it makes the Bishop sound more intelligent when he paradoxically identifies the terms that his adversary has opposed: 'faith means perpetual unbelief' (666). The readjustment of the empirical views of life and faith gives the Bishop's apology clarity and complexity and makes his rhetoric art. But in exposing his adversary's self-conceit and inconsistency for what they are, there is never any sense that Blougram is assimilating new insights as he proceeds, learning as much from his heckler as the heckler learns from him.

Since Blougram's apology is as carefully rehearsed as Newman's or Socrates,' it is in Gigadibs's interest to 'win' by 'losing': to concede defeat in the debate in order to gain success in his life. When the biblical and literal uses of the word 'sheep' converge at the end of the monologue, we are reminded once again how the acting out of a prepared script allows no counter-play to intrude. On his sheep farm in Australia, where he is urged to study his last chapter of St John – 'Feed my sheep' – Gigadibs will still be enslaved by flocks while Blougram rules as undisputed master of his fold.

Though F.H. Bradley's *Ethical Studies* (1876) appeared too late to influence most of Browning's monologues, there are important Socratic affinities between the two writers. The subversive turn in Browning's ethical thought occurs at the moment when the ethical moralist, the champion of 'my station and its duties,' is catapulted into the sphere of what Bradley calls 'ideal morality.' Here he must function as a Socratic practitioner of what might paradoxically (but more accurately) be called 'ethical immorality,' a Socratic effort to maximize personal value even at the cost of violating cultural mores or norms. The catalyst in this process is the Faustian overreacher, a revolutionary character like Browning's Paracelsus, who strains against the limits of mere custom or convention.

The hedonist who advocates 'pleasure for pleasure's sake' is a Don Juan who refuses like the lover in 'Le Byron de Nos Jours' or 'Two in the Campagna' to will an endless repetition of the sensuous moment. Instead of wanting one thing, sex, an infinite number of times, he wants to experience an infinite number of things in a single instant, like Faust. Browning's critique of Don Juan's bad faith and boredom resembles F.H. Bradley's and Kierkegaard's. Equally self-defeating are the empty precepts of an unethical moralist like Browning's prior in 'Fra Lippo Lippi.' Embodying Bradley's doctrine of 'duty for duty's sake,' the prior blocks the moral, artistic, and even the spiritual development of the monk. Even Browning's dull grammarian or his faithful but plodding poet in 'How It Strikes a Contemporary' marks the limits of Bradley's injunction to discharge the responsibilities of one's 'station and its duties.'

Two of the most eminent 'ethical immoralists' of the Victorian era are George Eliot and Robert Browning. Eliot lived out of wedlock with G.H. Lewes while his deranged wife was still alive. And Robert Browning eloped with Elizabeth Barrett against her tyrannical father's will. Given the extraordinary social circumstances of their acts of deliverance, however, the self-realization of Browning's Caponsacchi and of the Perseus-like saviours in 'The Glove' and 'Count Gismond' is ultimately just as ethical as Eliot's rewarding union with Lewes or Browning's heroic elopement with Elizabeth Barrett.

It is true that such deeds of self-realization are not conventionally moral. As assaults upon King Nomos or the dictates of mere convention, they may even seem immoral. Hence the paradox of a subversive Socratic hero or heroine who in defying the moral law may with some justice be called an 'ethical immoralist.' In F.H. Bradley's memorable words, 'man is not man at all unless social, but man is not much above the beasts unless more than social.'[15] Or as G.K. Chesterton says, in eloping with Elizabeth Robert had 'the same difficulty as Caponsacchi, the supreme difficulty of having to trust himself the reality of virtue not only without the reward, but even without the name of virtue.' The moral Socrates must be prepared to seem immoral. When the hour comes, he must be ready to walk 'in his own devotion and certainty in a position counted indefensible and almost along the brink of murder.'[16]

Hegel believes that, unlike Christ's parables or the analects of Confucius, Socrates' wisdom can be explained by the method of inquiry popularized by the Sophists. Indeed George Grote, praising Socrates as the greatest of the Sophists, favourably compares his rational methods to the quantitative moral analysis of the Utilitarians. In clearing away the intellectual idols denounced by Bacon, this rational Socrates brings to the study of ethics the same method of logical aggregates associated with Bentham and with the atomic philosophy Tennyson dramatizes in his monologue 'Lucretius.' Compared with the mysterious Crucifixion narratives in the Gospels, which are too profound for tidy minds to limit, even Socrates' death in the *Apology* is an intellectual morality play totally secularized and staged as an ironic comedy of ideas. The effect of such rationalism and irony is to reduce the mystery of the unknown Socrates to the flatness and fixity of a two-dimensional mask. He is the prototype of Ben Jonson's humour characters, including the male chauvinist caricatured by Amy Levy in her monologue 'Xantippe,' a Socrates who is incapable of moving beyond the obsessive 'self-ignorance' he exhibits or the subversive intellectual acts he seems impelled to repeat.

It must be conceded, however, that the Socrates I have just been describing has more in common with the apologetic seer of the *Apology* or with the buffoon of Aristophanes' comedy *The Clouds* than with the Socrates of the aporetic dialogues. The latter is the subversive Socrates, the ironist of pure negativity, who cannot in the end be reconciled with Grote's attempt to see him as a Greek Utilitarian or with Hegel's tendency to identify him with the most enlightened of the Sophists. Because the subversive Socrates is always trying to escape from intellectual bondage, he has to keep his exit routes open by remaining conscious at every moment that no single doctrine or creed has any ultimate claim on him. The best exponent of Socrates' 'negative independence of everything'[17] is the young Kierkegaard, whose academic dissertation *The Concept of Irony* preserves the contrast between positive and negative identity while associating the elusiveness with Socrates and the stability with Christ. Kierkegaard argues that the mystery of Socrates' identity goes deeper than the mystery of Christ's identity, since the philosopher has more negative capability. Compared with Socrates, even the most open community of honest and thinking Christians seems to cherish a passion for submission. Whereas Socrates 'returns' from the world 'empty-handed,' and his 'ironical personality is ... merely the outline of a personality,' Christ's relation to the world is 'absolutely real.'[18] To smash Narcissus's mirror Browning's David has only to proclaim his real identity as a member of the Logos, a body whose power is totally decentralized, as Northrop Frye says, because 'the whole is complete within each individual.'[19]

Monologues of doubt and deliberation assume that a Socratic inquirer gains a grip on truth by exposing logical fallacies in an adversary's arguments. But no one knows better than Socrates that a logician's soul may be icy and Olympian. To know truth is also to become a friend of Socrates, who lives and embodies truths he can never prove. Browning's Bishop Blougram is a deft logician but an unlovable cleric. David's intelligence may be baffled and defeated in 'Saul,' but his love is transparent. The best monologues, like the best Socratic dialogues, show that there are two roads to truth – through *elenchus* and through embodiment. Truth is disclosed not just through Socrates' paradox of learned ignorance. It is also achieved through his habit of open inquiry. We detect a flash of this habit in the disarming avowal, 'I would meet you upon this honestly' in T.S. Eliot's 'Gerontion' (56), and in all monologues whose swerves of voice and mood trace the way of elusive wisdom and hidden gods.

'Technology is the Promethean gift of Descartes' – the gift of method – 'realized as a way of life.'[20] To yield to the technological impulse is to lose philosophy's ancient task of pursuing the Socratic goal of wisdom and self-knowledge. By unmasking the truth of opposites in such unexpected places as the vernacular spirituality of Browning's Fra Lippo Lippi or the inspired folly of T.S. Eliot's Magi, the dramatic monologue recovers the classic function of the wise fool or ironist. Instead of seeing the world of objects as shadows in Plato's cave, the monologues now view them as reversible images of folly and wisdom, ignorance and knowledge, constantly changing position in a Socratic mirror. Whatever George Grote may say to the contrary about Socrates' invention of a method, Socrates' dialogues sponsor something profoundly more important than a method: the pursuit of wisdom and the quest for an examined life. As a charm to be used against the positivist's love of facts and objects, the dramatic monologue helps a technological society recover its origins in learned ignorance and Socratic humanism. Instead of exercising direct political control, Browning's poet in 'How It Strikes a Contemporary' operates secretly as God's spy. Peering sceptically behind his neighbours' masks, he affirms the value of lost wisdom and hidden powers.

3

Coleridge's Legacy: Naturalizing the Vocative

In swerving passionately from its inquisition of a personified dawn to an elegiac statement about the speaker's own oblivion and silence as a part of nature, Tennyson's monologue 'Tithonus' suddenly redirects the voice it evokes by trying to remove it altogether: 'I earth in earth forget these empty courts, / And thee returning on thy silver wheels' ('Tithonus,' 75–6). The defining trope of the dramatic monologue is not prosopopoeia, the figure of address that Tennyson's Tithonus uses to personify the dawn as the goddess Aurora. Nor is it *exclamatio* or *ecphonesis*, the 'Oh' of outcry that in Browning's monologue 'One Word More' functions as a rhetorical signpost of admiration and wonder: 'Oh, their Rafael of the dear Madonnas,/ Oh, their Dante of the dread Inferno' (198–9). The trope that sets the monologue apart from other genres is the swerve or turn of voice that rhetoricians identify with *aversio* or apostrophe: it is a more subversive and unpredictable figure of speech than either prosopopoeia or *exclamatio*. Several examples can be found in 'A Toccata of Galuppi's,' where tropes of deviation first direct the voice of Browning's Victorian Prufrock away from Galuppi's music to the dead musician himself. They then redirect that voice a second time by deflecting it from the dear dead women with the golden hair to the speaker's own mortality: 'I feel chilly and grown old' (45). Ironically, one of the monologue's most rending swerves occurs at the precise moment the speaker resolves, in his proud rationality, never to 'swerve':

> But when I sit down to reason, think to take my stand nor swerve,
> ... In you come with your cold music till I creep through every nerve.
> 'A Toccata of Galuppi's,' 31, 33

Douglas Kneale, the scholar who writes most discerningly about the difference between the swerve of voice associated with tropes of apostrophe or *aversio* and mere vocatives of direct address, takes Jonathan Culler to task for blurring the distinction.[1] Only if we support Kneale's attempt to distinguish between apostrophe and address can we trace the monologue to its genesis in the double auditors – both visible and hidden – of many Romantic elegies, odes, and conversation poems.

An important prototype of the monologue's swerves and deviations is Wordsworth's elegiac sonnet 'Surprised by joy,' where the apparent auditor, the young daughter who is addressed, is not an auditor at all.

> Surprised by joy – impatient as the Wind
> I turned to share the transport – Oh! with whom
>
> 'Surprised by joy,' 1–2

The first transport of feeling is dramatized by the dash before 'impatient' and the second by the dash before the soul-wrenching apostrophe: 'Oh! with whom.' The self-reproachful question 'But how could I forget thee?' (6) establishes the pattern of a subversive swerve or turn of voice followed by after-swerves or turns that are more wrenching each time they occur.

> – That thought's return
> Was the worst pang that sorrow ever bore,
> Save one, one only
>
> 'Surprised by joy,' 9–11

Every swerve of voice in this interior monologue helps the elegist revise his meaning by passing from the auditor he seems to be addressing to his most important auditor, in this case the mourner himself, the person he must tutor and try to console.

Wordsworth's apostrophic 'Oh' is the paradigm of all those swerves or turns of voice that in the best dramatic monologues keep deflecting attention from the silent auditor to the speaker. Instead of addressing Lucrezia, Browning's Andrea del Sarto is doing something more subtle and self-serving. By shifting blame to an auditor he has been too weak to influence in real life, he is trying to sound strong or heroic to an ideal auditor, God, and – ultimately – to himself. In the subversive swerve or turn that allows the Romantic elegist to pass from one auditor to another, we find an immediate and important precursor of the dramatic monologue's own vocal turns from applied to disinterested persuasion.

Jonathan Culler has shown how the lyric convention of apostrophizing nonhuman objects has come to seem increasingly remote to nineteenth-century and modern poets. Though a venerable lyric tradition of addressing the breeze, the dawn, or the nightingale affirms and celebrates the poet's words of power, only inmates of mental hospitals would actually talk to birds, trees, and doors – much less to holes in a wall, as Pound's speaker does in 'Marvoil.' We resist the poets' claims, and we feel embarrassed when they think they can change the natural world by doing magical things with words.

The single most important explanation of how the Victorian monologue dramatically displaces rapturous lyric apostrophes to nature spirits and daemons appears in John Keble's review of Lockhart's *Life of Scott*, and in Keble's *Praelectiones Academicae* (1832–41), also known as his *Oxford Lectures on Poetry*. Both works argue that all dramatic and epic genres are displacements of a poet's lyric impulse. Thus Virgil's epic the *Aeneid* is said to disguise a pastoral yearning, indulged most directly in the *Georgics*. A poet writing a lyric is under little restraint to 'any sudden burst of high or plaintive feeling' he may choose to indulge (Keble, 'Review,' p. 440). Such is not the case, however, with classical epic, where a persona is 'interposed, as a kind of transparent veil, between the listener and the narrator's real drift and feelings' ('Review,' p. 436). Keble's observation applies with equal force to a monologue like Tennyson's 'Demeter and Persephone,' where the great Earth-Mother's indictment of Zeus for the loss of her daughter acts as 'a safety-valve to [the] full mind'[2] of the grieving Tennyson, whose younger son, Lionel, had just died on his return voyage from India. Like the narrative structure of a prose romance by Sir Walter Scott or an epic action by Virgil, the classical monologue uses its mask to veil a deep confessional impulse.

Keble invites a critic to study the effects of the poet's dramatic displacements not only in the poet's naturalizing of the vocatives of direct address but also in his experiments with metre. In colloquial asides to a silent or an absent auditor, as in Coleridge's conversation poems, the speaker in a monologue often substitutes the irregular metres and casual idioms of 'talking poetry' for those exalted and formal apostrophes to the breeze, the ambrosial air, or other surrogates of the Holy Spirit that manage to keep nineteenth-century nature poetry so remarkably well ventilated.

Naturalizing the Vocative: Coleridge's Conversation Poems

Coleridge's conversation poems naturalize the ode and lyric by substituting, for formal apostrophes to seasons, places, and natural phenomena, the dramatic monologue's vocatives of direct address to a person. In 'This Lime-Tree Bower My Prison' (1797) Coleridge vacillates between both uses of the vocative: between address to his absent friend, Charles Lamb, and apostrophes to the sun, clouds, and ocean.

> but thou, methinks, most glad,
> My gentle-hearted Charles! for thou hast pined
> And hungered after Nature, many a year,
> In the great City pent, ...
> ...
> Ah! slowly sink
> Behind the western ridge, thou glorious sun!
> Shine in the slant beams of the sinking orb,
> Ye purple heath-flowers! richlier burn, ye clouds!
> Live in the yellow light, ye distant groves!
> And kindle, thou blue ocean!
>
> 'This Lime-Tree Bower My Prison,' 27–37

Though there are two auditors, the apostrophes to the nonhuman auditors are subordinated to the poet's address to his friend, for whose benefit these natural phenomena – no longer inanimate objects now, but actors – are invited to perform.

To apostrophize the natural objects as 'thou ... sun,' 'Ye purple heath-flowers,' 'ye clouds,' 'ye groves,' and 'thou blue ocean' is to bring them to life as dramatis personae in the theatre of the poet's mind. Coleridge commands the 'glorious sun' to sink in majesty, the purple flowers to shine, the clouds to burn, the grove to live in light, and even the ocean to kindle, so that his absent friend, Charles, a city-dweller and a stranger to such mysteries, may be 'Struck with deep joy' and 'stand,' as Coleridge has stood, 'Silent with swimming sense' (38–9). As a lord and sovereign over outward sense, the magician who apostrophizes these objects and commands them to act is already celebrating his power as a master of the revels, a kind of Nether Stowey Prospero.

In 'The Eolian Harp' (1795) Coleridge's hushed world of cottage, bean-field, and 'distant sea' (11) commemorates what Browning would call 'a good moment,' a triumph of apostrophic time over simple narrative.

Nothing external actually happens in the poem, because the speaker's vocative of direct address to Sara and his meditation on the harp internalize the action, changing every event into a drama in his own mind. The music made by the desultory breeze as it caresses the harp is valued only for the music of the world-soul that it awakens in the listener who uses synaesthesia and apostrophe – 'O the one life within us and abroad' (26) – to produce marvelling impressions of the 'Rhythm in all thought' (29) and the reversing chiastic flow of 'light in sound, a sound-like power in light' (28).

Even when the speaker registers Sara's gesture of 'mild reproof' (49), he mutes and controls it by using a negative verbal construction – 'not reject' – and a negative form of the adjective, 'unhallowed': 'nor such thoughts / Dim and *un*hallowed does thou *not* reject' (50–1; emphasis added). Both the vocatives of direct address to Sara and the apostrophes to the world-soul, 'the one life within us and abroad,' alert us to the transforming power not so much of Sara or the world-soul as of the poetic voice itself. But Sara is not just critical of the speaker's pantheism. Though she may reject as unorthodox his parody of grace in protest against the dogma of original sin, she is also slightly amused, I think, by his mental bombast and solemnity. For in failing to acknowledge the erotic value of her 'soft cheek' (1) and of the 'delicious surges' of the music's 'long sequacious notes,' as they 'sink and rise' (18–19), Coleridge's speaker is subtly but insistently misreading the music. In such a conversation poem we find a prototype of all dramatic monologues, whose most important disclosures are unconscious, and whose silent auditors are present mainly to provoke activity in the speaker and to delegate their potential power to *him*.

In 'Frost at Midnight' (1798) the silence and incomprehension of the speaker's auditor – the sleeping infant who is twice addressed as 'babe' – allow Coleridge to exercise prophetic authority without any fear of being reproved or checked by a critical listener like Sara. The speaker's vocatives of direct address to his son bring together two forms of discourse: the poet's private language and the 'eternal language' of God, who uses a form of divine chiasmus to 'teach / Himself in all, and all things in himself' (60–2). 'So shalt thou see and hear,' Coleridge prophesies, in a beautiful use of the auxiliary verb of exhortation and decree,

> The lovely shapes and sounds intelligible
> Of that eternal language, which thy God
> Utters, who from eternity doth teach
> Himself in all, and all things in himself.

Great universal Teacher! he shall mould
Thy spirit, and by giving make it ask.

'Frost at Midnight,' 58–64

Celebrating the future education of the child as a potential presence, Coleridge preempts the place of the 'God' and his 'secret ministry of frost' (72), which have been valued tutors of his own heart, by dramatizing his role as the Teacher's prophet.

Coleridge's conversation poem 'The Nightingale' (1798) uses a double vocative: an apostrophe to the bird and an address to two human auditors, the poet's sister and his friend. The most conversational feature of the poem is the speaker's self-critical reinvention of his meaning. No sooner has Coleridge quoted Milton's memorable description of the nightingale as 'most musical, most melancholy' (13) than he takes issue with it:

A melancholy bird? Oh! idle thought!
In nature there is nothing melancholy.

'The Nightingale,' 14–15

Since he disagrees with Milton, why does Coleridge not revise his first thoughts by removing the two adjectives he places in quotation marks?

I think Coleridge prefers to let his original impressions stand in order to dramatize the difference between a mere description of a bird and the drama of a mind trying to chart the exact truth about its subject. Properly appreciated, the nightingale 'Should make all Nature lovelier, and itself / Be loved like Nature!' (33–4). Only by degrees does Coleridge stumble on the truth that in the nightingale's strains a listener hears only the music he has already composed in his heart. Paradoxically, even in seeming to establish powerful relations between the speaker and the nightingale, the apostrophes to the bird – 'Farewell, O Warbler!'; 'Once more, farewell, / Sweet Nightingale!' (87, 109–10) – turn description into event by locating the bird in a region of Coleridge's mind. By internalizing birds and people that seem at first to be external, the vocatives and apostrophes of direct address substitute the unpredictable and always changing force of an event for the stable and unchanging accuracy of an objective description:

Well! –
It is a father's tale: But if that Heaven
Should give me life, his childhood shall grow up

Familiar with these songs, that with the night
He may associate joy. – Once more, farewell,
Sweet Nightingale! Once more, my friends! farewell.

'The Nightingale,' 105–10

As the drama in progress spills across the boundaries of the monologue's formal farewells, Coleridge finds that it can be kept alive only in
the memory of his son and in the minds of future generations of friends
and readers.

The vocative is the defining trope of the Victorian monologue, which
naturalizes the apostrophes of Coleridge's conversation poems by transforming them into a speaker's seduction of a silent listener. But behind
the vocative we can still hear the apostrophes of lyric poetry, and the
more audible these apostrophes become, the more aware we also are of
the ventriloquist who speaks through his puppets. By functioning as a
trope of deflection that 'complicate[s] or disrupt[s] the circuit of communication,'[3] apostrophes and vocatives raise important questions about
who is being addressed in a monologue and about who is being heard.
The dead musician whom the speaker addresses in Robert Browning's
'A Toccata of Galuppi's' (1855) is not a living person but a ghost, a
spectral presence. And that monologue's vocatives also make us aware
of another ghost: the ghost of the poet, who is the spectre or phantom
behind the mask.

A talking-song is to a soliloquy what 'acting out' is to acting, or
what lyric fantasy is to dramatic discovery. We 'overhear' the make-
believe of a lyrical 'talking-song,' but we 'hear' the self-consciously
plotted argument of a dramatic 'soliloquy.' Whenever we eavesdrop on
a speaker, we are likely to tune in to his lyric vagrancies and trespass
on his privacy. Even as speakers in dramatic monologues turn toward
empirical listeners, they may also turn away from them by addressing
dead musicians, imagined tombs, or the portraits of ghosts. Vocatives that are addressed to present auditors are replaced by lyric asides
to phantoms, natural objects, works of art, or other, less perceptible
entities.

In gesturing toward the portrait of his last duchess, Browning's Duke
is deflecting attention from his auditor. His marvelling lyric swerves – 'I
call / That piece a wonder, now,' 'Notice Neptune, though' ('My Last
Duchess,' 2–3, 54) – displace the Duke's ostensible rhetorical motive: his
attempt to gain a dowry by favourably impressing the envoy and the
Count. Dramatic monologues might be defined as poems in which lyric

absorption in inanimate objects like the Bishop of St Praxed's tomb or Fra Pandolf's portrait of the Duke of Ferrara's wife continually deflect a speaker's ostensible attempt to seduce an auditor verbally.[4] The speaker's undoing comes from the power of his swerves, usually signalled by deictics or vocatives, to turn aside and complicate his rhetorical appeals to an auditor.

These asides or swerves evoke not so much a powerful response to or feeling about the object addressed as an intense feeling for the subversive act of invoking itself. The function of the vocative or the apostrophe is to bend to the speaker's will the inanimate or dead objects that the speaker addresses. As Culler says, 'to apostrophize is to will a state of affairs, to attempt to call it into being.'[5] Since it also assumes a world of sentient forces or unseen powers, potentially responsive to human desires, apostrophes and vocatives always posit the power of a dramatic monologue to turn description into event and to make something unforeseen happen.

The Apostrophic Swerve: A Trope of Deviation

To naturalize a lyric convention that poets find increasingly venerable but remote, the dramatic monologue substitutes a human auditor for a nonhuman one. Instead of talking to the dawn, Tithonus addresses a beautiful woman, the goddess who becomes the silent auditor of his dramatic monologue. Birds, trees, and doors cannot talk back to the lyric poet who apostrophizes them. And neither can the auditor in a monologue. In both cases, the one-sided address is also a form of 'doing-by-saying,'[6] an exercise of the speaker's performative power in an attempt to influence the person who is apostrophized or addressed.

There is a close connection between the use of vocatives in elegies and monologues. We cannot literally talk to dead musicians, but because one condition of reading Browning's elegiac monologue 'A Toccata of Galupppi's' is to do just that, it is already too late to retract the rhetorical trope of conversing with a ghost once we register the fallacy it entails. An error is exposed and repudiated, repeated and perpetuated, at one and the same time. Like ghostly conjuring, personified apostrophe exposes its artifice at the very moment it invites acceptance as a fiction we live by, as an instance of what Coleridge calls 'poetic faith.'

One discursive germ of the dramatic monologue is a speaker's one-sided address to a silent auditor, which represents a humanized form of the standard lyric apostrophe. Another possible origin of the genre is the free indirect discourse – 'le style indirect libre' – of the social novelist. Without abandoning the pretence that the narrator is still speaking, free indirect discourse reproduces the inmost thoughts of a dramatic character. The swift changes in point of view, alternating between the narrator's commentary and the thoughts of the impersonated character, may be hard to plot in a novel. Yet instances abound in *Middlemarch*, as David Lodge has shown, and we can find several examples in Trollope's fiction.[7] Though the device exists in Austen's novels, and thus antedates not just George Eliot and Trollope but also the post-Romantic monologue itself, free indirect discourse plays an increasingly dominant role in Victorian prose fiction, whose narrators are often among the novel's most complex characters.

Traces of the poet all but disappear in a dramatic monologue. But they may still be discernible in the monologues' epigraphs, in the slippage of its masks, or occasionally (as in the postscript to 'Bishop Blougram's Apology' [1855]) in the poet's own intrusive commentary. The possible origin of the monologue in free indirect discourse explains the genre's status as ventriloquized lyric. In principle, the monologue is not 'monological' at all, in Bakhtin's sense. Its form is 'dialogical,' a supple and agile interplay between silent auditors, impersonated characters, and the poet who impersonates them.

To invoke a ghost is also to animate it. To withhold existence from a power we address is to contradict an invocation's first axiom of faith. If we successfully invoke and petition God, he may not only speak to us but also acknowledge our demands. Each answer to a prayer is implicit in its address; the Anglo-Saxon *biddan*, like the German *ersuchen*, is a verb of both entreaty and demand. When Childe Roland boldly summons up the dead comrades of his youth, he cannot in his next breath banish them to oblivion. Nor can Master Hugues apostrophize phantoms only to deny that they exist.

Whereas some dramatic action has to be developed in a stage play, nothing need happen in a dramatic monologue, because the monologue's address to a ghost or its invocation of a living person is itself the happening. What is dead can be conjured from the grave and what is living can be interred. Even when the speaker in 'A Toccata of Galuppi's' feels 'chilly and grown old' (45), he may also triumph over time by using invocation to turn the temporal transition from eighteenth-century Venice to Victorian England into a reversible movement from the age of Darwin back to the eighteenth century. Browning contrasts the one-way movement of narrative, where time has an arrow, with the reversible, two-way flow of a monologue's vocatives of ghostly address.

When Browning's amateur scientist conjures the ghost of the dead musician Baldassare Galuppi, he locates it in the time of the invocation. The time of the vocative is always a special time, the 'now' of an event rather than a mere descriptive moment that traces the path of a sequential narrative or story. Everything invoked in a monologue becomes an actor or stage prop in the improvised drama that the monologue is aspiring to become.

Though the monologue's origin in Romantic vocatives and apostrophes is a complex story, its main outlines can now be traced. As a trope of subversive swerving and deviation, an apostrophe always depends on a prior voice from which to swerve. Sometimes a poem may bear all the familiar hallmarks of apostrophe, including the interjection 'O,' and yet lack the deflection or swerve that is the defining feature of the trope. Though Shelley's 'Ode to the West Wind,' for example, abounds in rhapsodic 'O's, its impassioned address to the wind is sustained throughout: there are no significant swerves or deviations. Radically different is Wordsworth's sonnet 'It is a beauteous evening, calm and free,' which contains no 'O's at all. And yet the speaker's urgent imperative, 'Listen!,' and his two vocatives of direct address, 'Dear Child! dear Girl!,' deflect attention without warning, first from the outward to the inward ear, and then from the speaker himself to his silent auditor. Unless the reader responds to the speaker's exhortation to listen imaginatively, he will be deaf to the 'sound like thunder' of the 'mighty Being' (6, 8) who is audible only to those with the aptitude to listen in a new and deeper silence.

Just as daring as the swerve from quietude to thunder is the ritual blessing of the sestet, where the volta's swerve turns the sonnet into a miniature dramatic monologue.

> Dear Child! dear Girl! that walkest with me here,
> If thou appear untouched by solemn thought,
> Thy nature is not therefore less divine:
> Thou liest in Abraham's bosom all the year;
> And worship'st at the Temple's inner shrine,
> God being with thee when we know it not.
>
> 'It is a beauteous evening, calm and free,' 9–14

To be laid in Abraham's bosom (12) is a benediction usually reserved for people after they have died. The sonnet's second swerve allows the reader to realize with a shock that the young girl whom Wordsworth now addresses seems most alive when described as a soul who has passed into paradise.

Instead of imploring ambrosial air to fan the poet's brow or a wild wind to make him its lyre, 'Andrea del Sarto' shows how a painter who wants his wife to be tender to him swerves into moods of helpless attachment and self-pity that defeat his efforts to be amorous. Whereas Romantic apostrophes usually tame and harness the potent vocatives of prayer, the exquisite swerves of weak fatality and delay in Andrea's invocations to beautifully composed landscapes work the other way round by thwarting his pathetically flawed attempts to woo Lucrezia.

In each genre, however, the critical trope is one of sudden swerving or deviation. As Douglas Kneale explains, apostrophe should always be distinguished from a mere vocative of address: it must be understood 'as a *movement* of voice, a translation or carrying over of address.'[8] As we have just seen, Wordsworth in his sonnet 'It is a beautous evening' negotiates a double turn. First he deflects attention from the externalized setting to an invisible 'mighty Being' (6), and then he turns away from the 'thunder' (8) heard only by the inward ear to the child who hears only the words that are spoken to her. Reversing the movement of Wordsworth's poem, Andrea del Sarto turns aside from his proper or intended hearer, Lucrezia, to such absent or internalized auditors as King Francis, Michelangelo, and God, before addressing his most important auditor, himself. In dramatizing Andrea's dual role as actor and audience, the monologue incorporates multiple swerves and turns, not just as figures of direct address, but as tropes of subversive deviation that make Andrea the hidden (and most important) audience of his own performance.

Ghostly Conjurings in Browning's Monologues

Monologues are often praised for their dramatic immediacy. But as a genre that celebrates the vocative of direct address, the monologue commemorates a fictional time in which nothing dramatic or lyrically intense need actually occur. To evoke a ghost as a living presence is to apostrophize it. Though every ghost is a casualty of time, the invocation to a historical ghost also places it beyond time. Such is the double feat of the dramatic monologue, whose ghostly conjurings and commands to ghosts deny temporality in the very act of using tropes that acknowledge time's power.[9]

Monologues like 'A Toccata of Galuppi's' exploit what Culler calls the 'sinister reciprocity' of poems that 'capture the time of the conjurer and thrust it provocatively at the reader.'[10] Not only does Galuppi's music prefigure the Venetians' mortality, it also commemorates the moment of the speaker's own entry into the dismal fellowship of the dead. A temporal presence and absence have been replaced by a conjured presence and absence, as in Keats's harrowing lyric 'This Living Hand' (written 1819).

Ghosts feed on our blood – not on the blood of our empirical lives, which we are willing to sacrifice, but on the blood of our imaginative lives, which we are unwilling to lose:

Oh Galuppi, Baldassaro, this is very sad to find!
I can hardly misconceive you; it would prove me deaf and blind;
'A Toccata of Galuppi's,' 1-2

As the spelling indicates, the opening 'Oh' is not a genuine apostrophe, for there is no voice from which the invocation might swerve. Instead, the exclamatory 'Oh' expresses a strong reaction of astonishment and disapproval. The 'Oh' is both a puzzled interrogation and a harsh arraignment. The dead musician is put on trial even as the substitution of ghostly conjuring for linear narrative confers life on the dead and a deathlike chill on the living: 'In you come with your cold music till I creep through every nerve' (33). The sustained vocatives suspend the force of the dreadful stresses reinforced by long vowels, which toll incessantly like a knell: 'Death stepped tacitly and took them where they never see the sun' (30). For just as tacit as the fellowship of the dead is the death-revoking power of the invocations, which allow the musician and the scenes he evokes to stand before him as living presences.

Ghostly address is kept in the foreground by the repeated use of the vocative, 'you,' and by puzzled interrogations: 'do you say?' and 'what?' Just as free of historical and narrative time as the dead musician is the Rialto bridge, which seems frozen into a timeless present like a snapshot or the 'still' in a movie:

... 'tis arched by ... what you call
... Shylock's bridge with houses on it, where they kept the carnival:
'A Toccata of Galuppi's,' 7–8

Unconnected to the preceding and ensuing lines, the substitution of a description for a name situates the bridge in a vividly realized present. It sits in its own frame, captured by the shutter of the speaker's mind, which releases it for an instant from the flood of history.

Ghostly invocation may exhibit the paradoxical power ascribed by Harold Bloom to *metalepsis*,[11] the trope that by reversing the relation of before to after and of cause to effect allows the dead to live and the living to feel spectral. If the speaker's invocation of Galuppi's ghost is a mere arraignment, then it is the evasion of a censor who tries to repress his own fear of death by half scoffing at Galupppi's nihilism. But the Englishman's vocatives of direct address to Galuppi are also a metalepsis that produces the illusion of having fathered his own father, for Galuppi is the speaker's Venetian precursor, an artist of erotic nostalgia. And by resurrecting him from the grave of eighteenth-century Venice, the son's invocations of his spiritual and aesthetic father confer a kind of posthumous immortality on the composer whose own best music has a chilling, nerve-dissolving quality (33). For this reason, to appropriate the elegiac genius of Galuppi is also to reject what metalepsis in principle makes possible: the reversal of time's arrow. Or, as Bloom says, 'nothing has happened because nothing has changed, and the final grimness of Browning's eerie poem is that its speaker is caught in a repetition. He will pause awhile, and then play a toccata of Galuppi's again'[12] as a way of prolonging his own strange obsession with belatedness, with reaching out to mentors who are dead, to ghosts he loves but cannot understand.

Every time Browning wants to replace a temporal description with a feat of ghostly conjuring in his monologue 'One Word More,' he uses an exclamatory 'Oh' or a vocative like 'You and I,' which reminds us that he frames the poem as an address to his wife, Elizabeth. The concluding invocations to Rafael and Dante yield in the final line to another direct address: 'borne, see, on my bosom!' (201) The one song that Rafael composed is sung in Browning's brain; and the one angel that Dante drew is etched on his breast. But instead of merely announcing this miracle, Browning uses a striking shift in verb tenses – a swift progression from 'Drew' to 'see' (201) – to thrust his angel-etched bosom provocatively at both Elizabeth and the reader:

Oh, their Rafael of the dear Madonnas,
Oh, their Dante of the dread Inferno,
Wrote one song – and in my brain I sing it,
Drew one angel – borne, see, on my bosom!

'One Word More,' 198–201

A reader cannot literally hear Rafael's unsung melody, because Browning performs the song silently in the music hall of his brain. But in a daring attempt to cross the boundaries of space and time, Browning invites us to behold Dante's angel: Look, I'm baring my chest for you: don't you see the figure etched here?

The last line asserts what is clearly false; we might be expected to smile at its transparent fiction, for on Browning's exposed male chest we can surely see nothing, not even a tattoo. But when we read the monologue sympathetically, we probably see exactly what Browning predicts we shall see. If we 'bless' ourselves 'with silence,' as Browning does, then we create the kind of space in which ghosts can be conjured and the dead come back to life. Overcoming absence and death by an act of ghostly conjuring, we fulfil Browning's prediction: See, I hold out my chest to you. Look at Dante's angel. Though Browning knows the pictured angel is only a fiction, he uses the vocative 'see' and the two exclamatory 'Oh's to enforce this fiction as an event. In embracing a wholly invented or fictional time, in which doing is also a form of saying, we can temporarily suspend our disbelief that Browning is actually present and that the angel pictured on his chest is forever thrust out for us to see. As Culler says of Keats's poem 'This Living Hand,' Browning here 'predicts this mystification, dares us to resist it, and shows that its power is irresistible.'[13]

Praised by G.K. Chesterton as 'one of the most perfect lyrics in the English language,'[14] Browning's elegiac monologue 'May and Death' assumes the form of a one-sided conversation with a young man called 'Charles,' a pseudonym for Browning's dead childhood friend and cousin, James Silverthorne. The address to Charles is necessarily one-sided, and its vocatives of direct address indulge a longing for pathetic fallacy. If nature had mourned more wholeheartedly for Browning's friend – as it mourned for Milton's Lycidas – then three-quarters of its spring flowers would have died with Charles. Browning believes the fourth part should have died too:

> I wish that when you died last May,
>   Charles, there had died along with you
> Three parts of spring's delightful things;
>   Ay, and, for me, the fourth part too.
>
> 'May and Death,' 1–4

Since the death of Browning's young friend ought to have been accompanied by an absence of rhyming or consonance in nature, the survival of half of a ballad's conventional *a b a b* rhyme scheme in each tetrameter quatrain aptly marks a partial failure in sympathy. The rhyme of 'you' and 'too' traces a vestige of order in a world of loss and pain, where all symmetry or harmony seems temporarily suspended.

But in the second quatrain this fancy strikes the elegist as foolish. There is no reason why the consonance that still survives for other like-minded friends should not be celebrated in such formal pairings as 'arm in arm'; the linking of 'arm' and 'warm,' which creates a rhyme for the eye only; and the fully audible chiming of 'friends' and 'ends':

> A foolish thought, and worse, perhaps!
>   There must be many a pair of friends
> Who, arm in arm, deserve the warm
>   Moon-births and the long evening-ends.
>
> 'May and Death,' 5–8

Though the termination of the day may coincide with the termination of a line and quatrain, its closure is muted by the harmony of the rhyme words, which are themselves 'a pair of friends.'

Despite the absence of the telltale 'O,' the opening address to Charles is an apostrophe in all but name. For no sooner has the speaker given voice to his wild and wayward impulse to banish spring along with Charles than he revokes it as unworthy. The sudden silencing of his friend's voice is followed by a second silencing: by a removal of his own 'foolish' and subversive 'thought' (5). But just when the opening address to Charles is fading from memory and is all but displaced by meticulous courtesies to friends who are alive, four urgent optatives, each addressed to absent friends, renew the swerve of the opening apostrophe by redirecting the speaker's voice.

> So, for their sake, be May still May!
>   Let their new time, as mine of old,
> Do all it did for me:
>
> 'May and Death,' 9–11

The vagrant 'wish' of the first quatrain is now replaced by an imperious decree, whose fiat is made to sound imperial by crossing a line-break:

> ... I bid
> Sweet sights and sounds throng manifold.
>
> 'May and Death,' 11–12

By conjuring into being marvels of sight and sound on behalf of all absent friends, the elegist allows even the dead Charles to rise from the grave in a bold *metalepsis* that eases the wound of the mourner's own belatedness. Unobtrusively, the monologue's apostrophe to Charles and its subdued optatives reverse relations of before and after. Such tropes create the illusion of the dead youth's return to his former spring haunts by ritualistically and momentarily banishing three-quarters of the May flowers, then graciously revoking the decree by restoring all of them to life.

The most spacious syntactic units come at the end of the monologue, where two full quatrains are used to voice the mourner's culminating wish: his modest request that a certain spring plant with a red streak on its leaves might languish or even die this year. The plant is invoked in a full quatrain, then turned in the last stanza into the grammatical object of a short half-line petition, 'That, they might spare.'

> Only, one little sight, one plant,
>   Woods have in May, that starts up green
> Save a sole streak which, so to speak,
>   Is spring's blood, spilt its leaves between, –
>
> That, they might spare; a certain wood
>   Might miss the plant; their loss were small:
> But I, – whene'er the leaf grows there,
>   Its drop comes from my heart, that's all.
>
> 'May and Death,' 13–20

Just when the sundering of the elegist from his auditor is most complete, and the idea of sundering is even mirrored by the *tmesis* that separates the participle 'spilt' from the preposition 'between' that modifies it ('Is spring's blood, spilt its leaves between'), the distancing is spanned by the gracious run-on that crosses the space between quatrains. Even the distance between rhyme words begins to contract, as the internal rhyming of 'whene'er' and 'there' (19) echoes for the first time the word buried in the middle of the stanza's opening line, the pivotal verb 'spare' (17). The diminishing diction in phrases like 'their loss were small' and 'that's all,' which is the most contracted statement in the lyric, cannot disguise the minor marvel of the Ovidian metamorphosis that turns the drop of blood from the mourner's heart into the red streak on the leaf of the missing plant.

By personifying the dawn as Aurora, the return of spring as the reunion of Demeter and Persephone, and the beautiful valley of Ida as Oenone's mother, Tennyson in 'Oenone' (1832) uses classical mythology to turn the invocation of an ode or lyric into a dramatic monologue's more naturalized version of the same trope: the vocative of direct address to an auditor. No sooner has Oenone described the beautiful valley in Ida as 'lovelier / Than all the valleys of Ionian hills' (1–2) than she places it beyond space and time by addressing it as her mother:

> O mother Ida, many-fountained Ida,
> Dear mother Ida, harken ere I die.
>
> 'Oenone,' 22–3

Similarly in 'Tithonus' (1860), by invoking the dawn as a transcendent presence, as the luminous goddess Aurora, Tennyson's speaker confers an illusion of permanence on the tremulous twilight vista of 'Far-folded mists' retreating like images seen from facing mirrors down 'ever-silent spaces of the East' and 'gleaming halls of morn':

> I asked thee, 'Give me immortality.'
> Then didst thou grant mine asking with a smile.
>
> 'Tithonus,' 9–10, 15–16

Just as Keats's nightingale soars into a timeless world that Keats cannot enter, so Tithonus detaches the linear journey of his own return to earth from the circular trip of the goddess: 'Thou wilt renew thy beauty morn by morn' (74). Classical mythology's capacity to turn the apostrophes of an ode or lyric into the vocatives of a dramatic monologue may partially explain why Tennyson's greatest monologues are mythical in their origin. Moved by the traditional words and ancient symbols, as he is moved by the dignity and grace of the goddess, Tithonus has every right to affirm that his auditor, like his language, is beautiful.

As soon as the dark house, the doors, the yew tree, and the burial ship in *In Memoriam* (1850) are apostrophized as powers or daemons, the mourner can show that the most 'ghastly' elements are also the most 'ghostly'; however sinister and menacing, they are stubbornly alive. Section 7 of the great elegy opens as inert description. But when we must rapidly reconstrue the first five lines as an apostrophe in order to make sense of the grammar in line 6, the petition to the 'Dark house' to 'behold' the mourner clearly acknowledges that the house on Wimpole Street is a phantomlike presence, a genius of place, perhaps even a region of the mourner's own mind:

Dark house, by which once more I stand
  Here in the long unlovely street,
  Doors, where my heart was used to beat
So quickly, waiting for a hand,

A hand that can be clasped no more –
  Behold me

In Memoriam, 7.1–5

The assumption of life enforced by the mourner's invocation to the house is not put at risk by any disclaimer that he may make about the darkness of 'the long unlovely street' or about the desolation of doors that will never again open on his friend. The assertion of bleakness and despair oddly contradicts the mourner's faith in a living auditor, a faith that is implicit in his use of invocation and his petition of direct address to the personified house.

Even a casual study of Robert Lowell's manuscript revisions of 'Colloquy in Black Rock'[15] shows how a pivotal swerve away from mere description to a single unifying apostrophe to a god in hiding turns a diffuse meditation into a powerful dramatic monologue. In the same notebook Lowell uses to revise early drafts of the poem, he keeps pondering Aristotle's distinction between material and final causes. A concentrated meditation on the horror of sensory glut, 'Colloquy in Black Rock' shows what happens when a material world of 'watermelons gutted to the crust' (12) remains unshaped by final causes. Originally entitled 'Meditation in Black Rock,' the early versions of the poem desperately flail about in search of some unifying vocative of direct address. After experimenting with several auditors ('My children,' 'My judges,' 'My brothers'), Lowell finally decides to address his own heart: 'Here ... / My heart, you race and stagger' (1–2). Though the body predicts that its debate with the heart will terminate like all discussions in the 'detritus of death,' the discussion does not *end* there. For the word 'End' is promoted to the head of the second stanza: it is not the terminal word we expect it to be but a verb that registers the absurdity of regarding material decay as the 'end' or final cause of anything.

All discussions

End in the mud-flat detritus of death;
My heart, beat faster, faster.

'Colloquy in Black Rock,' 6–8

The second and third times the heart is invoked, the constatives of detached and critical description ('you race and stagger and demand,' 2) are replaced by urgent performatives: by accelerated imperatives to 'beat faster, faster' (8, 18). Accepting Randall Jarrell's advice to detach his fourth and final apostrophe to the heart by preceding it with a dash, Lowell secures the performative as well as the descriptive force of his two concluding verbs, which bring the pentecostal fire of a hidden god powerfully to life.

> and the mud
> Flies from his hunching wings and beak – my heart,
> The blue kingfisher dives on you in fire.
>
> 'Colloquy in Black Rock,' 24–6

Equally potent is Arnaut's apostrophe to the hole in the wall in Pound's monologue 'Marvoil.' The descriptive narrative at the beginning of the monologue falls into predictable patterns of chiasmus and reversal: 'I have small mind to sit / Day long, long day cooped on a stool.' But the monologue comes to life the moment it substitutes apostrophic time for narrative time:

> Wherefore, O hole in the wall here,
> When the wind blows sigh thou for my sorrow
> That I have not the Countess of Beziers
> Close in my arms here.
> Even as thou shalt soon have this parchment.
>
> 'Marvoil,' 40–4

The apostrophe to a hole may provoke a titter or ironic smile. What could be more absurd than turning a wall into a dramatis persona, like the rustic actors in *A Midsummer Night's Dream*, then apostrophizing a mere empty space in that wall? But in animating the wall's hole, which will survive as the troubadour's surrogate, sighing his 'sorrow in the wind' (46), the ritual address does more than evoke the speaker's love for the Countess of Beziers. In committing his praise of the lady to the wall's safekeeping, Arnaut's apostrophe also helps commemorate – and keep alive in the dwelling-place of memory – his posthumous identity as a bereaved lover and troubadour:

> Keep yet my secret in thy breast here;
> Even as I keep her image in my heart here.
>
> 'Marvoil,' 47–8

The symmetrical phrasing ('in thy breast here,' 'in my heart here') combines with the diffused personification to dramatize an empathic merging of persons.

Arnaut is celebrating the power of poetry and music to displace a temporal pattern of actual loss – the removal of the lover from his lady and their eventual separation after death – with a reversible alternation between absence and presence, loss and repossession. As long as the apostrophized hole keeps the lover's secret in its breast by embracing the parchment, the lover will be able to replace the one-way movement of a temporal sequence with the reversible movement of apostrophic time. Nothing else need happen in a monologue that apostrophizes a wall, because by preserving the lady's image in his heart the lover's apostrophe itself becomes the happening.

Ghostly Vocatives: The Genesis of the Monologue

The paradigmatic narrative of all ghostly conjuring is Jesus' call to Lazarus, 'Lazarus, come forth,' or Orpheus's call to Eurydice. In such dramatic monologues as Browning's 'An Epistle of Karshish,' De Tabley's 'Orpheus in Thrace,' and Tennyson's 'Demeter and Persephone,' the stories of Lazarus, Eurydice, and Persephone recount the raising of ghosts from the underworld, which is what Tzetvan Todorov would call the 'discursive germ'[16] of the genre in which such stories of resurrection appear. As the manner of writing a dramatic monologue becomes its most important subject matter, the fictive raising of the historical or legendary dead through invocation and personification introduces a mirror version of itself in a narrative about conjuring ghosts by means of deictics, apostrophes, or other words of power.

In Gustave Doré's etching of the resurrection of Lazarus, which is reproduced in the frontispiece, Christ's raised arm points to a hidden God, a creator who is as omnipresent but invisible as the poet behind the Arab's mask in 'An Epistle of Karshish.' The power of a hidden God to raise from death his own Son – the very sage who resurrects his figural type, Lazarus – is a power exercised by the poet whenever he breathes life into the bones of historical corpses. One of the etching's oddest features is the two-way flow of energy that keeps replenishing and drawing new sustenance from the pool of light at the centre. Does the force originate in Christ? Or is its source the incandescent Lazarus, the resurrected ghost whose eerie glow prefigures Christ's own resurrection? To write monologues is to exercise a shared or delegated power. Ideally, the creator's face should be as masked but transfixed as the face of Doré's Lazarus, which is not only turned aside from the viewer but also veiled in a radiant white shroud.

The voice we finally hear in a monologue is the voice of a ghostly conjurer who is not merely the poet Browning or the Nazarene sage who raises Lazarus from the underworld but a neuter voice behind the personal voice, what Hillis Miller calls 'the "it" behind any "he" or "she."'[17] The justification of such self-cancelling personification is the identity of the sage with God, 'the very God! think, Abib; dost thou think?' (304). The personification of God as the sage who raises Lazarus from the dead reaches beyond personification to an affirmation of miraculous identity. The sage not only personifies God: he *is* God.

Like the historical or legendary ghosts they summon, monologues always exhibit fragmentation and disfigurement. Their acts of spectral summoning presuppose the absence or death of what they resurrect. The talking eyes of the Bishop of St Praxed's mistress, the lifelike smile of the Duchess of Ferrara, Gandolf's leer, the Spanish monk's drinking of watered orange pulp at three gulps to confute the Arians, all are detachable elements floating freely in the air, like the grin of the Cheshire cat. Just as a mask substitutes a frozen face for a whole and mobile person, so a monologue often reduces real people to their skeletal parts. An act of spectral summoning projects an illusion of wholeness from a base of dismemberment.

The art of the monologue also exposes the fictive status of its truth-claims in the very act of urging those claims as a condition of reading the poetry. Perhaps this paradox explains why the monologue's art of endowing the inanimate with life even while exposing the personification as a poetic fiction accords so well with the deconstructive genius of the Higher Criticism. To read a monologue the way David Friedrich Strauss reads the Bible is to accept a trope or an enabling fiction as a regulative truth. Monologues that resuscitate historical ghosts are history-like fictions: in Browning's canon they are a secular version of the Gospels, which themselves live on the borderland between fiction and truth.

Of most interest to Browning's St John in 'A Death in the Desert' are the truths about Christ that are least attainable through historical criticism. And yet fictions about the Jesus of history are necessary in order to make the Christ of theology intelligible. The art of Browning's Christian apologists – St John, Bishop Blougram, and the speaker in 'Christmas-Eve' – is, if you will, a deconstructive art. For although these characters recognize that Jesus is not a figure of the past but of the present (a living being who speaks to us now), they also realize that to deconstruct the Gospels' history-like fictions is to rob those fictions of their regulative force, ending with 'Fichte's clever cut at God himself' ('Bishop Blougram's Apology,' 744). A Jesus who is too closely identified with someone we might want to be – a wise, compassionate, prophetic, charismatic figure – may be merely an idol, a flattering picture of his worshippers, perhaps, but not a portrait of God.

Resuscitation of a corpse is not to be confused with resurrection. A bodily resuscitation takes place in the external world. An authentic resurrection occurs within a believer: it is a performative rather than a descriptive act. As one scholar says, 'whatever the resurrection involved, it was clearly not ... a once-dead person coming back to life and resuming the conditions of ordinary existence until he or she dies again'; resurrection means 'entry into another mode of being, not restoration to a previous mode of being.'[18] The ghostly conjuring of a dramatic monologue resurrects a historical character: despite Browning's own metaphor, it does not merely resuscitate a corpse. To be resurrected is to enter into the consciousness of the one who resurrects. The poet of the monologues appropriates the historical character; the sensibility of each is altered as a result.

Though all monologues invoke and personify historical or legendary ghosts, the act of raising a ghost, like resurrecting a corpse, may be an act of black magic fraught with risk for both the conjurer and the ghost. The conjurer may be possessed by an evil spirit, as are Guido and the Duke of Ferrara, whose demons must be exorcised. Alternatively, the raised spirit may suffer the fate of Lazarus in Browning's monologue: in being raised from the dead, he may be spiritually razed or raped.

What turns out to be unreadable, however, is not the risky trope of invoking ghosts but the narrative from which such invocations have been banished, for invocation of a personified subject is, as J. Hillis Miller says, 'the inaugural trope of narration.'[19] Though the historical and legendary ghosts that the genre resuscitates are fictions of personification and illusions of presence created by vocatives of direct address to absent, dead, or silent auditors, it is equally true to say that without a willing suspension of our disbelief in such fictions we should never have the wit to read a monologue or the imagination to reconstruct it. Even as we surrender to the spell of the genre's summoning forth of historical and legendary ghosts, we simultaneously acknowledge our surrender to that spell for the mystification that it is: a bewitchment of our minds by means of words.

Keble's Legacy: Preserving Oracles in a Non-Theistic Age

In recuperating an archaic convention of lyric apostrophe by humanizing the object addressed, the Victorian dramatic monologue illustrates John Keble's theory of the mechanisms by which genres are disturbed, displaced, and transformed. The naturalization of lyric apostrophe is part of a Victorian attempt to provide a local habitation and a name for the Romantic poet's communion with nature-spirits and ghosts. The address of Browning's personae to human auditors instead of to west winds or birds is also in keeping with attempts in Victorian theology to venerate some eternal greatness incarnate in the passage of historical and temporal fact, especially in the anthropological theology of George Eliot, for whom the second great commandment, love of one's neighbour, all but supplants the first commandment, love of God. Idealist attempts to deify all humanity come to focus in the anecdote that Alan Sell recounts about Sir Henry Jones, the author of the most important nineteenth-century book on Browning: '"I," said Sir Henry, "I deny the divinity of Christ! I do not deny the divinity of any man."'[20] Versions of the monologue's humanizing displacement of rapturous prayers to an otherworldly God occur in two important German sources of Victorian moral theology: in Strauss's worship of a wholly secular community of faith and in Feuerbach's veneration of love as the most godlike human attribute: 'homo hominis deus est.' Both authors were made available to Victorian audiences through George Eliot's own translations from the German.[21]

Coleridge's conversation poems contain both the poet's one-sided conversations with silent auditors like Charles Lamb or Sara and his two-way conversations or dialogues with a divinely animated Nature. When the key to that second 'language' is lost in the Victorian age with the rise of Darwinian science, the externalized dramas of a dialogue with God, who 'doth teach / Himself in all, and all things in himself' ('Frost at Midnight,' 61–2), are internalized as the divisions of a mind deeply and mysteriously at conflict with itself. For the perfect chiasmus of God's teaching, the private language of the poet's heart substitutes what John Donne calls a 'dialogue of one' ('The Ecstasy,' 74).

The monologue's use of the first-person pronoun tilts the genre away from drama in the direction of lyric poetry, which is utterance without refutation, speech in which there is no space for any voice of dissent. That lyric tilt is also a deception, however – what Alan Sinfield calls a 'feint'[22] – for even in using the first-person pronoun the poet detaches himself critically from his speaker, as if he were writing half of a two-way conversation, or Donne's 'dialogue of one.' Precisely because the auditor is mute, the monologue can indulge fantasies that defy the critical testings of a dialogue or play. But because the trace of dialogue still survives in a monologue's silent or absent auditor, the genre is never as solitary or isolated as a lyric poem.

Apostrophe is a Janus-like trope; it is at once a turning away or deflection and a direct calling – a vocative of immediate address to an auditor. It might be thought that in naturalizing apostrophe, the monologue preserves only the second of the trope's two divergent functions. But apostrophe's art of deflection leaves its trace on the monologue, even when an intensely imagined otherness is gestured at or pointed to without being directly addressed. This swerve occurs whenever a speaker turns aside from an auditor to marvel at a work of art like the Bishop of St Praxed's tomb or Fra Pandolf's painting of the Duchess of Ferrara, or even at an ideal witness like the Christian God envisaged by Karshish or David. Alternating between the swerve of a deflection and the direct address of a vocative, apostrophe's two-way flow alerts us to the odd fact that the speaker's conscious motives are seldom his deepest or most important motives.

I have argued that, like Coleridge's conversation poems, Browning's and Tennyson's dramatic monologues are poems of one-sided conversation in which a speaker's address to a silent auditor replaces Shelley's vocatives of direct address to the west wind or Keats's apostrophes to autumn. In naturalizing a venerable convention of lyric apostrophe by humanizing the objects addressed, Victorian monologues are also designed to preserve intact the poet's words of power. The dramatic monologue becomes an ascendant genre in post-Romantic literature partly because it is better equipped than lyric poetry to oppose the dogmas of a secular and scientific age in which an antiquated belief in 'doing-by-saying' (including a belief in oracles, prophecies, and knowledge as divination) is in rapid and widespread retreat.

4

The Dangerous Legacy of Keats and Fox: The Trespass of Intimacy

All the leading Victorians have troubling shadow selves. Browning, for example, is an ethical immoralist who shows in his poem 'The Statue and the Bust' that the only way to achieve ethical integrity is to violate the moral codes of a society that condemns adultery. Tennyson, a celebrant of empire who also sees it on the brink of collapse or decline, realizes that the most solid and enduring institutions, like the great globe itself, are insubstantial and fugitive. Arnold is a romantic classicist, and Pater a Victorian antinomian. Newman and Hopkins are at once sceptics and believers. Even in promoting the greatest happiness of the greatest number, J.S. Mill precipitates a crisis in Utilitarian thought by following his individual bliss as an advocate of liberty. Because the eminent Victorians are notoriously self-divided, often at war with themselves, they seem to feel a temperamental affinity for the dramatic monologue, a genre that keeps its speakers in touch with their shadow selves by cultivating the genius for impersonation that Keats associates with negative capability and the mind's capacity to proliferate itself endlessly through self-created roles.[1] Displaying a generous hospitality to life's variety and risks, poets as diverse as Chaucer, Whitman, Browning, and Pound enlarge our sensibilities by making us intimate with quacks, voyeurs, and charlatans. Often our intimacy with these characters is in direct ratio to their trespass on our privacy, to their assault upon our sense of who or what we are.

Fox's Vishnu: Breaking Taboos in Whitman and Lowell

In an 1831 review article of Tennyson's early poetry, W.J. Fox argues that Tennyson finds equivalents of his interior mental states in an external world. The people and objects he impersonates are resistant enough for the exercise of the poet's conscious energy but still placable enough to be dominated by the poet as a vagrant god, a kind of 'transmigrating Vishnu.'[2] Though Fox illustrates his theory by analysing Tennyson's monologue 'Mariana,' we are most aware of the poet's godlike transmigrations in poems that were not yet written when Fox published his essay. I am thinking of monologues by Browning, a close friend of Fox, who was almost certainly familiar with Fox's *Westminster Review* essay, and of later monologues by Whitman and Robert Lowell. These poems simulate the activity of a person imagined as virtually real: Lowell's backwoods Persephone in 'The Mill of the Kavanaughs,' for example, or the ubiquitous voyeur in Whitman's 'Crossing Brooklyn Ferry.' Behind their speech and manners we are also aware of the poet himself, a cross between Vishnu and Keats's poet of negative capability, who is willing to trespass on our privacy and even break taboos in order to become intimate with us.

A condition of our reading a dramatic monologue is our intimacy with the speaker. 'Intimacy,' I think, is a better word than sympathy, because 'sympathy' may imply a suspension of judgment that is alien to the genius of the genre.[3] We often feel closer to the speaker in a dramatic monologue than we anticipate or even desire. The trespass of intimacy in a dramatic monologue often turns the reader, like the speaker, into a male voyeur. Porphyria's lover, Browning's Duke of Ferrara, even his painter in 'The Lady and the Painter' dehumanize a woman by treating her as an object of specular gaze. In William Morris's 'The Defence of Guenevere' the woman herself connives at such voyeurism by inviting her male judges to view her as a beautiful object. She speaks as if it were possible to reduce ethics to aesthetics and redefine virtue and vice as matters of good or bad taste.

In Browning's monologue 'One Word More,' the sexual roles are reversed. In tantalizing his auditor with the prospect of trespassing on another person's intimacy, or with the thrill of seeing something strange and singular (the psychological equivalent of Dante's lost painting or Raphael's century of sonnets), Robert performs a male striptease for Elizabeth. Strip off my shirt, he says in effect, and you will see for the first time what is written on my chest. Browning practises a more subtle and diffused form of striptease whenever a speaker like Karshish or David perfects a rhythm of postponement or a rhetoric of delay. In such speakers Browning refines a version of the metaphysical striptease that his mentor Carlyle performs in *Sartor Resartus*, where Teufelsdröckh ventures to remove from the body of nature the last living garment of God himself.

Though a reader may trespass on the privacy of speakers when they are caught off guard, stripped of their masks, or made physically or psychologically naked, a speaker may trespass on the reader's privacy, too. In 'Crossing Brooklyn Ferry' Whitman may make himself more intimate with us than we wish by prying into our secrets. And in the monologue that Robert Lowell writes for Hart Crane we may feel our privacy invaded when we are challenged to lay out our heart for the poet's keep and even to get into bed with him. Hart Crane rapes his more innocent male readers by turning them into homosexual partners like one of the many sailors he has stalked.

To mime a life of sexual deviancy, Lowell uses a metrically irregular form that appears to abandon any rhyme scheme in lines 7 to 11, even though the return of rhymes in the last four lines subtly amends that impression of deviant behaviour.

> I,
> *Catullus redivivus*, once the rage
> of the Village and Paris, used to play my role
> of homosexual, wolfing the stray lambs
> who hungered by the Place de la Concorde.
> My profit was a pocket with a hole.
> Who asks for me, the Shelley of my age,
> must lay his heart out for my bed and board.
>
> 'Words for Hart Crane,' 7–14

The epigram 'My profit was a pocket with a hole' sends us, like the speaker's wayward rhymes, in search of a hidden meaning. We are reminded that his only identity consists of self-created poses or masks. Because everything has passed through him indiscriminately, he is intimate with everyone. Indeed if there were no hole in his personality, if he were not also hollow at the centre, his identification with his auditors would be less promiscuous, and so less complete. To be everyone's comrade he has to be a labile chameleon, a nonmoral artist of negative capability, a creator who has no genuine identity of his own. Because a self so protean and fluid must recreate itself from moment to moment, it also depends upon the intimacy of readers who have enough empathy with Crane to embrace him as a comrade, even as a sexual partner. Clearly, it is easy for readers to feel closer to such an intrusive presence than they want to feel.

Like Prospero, Whitman's speaker in 'Crossing Brooklyn Ferry' fears his ending is despair unless his future auditors can confer on him the grace of a posthumous existence, extending as far into the future as the poet himself peers into 'the dark backward and abysm of time.' The only way these readers can experience New York harbour from the future side of the poet's words is by allowing Whitman to flood their consciousness, trespassing on their privacy, until he becomes more intimate with their inmost secrets and desires than they are.

The wall of newspaper print that inundates the reader like a flood-tide has no power to stay the Heraclitean flux unless an elusive 'what,' barely intimated as the most secret of the reader's desires, obliquely proves what no homily or overt argument can hope to prove: the immortality of the soul: '*What* I promis'd without mentioning it,' '*What* the study could not teach' (99–100, my emphasis). Like Whitman's lines before they are read, future readers are celebrated as 'dumb, beautiful ministers' (126). Because their secret knowledge of the soul's immortality is knowledge of a truth that they and Whitman lovingly believe into existence to bring about the future, it is also a secret that binds them to the poet with obligation and affection.

Whitman uses his poem as a broadcasting megaphone, amplifying his voice so that future generations can hear. Like a newspaper with mass circulation, his poem is at once the most solid and most diaphanous of forms. Though he marshals his name lists like a phalanx of troops, he fears that his massive inventories will soon become as obsolete as yesterday's newspaper. Like the river that flows 'with the flood-tide' and ebbs 'with the ebb-tide' (101), his massed anaphoras may be as evanescent in their porous bulk as an epic swollen with antiquated lore.

To establish a two-way flow between himself and his readers, Whitman allows his tricky genitive phrases to fluctuate between objective and subjective forms. If we construe 'the life, love, sight, hearing of others' (12) as an objective genitive, then we may infer that Whitman is perceiving and sustaining his universe. But if the genitive is subjective, the reverse is true: both Whitman's contemporaries and posterity, including the present reader, are artists and architects: they are to Whitman what God is to Berkeley, the power that keeps the poet alive in the dwelling place of their memory. In dramatizing a relentless progression in intimacy, Whitman even crosses the boundary between the living and those yet unborn by introducing the cross figure, chiasmus: 'you,' 'me,' 'I,' 'you.'

Closer yet I approach you,
What thought you have of me now, I had as much of you – I laid in my stores
    in advance,
I consider'd long and seriously of you before you were born.

'Crossing Brooklyn Ferry,' 86–8

As the roles of the poet and his reader are gradually reversed, Whitman's celebration of the auditor as saviour both exalts his audience and reminds it of its own belatedness.

The bold *metalepsis* that reverses the roles of speaker and auditor raises Whitman's ghost from its grave and confers a kind of spectral half-life on the reader: 'Who knows, for all the distance, but I am as good as looking at you now, for all you cannot see me?' (91). As Jonathan Bishop says, 'each of us becomes the savior of "I" – and so the presence longed for, unseen except by faith, yet surely there. Hence the shiver it is impossible not to feel' as we read:[4]

We understand then, do we not?
What I promis'd without mentioning it, have you not accepted?
What the study could not teach – what the preaching could not accomplish is
    accomplish'd, is it not?

'Crossing Brooklyn Ferry,' 98–100

There is no thought so private and no feeling so intimate, Whitman boasts, that he has not already entertained it generations before we were born. In his role as the archetypal voyeur, the ghost we ourselves have raised is 'as good as looking' at us now, even though we cannot see him and so cannot recover our autonomy by returning his gaze. Like W.J. Fox's poet, Whitman's voyeur seems forever searching for some revelation which is inside him all the time. Whitman's true subject is himself, his transmigrating soul, which in its myriad facets can be seen only as it is reflected from posterity like an image of the god Vishnu recomposed by mirrors.

The Trespass of Chaucer's Pardoner: A Double Audience

Though Jean-Paul Sartre says 'one writes' either 'for one's neighbors or for God,' T.S. Eliot praises George Chapman's ability to create double worlds by writing for both audiences simultaneously.[5] While a dramatic character is addressing other characters on the stage, he is also addressing imaginary auditors in an idealized world that applies its own superior standards to the drama. Chaucer's Pardoner trespasses on the intimacy of such a double audience when he invites a group of ideal readers (or connoisseurs of rhetoric) to applaud the verbal daring with which he puts his homiletic skills to the test by asking his ostensible audience – the pilgrims – to buy relics he has just admitted to be fake.

The Pardoner's double audience collapses into a single audience only in lines 941–2 of *The Pardoner's Tale*, where he finally removes any ambivalence about whom he is addressing:

> I rede that oure Hoost heere shal bigynne,
> For he is moost envoluped in synne.
> Com forth, sire Hoost, and offre first anon,
> And thou shalt kisse the relikes everychon
>
> *The Pardoner's Tale*, 941–4

Though it is dangerous to single out a member of an audience for special reproof, the Pardoner calls directly on the Host, making a bold joke at his expense. 'Come forth and kiss my relics,' the Pardoner taunts the Host, 'and pay for them.' This is the Pardoner's crowning dramatic effect. When Bessy Cranage feels singled out by Dinah Morris in *Adam Bede*, she swoons and faints. But the Host is too hardy to faint, and lashes back with unexpected animus. The Host feels as violated as the reader may feel, and springs to life as the Pardoner's outspoken challenger and heckler.

As the dialogue of an open dramatic exchange supplants the closed monologue of the story-teller, who cannot with propriety be jeered or interrupted unless he commits the unpardonable sin of boring his audience, the Pardoner finds he can longer work his spell. The irreverent Host proclaims that the only fitting emblem for the Pardoner's debased words is his shrivelled testicles, whose proper shrine is a hog's turd.

Just as the Pardoner is collapsing before the reader into two-dimensional flatness and is seen only as an object of sexual joking and ridicule, the double ironies return. Even when the Pardoner concedes that Christ's pardon is better than his own, are we to applaud his self-criticism? Or are we to censure him for turning an apparent streak of honesty to dishonest ends? Who is being censured at the end of the Pardoner's Epilogue, the Pardoner or the Host?

At first we assume that the Pardoner's role-playing deserves to be censored. Acting out a sexual fantasy for which he is peculiarly unsuited, the Pardoner tempts the Host to strip bare his mask. The Host knows how to strike back where it hurts most, where the Pardoner's patently protective fictions about whoring and wenching have made him most vulnerable. Though the Pardoner sings lustily of amorous adventures in the *General Prologue* ('Com hider, love, to me!' 672), a woman is unlikely to find much in this clerical Don Juan to attract her. His erotic role-playing is compromised by his weak voice and unmanly appearance: he seems to be either a gelding or a mare.

The Pardoner's silence is not a silence of sullen reserve, however, but a silence of shock, impotence, and bitter resentment: 'So wrooth he was, no word ne wolde he seye' (*The Pardoner's Tale*, 957). Like the reader and the Host, the Pardoner himself feels violated: he has been attacked where it hurts most. The Host has trespassed on too private a domain: he has broken a taboo. As the eloquent tale-teller is struck speechless, the cruelly retaliatory Host becomes suddenly resentful that the Pardoner is unwilling to joke with him and continue their playful dialogue. But what can the Host expect? Has he not suspended the conditions of further verbal play by hitting below the belt in a scurrilous *ad hominem* attack?

Readers are uncertain whether Chaucer, the poet behind the masks, is secretly on the side of the transparent role-player, the clerical Don Juan who is pathetically unsuited for his role, or on the side of the Host, the ruthless exposer of hypocrisy and bad faith. Just as the Pardoner is stung by the obscene brutality of the Host's attack, so the Host is stung by the Pardoner's apparent overreaction to his jest. He is resentful that his sparring partner should withdraw from the verbal contest at the very moment the victory seems within the Host's reach:

> I wol no lenger pleye
> With thee, ne with noon oother angry man.
>
> *The Pardoner's Tale*, 958–9

Has the Host's response been too devastating, or is he justified in being out of temper with the sullen Pardoner? The double irony is delicately sustained, for the Pardoner and the Host could each argue with some display of logic that an impartial and judicious observer like the Knight secretly approves of *him*. Chaucer refuses to tip his hand, however. Even when the poet behind the masks allows his surrogate, the gracious Knight, to assume the conciliatory role now forfeited by the Host, the poet carefully maintains his own judicious distance and reserve.

The Pardoner violates a double space: he trespasses on the space of the

Host and other pilgrims when he presumes on their credulity by inviting them to buy his relics; and he trespasses on our intimacy by becoming too confessional with *us*. The unconscious liar who speaks in bad faith is never more dangerous than when cultivating a talent for openness and candour that trespasses on our sense of privacy and on our moral and sexual taboos. The Pardoner's double audience allows a double trespass to occur. Just as the Host turns the tables on the Pardoner by trespassing on the story-teller's space when he heckles and abuses him, so the reader turns the tables on the Pardoner by sharing sexual jokes at his expense with both the Host and Chaucer, the narrator of the *General Prologue*.

Because the Pardoner, like all role-players and practitioners of negative capability, enjoys the power of ambivalence, of the living contradiction, we may at times feel violated by him. A holy man without religion, a lecher without the sexual power to be lecherous, a blasphemer who denounces blasphemy, the Pardoner trespasses on the taboos of both his audiences. We have to concede, however, that the sword cuts two ways. The abusive licence that the Host has taken with the Pardoner has also traumatized *him*: when people trespass on each other's privacy no one is inviolable.

Keats's Dangerous Legacy: Intimacy with Speakers Unsuited for Their Roles

Unless Keats's poet of negative capability is a free democrat of the spirit like Chaucer or Whitman, a 'transmigrating Vishnu' (in Fox's striking phrase) who can impersonate such 'elemental beings as Syrens ... mermen and mermaidens,'[6] he will grow too godlike in his office. Open to the indignities of even his lowliest incarnations, Fox's Vishnu must learn to receive as well as give. In sharing free intimacies of consciousness with such beautiful losers as Browning's Andrea del Sarto and Lowell's eccentric Mother Therese, the true impersonator must have the versatile sympathies of a Chaucer or a Whitman. Though such a poet may learn from his impersonations by taking back from them more than he is conscious of putting in, there is a danger that in gaining the whole world the artist of universal empathy will lose his own soul. Keats believes that in creating a Iago as well as an Imogen Shakespeare forfeits an authentic identity of his own. In a letter to Elizabeth dated 11 February 1845, Robert Browning expresses a similar distrust of his early 'scenes and song-scraps.' For their prismatic diffusion of the Shelleyan poet's 'pure white light,' he resolves to substitute 'R.B. – a poem,' a visionary testament in which the prophet or seer can speak in his own person without the aid of any mediating mask.

The genre that best explores the dangers and challenges of negative capability is the dramatic monologue. Perhaps because the only personality worth expressing in art is a product of contrivance and disguise, readers are paradoxically more intimate with the dramatic poet who ventriloquizes through Andrea del Sarto and Fra Lippo Lippi than with the immature confessional poet of 'Pauline.' I want to show in this chapter how the failure of a dramatic speaker to establish intimacy with an auditor may be a necessary though not sufficient condition of a monologue's capacity to establish intimacy with the reader. If Browning's Englishman in Italy is trying indirectly to seduce Fortù, he is too devious to be a successful lover. Precisely because he talks too much about himself to woo Fortù, he seduces us, who are intrigued by his covert power plays and thinly disguised sexual fantasies about towering mountains and 'soft plains' cowering below them (181–91). Similarly, though Andrea del Sarto talks too much about himself to interest Lucrezia, who keeps tuning out, his habit of revealing more about himself than he is conscious of revealing makes him highly successful in seducing the reader.

Occasionally, as in 'How It Strikes a Contemporary,' where Browning's speaker spies on a spy, the trespass of intimacy becomes self-duplicating and reflexive. The most intimate details of the poet's domestic life with his dog and maid are an object of the speaker's intrusive gaze. But because the poet himself passes through the world incognito, becoming more intimate with other people's secrets than they might care to acknowledge, he is also the ultimate voyeur who returns the speaker's gaze by gazing on everyone else. Because the speakers in many monologues are pulled two ways at once, their incapacity to pursue wholeheartedly any single course of action unsuits them for their roles. Far from alienating us, however, their indecision and vulnerability make us oddly intimate with them.

We feel close to the lovers in Browning's little monologue 'A Woman's Last Word' because each is exposed and made vulnerable.

What so wild as words are?
  I and thou
In debate, as birds are,
  Hawk on bough!

                      'A Woman's Last Word,' 5–8

The woman concedes that if her truth is her partner's falsehood, then it is her falsehood, too. Instead of aspiring to the hubris of imagined godhead, like Eve, the woman is content to forgo knowledge by using cognate or married words to achieve a 'marriage of true minds': 'I will speak thy speech, Love, / Think thy thought' (27–8). But just when the woman seems about to make modern feminist critics wince, she recovers her authority by deferring till tomorrow her promise to lay both 'flesh and spirit' in the man's 'hands' (31, 32).

Between the eighth and ninth quatrains the male lover apparently asserts his rights: let us be actively amorous, he suggests. But in reminding him of her earlier use of the auxiliary verb of volition – 'I *will* speak, ... think ... and meet' (my emphasis), the woman once more tilts the balance of power in her direction. She will have sex the next night, not now.

> That shall be to-morrow
>   Not to-night:
> I must bury sorrow
>   Out of sight:
>
> – Must a little weep, Love,
>   (Foolish me!)
> And so fall asleep, Love,
>   Loved by thee.
>
> 'A Woman's Last Word,' 33–40

Using for the second time the verb of volition rather than a simple future tense ('That shall be to-morrow'), the woman gently dramatizes the fact that, though the last word – a tender use of the pronoun 'thee' – is literally a reference to the husband, it is also *her* word. Even in being self-deprecating ('Foolish me!'), she has been able to perfect the Keatsian art of negative capability without forfeiting a will and selfhood of her own.

Just as the proprietor of a portrait exercises control and power over the female model who is looking at him while the picture is being painted, so in Browning's monologue 'Andrea del Sarto' Lucrezia's true lover is the friend for whom Andrea offers to paint his picture, not Andrea himself. Ironically, the reader and the absent 'Cousin' are both more intimate with the model, Lucrezia, than is Andrea, her husband. In painting a picture for his wife's friend, Andrea half recognizes the disquieting truth that the lover is not usually the man who appears with the woman in the portrait but the spectator-owner at whom the woman is directing her gaze.

Our intimacy with the court lady in 'Count Gismond' is a result of
similar conventions. Has she been as intimate with her husband as with
the man who accuses her of being his mistress? 'Nakedness reveals
itself. Nudity is on display,' claims John Berger.[7] In Morris's monologue
'The Defence of Guenevere,' the queen is made figuratively nude because she is put on display as an unmasked subject. That is exactly how
her cousins want to treat the court lady in 'Count Gismond.' They want
to strip her of her moral masks, putting her fornication on display as an
alternative mode of dress. Berger says 'the nude is condemned to never
being naked. Nudity is a form of dress.'[8] The cousins in 'Count Gismond'
want the woman to wear her guilt as a humiliating public mask, a badge
of shame, like Hester Prynne's scarlet letter in Hawthorne's novel. She is
made nude instead of naked.

We are most intimate with the lady when she proves unsuited for the
role in which her deliverer has cast her. When her son's 'black / Full eye
shows scorn' (122–3), his glance seems too similar to her slain accuser's
own scornful look to dispel altogether the possibility that Gauthier is
indeed the father. The use of aposiopesis – 'Pass the rest' (107) – is not a
mere concession to privacy, reserve, or even to the silence that belongs to
the mystery of love itself. Her silences may veil something sinister. Not
only does she know she is guilty: she knows that her deliverer knows,
too. The knowledge of husband and wife is multilevelled and reflexive.
Nothing in Browning's monologues is quite so touching or affecting as
these untheatrical moments, which reveal intimacies of consciousness
too complex and subtle for a stage play to dramatize.

A lover may feel less intimate with the woman he is trying to woo
than readers themselves may feel with the unsuccessful wooer. In his
monologue 'Dompna Pois de me No'us Cal,' Pound's lover decorously
keeps his distance from the woman who spurns him. In each stanza the
end words that stray in search of long-deferred rhymes match the withholding of the lady's earnestly petitioned favour.

> Lady, since you care nothing for me,
> And since you have shut me away from you
> Causelessly,
> I know not where to go seeking,
>
> 'Dompna Pois de me No'us Cal,' 1–4

The honesty of the lover's admission – 'since you care nothing for me' –
is qualified only by the one-line isolation of his dactylic 'Causelessly,' as
if his rejection were truly a wonder to ponder and question. In his lady's

absence, he resolves to love in imagination a composite perfection, a patchwork of all the excellent qualities he has admired in women. But at the end of the monologue he deftly enforces intimacy with the lady who professes to be indifferent to him by suddenly shrinking the physical space between them.

> And yet I'd rather
> Ask of you than hold another,
> Mayhap, right close and kissed.
> Ah, lady, why have you cast
> Me out, knowing you hold me fast!
>
> 'Dompna Pois de me No'us Cal,' 66–70

The artful pretence that a mere petition to this lady is a more erotic experience than embracing and kissing any other woman leads to a surprising growth in intimacy in the final line. The taunt that even in casting her lover out this woman is holding him fast is the lover's ultimate trespass on the intimacy of an absent admirer who merely pretends (he claims) to be aloof and withholding.

Intimacy and Silence in Elizabeth Barrett Browning's Monologues

To have power in a monologue is to have access to intimacies of consciousness. But because silence has its own subversive strategies, this power of intimacy is not to be confused with a will to monopolize conversation or to occupy the spotlight in the manner of Chaucer's Wife of Bath, whose axiom of faith is 'loquor ergo sum.' On the contrary, power often resides with an actively silent auditor like Fortù in 'The Englishman in Italy' or with the defiant or bored Lucrezia, whose silence holds consciousness like a sum of power in reserve. Though power in a monologue is exercised by those who have consciousness, Barrett Browning knows better than most poets that consciousness may express itself in silence as well as words.

Her monologues ingeniously experiment with several forms of silence. Communing with an audible silence in nature, the sister in 'Bertha in the Lane' experiences a moment of plenitude and possession.

> And the Silence, as it stood
> In the Glory's golden flood,
> Audibly did bud – and bud
>
> 'Bertha in the Lane,' 11. 5–7

But if she is at first too happy to speak, she is soon too pained. Though the phrase 'he esteemed me' sounds affectionate and kind, Robert plants it on her as an epitaph. To gear down his love into the tamer language of esteem is to deliver a death blow from which the sister cannot recover: it is the begining of her end.

Like the word 'esteem,' almost every important phrase in the monologue looks two ways at once. Does the speaker truly think that silence is her destiny? Or is she merely trying to win pity for her plight? Though her dying at noon is the soul of pathos, it is too contrived to seem real. Too reticent to speak on her behalf, Bertha's sister has never fully lived. Only in stanza 15, halfway through the poem, do we discover that the person who stole away the speaker's love is her auditor, Bertha, the young sister whose wedding dress she has just finished sewing. The betrayal that produced a mere silence of loss and dispossession at the time it was overheard now produces a flood of words.

When Bertha's older sister finally concedes the full magnitude of her loss, which is nothing less than life itself, the monologue we are reading turns out to be far closer than we first suspect to an elegy like Hardy's 'Who Is Digging on My Grave?' As the poem switches genre, we realize that most of its elegiac sentiment has been purified by an irony that is sharper for being understated and more poignant for being masked.

Because the monologue is full of unheard words, we are half tempted to voice the unspoken thoughts behind the words we actually hear, as in the closing triplet in stanza 2.

No one standeth in the street? –
By God's love I go to meet,
      Love I thee with love complete.

'Bertha in the Lane,' 2. 5–7

Though the sister appears to say, 'By God's love, I love you completely,' that may not be what she means. We may squint at the adjective 'complete,' taking it as a misprint for 'compete.' There are simply too many competing 'loves,' three in two lines, to be sure of the meaning. Indeed the words behind her words suggest that the competition among so many 'loves' may seriously impede the vaunted completion. Nor may the sister's embrace of Bertha be as disinterested as we first assume. Is the speaker genuinely solicitous of Bertha, or is she merely trying to torture her sister by playing a heroic role?

In Barrett Browning's monologue 'A Year's Spinning,' a poetry of unheard words and silences invites each reader to reconstruct another narrative of betrayed love. As a ballad recast as a dramatic monologue, the poem is in search of a missing auditor. The two people who once spoke to the spinner – the mother who cursed her for being seduced by a faithless lover, and the lover himself – are now silent. The mother has died denouncing her daughter from her deathbed, and the lover has abandoned her.

The multiple meanings of 'spinning' are kept alive by the monologue's ballad-like refrain ('But now my spinning is all done'), which keeps changing meaning from one stanza to the next. Though the spinning wheel stops when the thread of the spinner's life has been spun and cut, the speaker has also spun in a different sense. When her faithless lover delved and she spun for nine months the thread of a third life, the product of all her laborious spinning was a stillborn child.

Though the monologue uses a demanding *a b a b b* rhyme scheme, its many imperfect rhymes – 'on,' 'sun'; 'spun,' 'known'; 'drown,' 'groan'; 'stone,' 'one' – mime the imperfections of the spinner's own life. Enclosed in her monologue's silence, the dying spinner is as isolated in death as she was in childbirth, when the silent, stillborn infant could hear nothing, including its mother's groan.

'The Lady's Yes,' a little monologue by Barrett Browning on what J.L. Austin calls the doctrine of the Infelicities, shows that silence may be preferable to infelicitous speech. If the petition 'Love me,' uttered at a boisterous party, sounds like a mere jest or a line delivered in a stage play, its force is nullified. As Barrett Browning's version of her husband's poem 'The Glove,' the monologue shows how the language of courtship is invalidated. The proof that nothing has changed is the woman's failure to love the man in the cold light of morning. If the colour cast by candlelight is a mere enchantment, then its magic is spurious. The traps that are always lying in wait for Barrett Browning's women sometimes spring shut on the men who set them.

The speaker tries to script a second drama, in which the rituals of lovemaking might be more propitious. If she were courted as Bertram courts Lady Geraldine, her lover's 'truth' might make the woman 'true.'

By your truth she shall be true
   Ever true, as wives of yore,
And her Yes, once said to you,
   SHALL be Yes for evermore.

'The Lady's Yes,' 25–8

Though her use of the auxiliary verb 'shall' wavers between a prophecy or decree and a simple future tense, her final capitalized use of the same auxiliary – 'SHALL be Yes' – subsitutes for her wooer's failed performative use of words an authentic example of 'doing-by-saying,' in which an appropriate response is implicit in the petition itself.

In the monologue 'Lady Geraldine's Courtship,' written to a fellow student by the poet Bertram, a personified Silence is one of the main dramatis personae. At the centre of the monologue is a garden where no music can be played except the song of the fountains, and where the presiding genius is a statue of Silence holding a rose. Just as most observers see only the limply grasped rose and mistake the visible flower rather than Silence for the true subject of the sculpture, so few interpreters can grasp the ironic disparity that exists between the words they hear and the intimacies of consciousness that must be lived inwardly rather than spoken or outwardly expressed. Geraldine tells Bertram that, instead of substituting names for things, she will use silent-speaking words to name what is otherwise unnamable. Like the statue of Silence, she will not blurt out her meanings for every uninitiated auditor to profane, but will speak them obliquely. When her intimations prove too subtle for Bertram to grasp, Geraldine returns at night, as in a dream, to tutor her lover in a new and silent language of the heart.

As a poet of silences herself, Geraldine speaks in oracular phrases that look two ways at once. Like her one-word response to her lover's petition, Geraldine's important utterances are capable of a double interpretation. Especially equivocal is her pivotal vow never to 'blush to think how [the man she marries] was born' (264). The most obvious meaning is that she will never concern herself with the accident of birth, since true wealth and rank are of the spirit. But the poet's rival, the rank-bound earl, could argue with some display of logic that Geraldine is also saying the opposite: she is vowing never to be embarrassed by the low rank of a socially inferior husband.

Everything in the monologue is Janus-faced, including its title, which may hide a subjective genitive behind its ostensibly objective form: instead of wooing Geraldine, the student-poet is wooed by the Lady. In a delicate rewriting of Lady Booby's seduction of Joseph Andrews in Fielding's novel, Elizabeth Barrett has also produced a Victorian version of the Duchess of Malfi's courtship of her steward Antonio.

Wavering between elation and despair, and swung or tossed between the troughs and crests of his spacious anapests, Bertram dramatizes the intervals separating the mountain peaks from the valley.

She was sprung of English nobles, I was born of English peasants;
What was I that I should love her – save for feeling of the pain?
'Lady Geraldine's Courtship,' 15–16

In allowing the social divide to become the metrical divide of the pregnant pause, dash, or medial caesura, the verse form does all it can to
dramatize the gap between the low and the nobly born. The humiliated
Bertram becomes a living oxymoron: he is burned by intense frost and
scorched by the cold scorn of those who patronize him. Despite the
pretence of social equality when Geraldine exalts the low-born poet as a
king in hiding, nothing can dissolve 'the pale spectrum of the salt' that
banishes Bertram to the lower regions of the dining table.

The statue of Silence in the garden dramatizes the truth of incognitos:
genuine nobility assumes a mask of silence by pretending to be less
exalted than it really is. Even as Bertram momentarily turns aside again
from the goal he is sworn to reach, he uses a final *occupatio* to remind
Geraldine that his appeal to her is one part speech to three parts silence.
The oxymoron that his strength is his weakness and his weakness his
strength parallels the culminating paradox in 'Saul.' As a poet of the
unheard word or silent meaning, Bertram manages to defer outcomes by
imagining non-conversations and alternative dramas that might more
suitably have taken place. Since words can be found only for what is
dead in the heart, intimacies of consciousness are most potent when
every absence or silence is understood to be meaningful. The best monologues bring great energy to bear on things that happen outside the
poem: the consummation of Bertram's love for Geraldine, the reunion of
the absent Angelo with Tennyson's Mariana, the report of Browning's
envoy to his master the Count.

Though it is clear that Geraldine has always accepted Bertram and
that the one most in need of persuasion is the lover himself, it is not
certain whether the apparition of an abased Geraldine, who stoops to
rise, is a vision or a waking dream. When Geraldine says, ' 'tis the vision
only speaks' (408), does she mean that Bertram's dream is like Adam's in
Paradise Lost and like Porphyro's in 'The Eve of St. Agnes'? Does he
awake to find it true? Or does she mean that she loves Bertram only in an
imaginary world? Is only an ideal Geraldine worthy of him?

Intimacies of Evasion: Off-Stage Acting in Browning and Jarrell

By postponing the shock of making painful discoveries, even a speaker's dishonest or evasive use of negative capability and role-playing may forge strong ties of intimacy with a reader. Though we come closer to Andrea del Sarto's inner consciousness than we ever do to the Duke of Ferrara's, the effect is not only to confirm our sense of Andrea's duplicity as a role-player. The more intimate we become with him the more we also realize that a wish to think well of himself governs everything he says. As an off-stage actor, he is so concerned to be tender to his wife that his anticipated solicitude acquires the force of psychic truth. And yet as he shifts from self-pity to self-censure, from pride in his own technical facility to contempt for Raphael's draughtsmanship, the line between private fantasy and historic fact begins to blur. His solid grasp of the truth that he has betrayed King Francis and is a lesser artist than his great contemporaries gradually gives way to his creation of a counter-reality that is as disingenuous as it is consoling. And yet even to speak of his self-deception or bad faith is to remove ourselves from his monologue by moralizing it and by making distinctions that apply in a more epistemologically stable world than the one Andrea inhabits. His description of his life as a 'twilight-piece' is more than a metaphorical way of speaking; it depicts literally the world he lives in and continues to reinvent. His 'twilight-piece' is a fiction he lives by: though he invents it, its illusions are palpable sensations to be touched and seen on the darkening air through a strange veil of sight.

Alternating between high-sounding axioms that are also deceptions – 'I feel ... [God] laid the fetter: let it lie!' (52) – and serenities that are lies – 'I am grown peaceful as old age tonight' (244), the restless Andrea continues to hide more than he reveals. The moral unease in the monologue comes from the fact that his consciousness and conscience are inversely related. The more inclusively Andrea sees in a fully human sense, the less inclined he is to use Lucrezia as a scapegoat. But the more guilty he feels about stealing Francis's money and squandering his talent as an artist, the more tempted he is to narrow his aesthetic and intellectual responses into a purely moral attitude that transfers blame to Lucrezia.

Andrea's evasions are his opium: his protective fictions postpone the truth indefinitely. By contrast, Browning's lover in 'Two in the Campagna' and Randall Jarrell's traumatized child in 'The Truth' achieve a measure of catharsis by using their evasions only to defer more knowledge than they can handle at the moment. The lover's obsessive imagery of naked flowers and mounted orange cups in 'Two in the Campagna' creates a persistent unease by signifying both his fascinated longing for sexual intimacy and his sudden flight from it. Such metaphors tend to spread when the knowledge sought is both desired and feared, as in Jarrell's monologue 'The Truth,' where the boy who passively endures the traumas of war knows more than he knows he knows: he can experience his harshest truths but never speak them. Dramatizing a disjunction between sensation and knowledge, Jarrell explores the child's terrifying powers of discernment. Hovering between childhood innocence and a tragic knowledge of war's horrors, the boy is suspended uneasily between incomprehension and knowledge, like Henry James's Maisie. Recalling traumatic events of his childhood, the boy's repetition of key phrases – 'my father went to Scotland,' 'And it was light then – light at night' – makes the emotional weight almost unbearable.

In acting out a fantasy of evasion, the mother uses discreet lies that are powerless to make the underlying horrors of their domestic tragedy any less horrific. When the seductive euphemism, he 'went to Scotland,' is repeated, its deception is casually exposed in the italicized amendment: 'They *said* he went to Scotland' (1–2). As the sense impressions of the self recorded become well confused, the boy thinks he hears the dead dog barking, though it is actually his mother crying over the dead body of his sister. Pronouns and antecedents are wrenched out of context with as much rude surprise as the jolted child, who wakes up at night to endure a living nightmare.

> I heard Stalky bark outside.
> But really it was Mother crying –
> She coughed so hard she cried.
> She kept shaking Sister,
> She shook her and shook her.
> I thought Sister had had her nightmare.
> But he wasn't barking, he had died.
> There was dirt all over Sister.
> It was all streaks, like mud. I cried.
> She didn't, but she was older.
>
> 'The Truth,' 11–20

The simple descriptive jottings, locked into place by anaphora – 'She coughed,' 'She kept,' 'She shook' – sort oddly with the child's inability to understand anything he sees. When minor truths about the dead dog intrude, the major ones fail to come into focus for the child. Instead of attaching itself to the dead 'Sister,' the capitalized word in its immediate vicinity, the repeated pronoun 'he' ('he wasn't barking, he had died') circles back six lines to attach itself to the only possible male antecedent, the dog Stalky.

Equally sinister in their widespread dispersal and echoing are the rhymes of 'cried,' 'died,' and 'cried.' Like these widely separated rhymes, the grammar is in desperate search of connections. Jarrell uses his poignantly controlled use of double point of view to show how the child can still not understand what the adult speaker grasps immediately. The confused boy thinks that his dead sister, being older, is just behaving more stoically and bravely than he: 'There was dirt all over Sister. / ... I cried / She didn't, but she was older.' Savouring the sad irony, the retrospective speaker can now register the terrible error of all his inferences.

The shocking conflation of two internal rhyme words, 'It was light. At night,' dramatizes for a second time that, as London burns, the nighttime skies are all lit fitfully by a blackened sun.

> I didn't get one single thing right.
> It seems to me that I'd have thought
> It didn't happen, like a dream,
> Except that it was light. At night.
>
> 'The Truth,' 23–6

Since 'night' loops back to rhyme with 'right' – 'I didn't get one single thing right' – we are gently pressured to consider how 'right' such placements are. In the surreal coupling of two internally rhymed antonyms, the insistent chiming of 'light' with 'night,' Jarrell concentrates all his effort in one fierce act of sight.

As visual snapshots flicker before the eye in a grotesque cinema of the mind, each fragment offers some new slice of horror. In a swift progression in destruction,

> They burnt our house down, they burnt down London.
> Next day my mother cried all day, and after that
> She said to me when she would come to see me ...
>
> 'The Truth,' 27–9

Removed to a mental ward, the child discovers that everything that comes after that moment of truth is bathetic. The future can hold no new terrors for him: 'The war now is nothing.' That can mean either that the war no longer terrorizes him or that it is synonymous with blankness, annihilation, the void, the removal of all value and feeling from his life. Now that father, sister, and dog are all gone, the future may be terrible beyond speech. Or it may be merely banal.

The flashover point and the sudden breaking in of repressed truth coincide with the mother's gift of the toy dog, a substitute for the dead Stalky and also for a whole family – father, sister, and even the sanity, balance, and innocence of the speaker's childhood, which dies on that day. How can such intensities of consciousness end in a small grave? It is no wonder that the stolid opacity of the mother, made stupid or mad with grief, should be dramatized by the immobility of the terminal words, 'when she didn't know,' which are twice repeated without change.

> I asked her what was its name, and when she didn't know
> I asked her over, and when she didn't know
> I said, 'You're not my mother, you're not my mother.
> She *hasn't* gone to Scotland, she is dead!'
>
> 'The Truth,' 47–50

Confusing his dead sister with his mother, the speaker allows his auditor to become his true mother again only when he twice denies her identity. She returns to him at the moment she drops her own protective masks and mourns with him openly for the first time. At the centre of Jarrell's war monologues is 'some child, some helpless person,' as Robert Lowell observes. 'They dream through entranced scenes and images, memories, and petty plots, almost the peasant kingdoms of the Brothers Grimm. Always at one's elbow, however, is the real modern world with its brilliant and terrible technology and methods.'9

Since everything happens twice, repeated words keep being used in an altered sense. 'She is dead' is amended to 'Yes, he's dead, he's dead,' as the mother shows the same disrespect for pronouns and their logical referents as the son had shown earlier in his confusion of his dead sister with their dead dog, Stalky.

> And she said, 'Yes, he's dead, he's dead!'
> And cried and cried; she *was* my mother,
> She put her arms around me and we cried.
>
> 'The Truth,' 51–3

Equally evasive is the son's transfer to the dead sister of the phrase first used to describe the father, who is said to have gone to Scotland. But in correcting the son, the mother completes the rite of mourning with a felicitous acknowledgment of the long-withheld truth: 'Yes, he's dead, he's dead!' Though in context the line is a logical *non sequitur*, it is the only fitting conclusion to a monologue of fatal disconnections. The shocking change in pronouns from 'she is dead' to 'Yes, he's dead, he's dead!' brings repetition of a different, more therapeutic kind: 'And cried and cried.' Only in the last three lines can the dead be properly mourned. As a rite of the heart's private grieving, this mourning is not to be confused with the staged performance of a public funeral. For the stupid immobility of the twice repeated 'didn't know, didn't know,' the final repetition, with its simple parataxis, substitutes a far more affecting drama. It marks the delicate pause, the moment of transition, when the acting out of protective fantasies and roles can at last be challenged and the harsh truth accepted for what it is.

One of the paradoxes of intimacy is dramatized in Randall Jarrell's own favourite monologue, 'Burning the Letters,' whose speaker, a young war widow, is closest to her husband when most removed from him in space and time. The poem's intimacy is a product of what Kierkegaard calls recollection as opposed to mere remembrance. By interpreting and transforming the past as well as preserving it, the war widow hopes to be most in touch with her husband when performing the outwardly cruel and senseless act of burning the one remaining bond between them. Consigning the letters to a fiery grave is like cremating a body, a more material relic than 'those fallen leaves which kept their green, / The noble letters of the dead' in *In Memoriam* (95. 23–4). With a dog tag welded to the breastbone in a horrible incineration, the mutilated male corpse is not, she realizes, the warm and breathing man she loved and married. With his young face and questioning smile, he continues to live only in her recollection of him, in that court of memory which is the last home left to him.

As Robert Lowell says, Jarrell has an 'almost mythical feeling for the sorrows of the helpless. The soldiers and pilots he wrote about were his old companions and ex-aviation students.'[10] The intimacies of their suffering and the grief of those who mourn them are the one truth he knows. When the grieving widow wakes from the nightmare of a dying God, a nightmare that is still full of purgatorial possibilities, she faces something even blanker.

> In the darkness – darker
> With the haunting after-images of light –
> The dying God, the eaten Life
> Are the nightmare I awaken from to night.
>
> 'Burning the Letters,' 40–3

Instead of simply awakening 'tonight,' she wakes 'to night.' To the eye that scans the words on the printed page the revision is decisive. The darkness of a mere void or blank is bleaker than anything she has met in her nightmare.

Though the widow's tearing up and burning the relics is a heart-rending parody of the fraction or breaking up of Christ's body in the Eucharist, her most searching intimacies are also a paradoxical result of trying to end intimacy altogether. Reversing the action of *In Memoriam*, where the mourner's soul is wound in Hallam's as he reads the dead man's letters, the widow is a victim of unconscious self-deception. Like Matthew's chronicler in Wordsworth's elegy 'The Two April Mornings,' she understandably forgets that when we try too hard to banish ghosts they have a way of coming back to haunt us. As Macbeth is haunted by Duncan's ghost and Wordsworth by Matthew's, so the war widow's husband, we feel, will not stay safely in his shroud but will roam out of his fiery grave to take possession of her and derange her. Jarrell does not touch up his monologues: all his speakers' flaws and twists are seen, but in the end our intimacy with them is unlimited.

Intimacies of Invention: The Fantasies of Jarrell's Speakers

In the protective intimacy of their dramatic monologues, Randall Jarrell's speakers are continually indulging in fantasies of self-invention. To escape from the boredom and the horror of a life that is vaguely leaking away from her, the middle-aged housewife in 'Next Day' combines fantasies of sex and death. More inventive are the fantasies that assimilate the black woman in 'Gleaning' to the biblical Ruth and the woman at the Washington Zoo to the mythical Leda.

Part of the lonely crowd and urban nightmare, the housewife in 'Next Day' not only looks over people but also ignores them. And because she cannot contemplate herself too steadily in the mirror of inhuman faces in the supermarket, she retreats into the proverbial wisdom of an *aperçu* that blocks out more experience than it explains.

> flocks
> Are selves I overlook. Wisdom, said William James
>
> Is learning what to overlook. And I am wise
> If that is wisdom.
>
> 'Next Day,' 5–8

Even her innocent gesture of looking over people becomes slightly more sinister when pressure is put on the repeated verb. Wisdom is overlooking, both in the sense of wisely surveying and tactfully omitting. And that is precisely what an aphorism does. Because it sheds detail in favour of a generalizing truth, the woman half doubts the aphoristic force of William James's own wise saying about wisdom.

It bewilders and hurts her that the young grocery boy fails to turn her into an object of his virile gaze. Preferring a time when there was no 'overlooking' but only an intense 'looking over,' she recreates an odd and teasingly self-reflexive drama in which she imagines young men imagining her undressed, 'holding their flesh within my flesh, their vile / Imaginings within my imagining' (24–5). Trying desperately to break out of her domestic routines, Jarrell's woman wants to 'look over' the drabness and boredom, if only by peering over the edge of stanzas and lines. When there are no run-ons and a sentence ends at the close of stanza 2, the sense of loss can be heartbreaking:

> What I've become
> Troubles me even if I shut my eyes.
>
> 'Next Day,' 11–12

At other moments an 'ecstatic, accidental bliss,' a 'blind / Happiness,' transports her in rapture across line breaks and stanzas. Only when such transports fail and she is locked within stanzaic forms and lines, as she is locked within the unvarying days of her life, does desolation seem complete.

In the penultimate stanza of the monologue the woman's body that the male voyeur has undressed becomes the 'undressed, operated-on ... body' of her friend's corpse, on view at yesterday's funeral. Even as she recalls her dead friend's praising her as 'exceptional,' that adjective is made to seem its opposite by becoming the one terminal word in the last stanza that is not exceptional, because it is used not once but twice.

As I think of her I hear her telling me

How young I seem; I am exceptional;
I think of all I have.
But really no one is exceptional,
No one has anything, I'm anybody,
I stand beside my grave
Confused with my life, that is commonplace and solitary.

'Next Day,' 54–60

Unlike the twice-repeated use of the adjective, the four concluding syllables of the last line are truly 'exceptional' in their hypermetric isolation.
Though she wishes she could overlook a number of grim facts, including
the face revealed to her from the rear-view mirror, by the end of the
monologue she is completely honest and has lost her power to overlook
anything. As she stands beside the grave of her youth, as she stood
yesterday beside her friend's corpse, she composes her own epitaph in
the last and most appalling lines to be spoken.

In a feminist version of Browning's 'Fra Lippo Lippi' and Tennyson's
'Ulysses,' Randall Jarrell's monologue 'Gleaning' celebrates the hunger
for experience of a black woman who brims over with a voracious
appetite for sexual union with an apocalyptic 'last man, black, gleaning,'
who is to come to her at sunset to possess her in the field. Though the
black woman has gleaned bounties from the lord of the fields, who has
made her his wife or mistress like the biblical Ruth, she longs for more.
Having reached that point in her life when everything she ever wanted
is no longer enough, she is still as dissatisfied as the woman in 'Next
Day,' whose life seems all post-mortem, all 'after the funeral.'

Just as the woman at the Washington Zoo wants to be changed by a
vulture-man, so this black woman yearns to have the residue of her life
crushed out of her by a male lover. The double crushing of the body and
its essence are her equivalent of the cider press in Keats's 'Ode to Autumn,' which alone has power to extract the oozing substance of both
the declining year and its bounty.

In the last light we lie there alone:
My hands spill the last things they hold,
The days are crushed beneath my dying body
By the body crushing me.

'Gleaning,' 23–6

In fact, there is no weight upon the woman, who is merely bending over her soup spoon by the kitchen fire. But all her victories are victories of imagination. And in her sexual fantasy, as she helps spill the seed from the body that crushes and embraces her, so intense is the weight and pressure on her that she can both feel and not feel the life force that simultaneously frees and oppresses her.

Surrounded by foreign women dressed in saris, the speaker in Jarrell's monologue 'The Woman at the Washington Zoo' seems dull and unexciting by comparison. Because she is oddly imprisoned, she feels as if she were on the other side of the cage, on display – not as a leopard or exotic cat, but as some mere pitiable drudge of an animal. The empty internal rhymes ('dull null') and chiming couplets mock the predictable hollowness of her life:

> this dull null
> Navy I wear to work, and wear from work, and so
> To my bed, so to my grave, with no
> Complaints
>
> 'The Woman at the Washington Zoo,' 5–8

As a frail memorial that is also her tomb, even the dull repetition of immovable end words – 'neither from my chief, / The Deputy Chief Assistant, nor his chief' – dramatizes the boredom of the life that oppresses and exhausts her.

But in casting the vulture as the fierce lover she should have known, her language becomes suddenly aggressive and predatory:

> Take off the red helmet of your head, the black
> Wings that have shadowed me, and step to me as man:
>
> 'The Woman at the Washington Zoo,' 25–6

To be empowered the woman must be treated as masterfully as the fawn whom the wild stag subdues or as the purring lioness whom the male lion tames. As Jarrell's version of Yeats's 'Leda and the Swan,' the monologue ends with a call for metamorphosis. Once young and sexually alluring, like the woman in 'Next Day,' she asks to be raped.

> You know what I was,
> You see what I am: change me, change me!
>
> 'The Woman at the Washington Zoo,' 29–30

To put on the god's knowledge with his power, the woman needs to be possessed by a male vulture, just as Leda was possessed by Zeus disguised as a swan. Eager to grab some joy and freedom in her life, she has a psychological hunger to belong to someone and to know she has made a difference. In such half-mythic monologues, lonely and estranged people of both sexes may find that their most intimate fantasies are not so much mirrored as invented.

The Trespass of Intimacy: Is Closeness A Result of Detachment and Reserve?

Deep forms of caring and intimacy are not to be confused with the self-annihilating kind of empathy that allows Browning to efface his personality by emptying himself into the Spanish monk or into the court lady in 'The Laboratory.' Indeed the self-annihilating kind of empathy and the more intimate forms of identification appear to exist in inverse ratios. A reader is less gripped by Andrea del Sarto in a purely empathetic way, far less carried away by him, than by the raucous swearing song of the Spanish monk or by the hypnotic incantations of the court lady in 'The Laboratory.' Yet Browning himself never felt particularly intimate with these last two speakers. He dismisses his early monologues as 'scenes and song-scraps,' 'mere and very escapes of [his] inner power.'[11] In 'Andrea del Sarto,' by contrast, a poem Browning deeply cared for, the viscera and pulses are much less involved. The less physically swayed he is, the more Browning's own sense of failure and betrayal can become engaged to create the conditions of deep caring and concern.

To explain why intimacy in Browning's monologues is often a result of detachment and reserve, I want to digress for a moment to show how Janey Morris is moved to eloquence when her intimacy with Dante Gabriel Rossetti allows her to talk about an apparently different subject altogether. Rivalling in power her husband's best dramatic monologues, Jane Morris's most searchingly intimate letter is not even written to the man she is close to: it is written to Ford Madox Ford.[12] After plunging *in medias res*, 'Have you had any news?,' the correspondent fails to provide any context for her inquiry but refers instead to a letter she received last Friday from Mr Scott. Just as urgency seems to subside, it returns with redoubled force in her complaint that Mr Scott has told her nothing more, even though she has written to him twice. Reviving the full force of the letter's opening question, the dreadful dreams she had the previous night culminate in her determination to return to London the next day. Only when Jane is on the third page of her four-page letter does she provide the clue that allows a reader to piece the puzzle together. Anxiety about her friend Gabriel's health is introduced almost as an afterthought in response to a query about a ring Jane has loaned him:

Gabriel had several of them to paint from, but I don't know which he had just when he fell ill – I had one about the date you say with a red stone but it had blue gems round it, and I think could not be the one you spoke of

There are no periods in the letter. When Jane is not posing a question, she is connecting short sentence fragments with dashes. But nothing she writes in her direct correspondence with Gabriel is half so intimate or affecting.

Each phrase of her repetitious valediction – 'With affectionate regards to all / Yours affectionately, / Jane Morris' – is as pregnant with unspoken meaning as the coda of Browning's 'An Epistle of Karshish' or the gloss that concludes 'A Death in the Desert.' Such 'shadow-letters' and 'shadow-monologues' compose a palimpsest of texts: below Jane's or Karshish's actual words we glimpse a trace of what each would like to say to Gabriel or to Abib if more transparent speech were an option. The surface chatter about rings and unanswered letters cannot disguise the deeper intimacies of unconscious revelation, which come only in the confused limpidity of her postscript and in the letter's many desperate displacements of anxiety and concern.

Intimacies of reserve may be achieved through a subtle use of *paralipsis*, the trope of denying that any intimacy is possible. In *La Saisiaz*, for example, we are closest to Browning in the last line of his elegy – 'Least part this: then what the whole?' (618) – where a mask of reserve is suddenly drawn over secrets he might share. It is also easier to be intimate with a reserved ironist like Fra Lippo Lippi, who pretends to be worse than he is, than with a saintly self-promoter like Tennyson's St Simeon. As a painter of the flesh, which is God's best gift, Fra Lippo is a holy man who conceals his holiness. As G.K. Chesterton explains, 'the saint has an unfathomable horror of playing the Pharisee.'[13] The secrecy that often accompanies sanctity helps explain the close connection between intimacies of consciousness and the disguises assumed by such champions of reserve as the poet who travels incognito in 'How It Strikes a Contemporary.' As a knight of the hidden inwardness, the ironist is afraid of profaning his faith by expressing in outward form the drama of his life.

Indeed, if the hapless husband in Edward Thomas's love monologues did not feel so unsuited for the conventional requirements of his role, we should be less deeply stirred by him. Thomas's monologues owe their power to a wrenching sense that the lover's truest expressions of intimacy are also a trespass or intrusion. In the monologue 'And You, Helen,' the bountiful giver proves suddenly unsuited for his task, incapable of making a gift – even of himself – to his beloved. Though the couplets seem an imperfect medium in which to dramatize the very imperfect coupling of the husband and wife, they do at least implicitly concede that Helen is *sui generis*, incapable of rhyming with anyone but herself.

> And you, Helen, what should I give you?
> So many things I would give you
>
> 'And You, Helen,' 1–2

The most startling and intimate words offer to undo the marriage poem by giving the wife her freedom.

> I would give you back yourself,
> And power to discriminate
> What you want and want it not too late,
> Many fair days free from care
> And heart to enjoy both foul and fair,
> And myself, too, if I could find
> Where it lay hidden and it proved kind.
>
> 'And You, Helen,' 16–22

Though the hypermetric line – 'What you want and want it not too late' – poignantly laments the belatedness of what is 'late,' the true surprise is the discovery that the most intimate words in the monologue are words that deplore a total lack of intimacy. The husband's soul is so profoundly hidden and may prove so unkind when found that he is deeply uncertain whether he has any self to offer.

In 'After You Speak' Thomas's lover trespasses on the private thoughts of his auditor by presuming to read her mind. Though she speaks words of rejection, her eyes tell a different story.

> My eyes
> Meet yours that mean –

With your cheeks and hair –
Something more wise

'After You Speak,' 4–7

The harmony of the monologue's first achieved rhymes ('eyes' and 'wise')
affirms the wisdom of the talking eyes. Though the lover may be misin-
terpreting the woman's rejection of his love as an acceptance in disguise,
the one-word lines that celebrate his surge of elation as 'A mote / Of
singing dust / Afloat / Above' (19–22) are charged with feeling. At such
a celebratory moment we are as close to the speaker in his wavering
ecstasy as we are to Donne's lover in 'The Canonization.' The alchemy of
transmuting her sexual passion into love – 'I know your lust / Is love'
(25–6) – allows Thomas's lover, like Donne's, to rise from blunt candour
and satire to an ostentation of his love in some of the most honest poetry
in the language. The monologue wins sympathy for the lover precisely
because his reading of the woman's mind is fraught with risk and may
make him too honest to succeed in his appointed task.

In Thomas's monologue 'No One So Much As You,' the lover's many
confessed inadequacies make us feel even closer to him. So personal and
wrenching are his several admissions of failure, even where he most
wanted to succeed, that we seem always on the threshold of trespassing
on his privacy, violating some secret apprehension or fear.

None ever was so fair
As I thought you:
Not a word can I bear
Spoken against you.

'No One So Much As You,' 9–12

Though the repetition without change of the end-word 'you' dramatizes
the truth that his beloved is the one abiding element in his life, the
lover's use of the phrase 'I thought' also concedes that everything he
celebrates in her hinges on reckless trust and surmise. What he has done
and said seems coarse and weak compared to the unspoken words he
has held in reserve. And yet his love's decline into mere gratitude and
his manhood's contraction into the half-comic spectacle of a solitary pine
tree cradling a dove invite the most appalling reflection of all.

I at the most accept
Your love, regretting

That is all: I have kept
A helpless fretting

That I could not return
All that you gave
And could not ever burn
With the love you have,

Till sometimes it did seem
Better it were
Never to see you more
Than linger here

With only gratitude
Instead of love –
A pine in solitude
Cradling a dove.

'No One So Much As You,' 25–40

Initiating a series of cross-overs between quatrains, the lover voices the disturbing thought that it were better to be dead than to fail once again as her lover. That dark fear is allowed to gain incremental force by crossing successive stanzaic breaks until it casts its shadow over everything else in the poem.

It may be presumptuous of the husband to take for granted his wife's generosity, especially since he has no hope of reciprocating her bounty or of being her equal in ardour, courtesy, or grace of self-command. But if he is tactful enough to commemorate her in silence, who can possibly take offence?

Both an oddly aborted love poem and a projected elegy, Thomas's monologue 'P.H.T.' concedes that its speaker may not 'come near love' for his father until his father is dead. Using the same stanzaic form and metre as 'No One So Much As You,' the monologue reverses the situation of the other poem by envisaging, not the speaker's death, but his listener's.

To repent that day will be
Impossible
For you, and vain for me
The truth to tell.

I shall be sorry for
Your impotence:

'P.H.T.,' 5–10

Tremulous with indecision, the syntax looks two ways at once. Does the phrase 'The truth to tell' reach forward to the next quatrain – 'to tell the truth, I shall be sorry'? Or does it reach back to the previous line by providing an infinitive phrase for two grammatical subjects: the pronouns 'you' and 'me': 'Truly, I shall find it vain and you shall find it impossible to repent'?

'Going hence,' the son discovers, may even include a going beyond the boundaries of the quatrain, which is like a crossing of the divide between life and death. The son's reflection that his father can 'undo no more' only when he is dead sounds bitter and accusatory. But the speaker's most heartbreaking discovery is that he is so unsuited for his task of paying tribute to the people who are closest to him in life that he may have to wait until such people are dead before he can put into words what a full heart has to say.

You can do and undo no more
When you go hence,

Cannot even forgive
The funeral.
But not so long as you live
Can I love you at all.

'P.H.T.,' 11–16

The discovery that someone can be loved only from the far side of the grave is unanticipated and shocking. We feel most intimate with this wayward son when he calls his very words to his father an offence, a trespass to 'forgive' like 'the funeral.' The son realizes that his failed eulogy may presume upon patience and good will. But just when rhyme and metre are being thrown to the winds, sanity returns in a little fragment of muted rhyme that allows 'all' to echo 'funeral.' The monologue's plain script goes with the plain speech of someone who is touched to poetry only when he thinks of his father as a stranger he can reach out to and love without ever hoping to like or understand. The tough intimacies of such a monologue are as tenacious and frail as dandelion seeds. Reading Thomas is like listening to a conversationalist who makes all other conversation sound fraudulent.

When a strong connection exists between the poet and another person, the sense of their intimacy tends to increase as the physical distance between them widens. In his elegy *La Saisiaz* Robert Browning can evaluate his love for Elizabeth only when the distance of two deaths – his wife's and his friend Anne Egerton Smith's – brings the greater of these two losses into poignant focus for him. Conversely, Andrea's 'close-up' of Lucrezia's face has the curious effect of increasing psychic distance at the same time it reduces physical distance. Even in celebrating the marvel of the instant when he and his future bride crossed the thin divide separating friendship from love, the husband in Browning's 'By the Fire-Side' is struck by the precious slightness and precariousness of that breakthrough and by his sense that the outcome could easily have been different: 'the little less, and what worlds away!' (192).

Since God himself culminates in the 'moment, one and infinite' ('By the Fire-Side,' 181), the husband feels he is unlikely to know more of the divine in the lapse of all the ages. Half at war with reason in his zeal for that moment, he uses his extravagant talking-song to write a small part of his life in italics. Even though such a moment may be too fragile or transient to last more than an instant, and so is the opposite of everlasting, it is nevertheless in some sense eternal. By dying on purpose to the rush of time, Browning's speaker is able to stand outside his life. Thinking of himself as an eternal witness and hence as timeless, he becomes more alive in his present moments. As intervals of space and time increase the distance separating the aging husband from the good moment of his youth, the psychical distance between the two time frames also begins to diminish. Like the empathetic artist of roles, the husband in 'By the Fire-Side' also gains the greater intimacy that can be experienced only in some sort of middle space, halfway between projection of his own values and empathy with the moment's essential transience – with its tendency to seriously, sadly run away, as Frost protests, to fill the abyss's void with emptiness.

In his monologue 'Lucretius,' parts of *In Memoriam*, and much of *Maud*, Tennyson replaces the 'moment, one and infinite' of 'By the Fire-Side' with moments of fatal disconnection. An owner of the 1831 seventh edition of *The Christian Year*, Tennyson is an agnostic John Keble, whose liturgical calendar in *In Memoriam* substitutes for scripture's figural types an estranged typology of vanished biological species preserved in the fossil record. He also provides the best epistemological equivalent of J.S. Mill's associationist psychology, which dissolves the chronicles recorded in a medieval Book of Hours into a book of discrete atomic moments. But because a book of moments is not a living testament, Tennyson uses his internal monologues to bind the moments together and attach his affections to well-beloved people and places. To this end he also allows his unforgettable early morning visit to the 'Dark house' in 'long unlovely' Wimpole Street (7.1–2) and his last leave-taking of the 'Unwatched' and 'Unloved' rectory garden at Somersby (101) to show us his own heart and pierce us.

In *In Memoriam* the great chain of being in Pope's *Essay on Man* has turned into an escalator: the 'altar-stairs' that move up to God also slope down to darkness. Though the dangerous Platonic love between Tennyson and Hallam and between Dickens's David Copperfield and Steerforth is as intimate and furtively erotic as anything explored in Browning's monologues, it is also fraught with risk and trauma. It is only a short step from the eros that urges the soul toward attainment in *In Memoriam* to Santayana's dismantling of the *Symposium*'s ladder of love and the subsequent downfall of Oliver and Jim in his novel *The Last Puritan*. The skid down the slope to darkness finds its most disturbing equivalent in the downward spiral of Oscar Wilde's Dorian Gray, a 'Faust of love' whose aspiration veers toward cold opportunism and indifference.

Double Ventriloquism: Disarming the Censors

Browning's two great monologues on art, 'Fra Lippo Lippi' and 'Andrea del Sarto,' have, I think, been consistently misread. Their design becomes clearer if we place them beside a companion monologue, 'Pictor Ignotus,' which is the lament of a Salieri among painters, rapidly being eclipsed by a Renaissance Mozart. Though not exactly obscure, Fra Lippo and Andrea pale in the presence of their famous contemporaries. Rather than acknowledge his defects like the more honest Pictor Ignotus, each painter is trying to transfer to scapegoats, who are often disguised as censors or critics, responsibility for both their artistic and human failings.

Pictor Ignotus is a Casaubon figure: we can feel the chill descend on his fantasies of greatness, like a touch of death. Just as he feels pushed to the side of his life by the youthful painter who should have sat at the painter's feet as a grateful apprentice, so Fra Lippo foresees the greatness of Hulking Tom, the youth named Guidi, who will soon overtake and eclipse him. Being pushed to the side of one's life is Philip Larkin's definition of growing old. Because most of us, if we live long enough, will see our pictures die – 'surely, gently die' – as we are pushed to the margin of our profession by younger rivals, many of us may come to feel surprisingly intimate with these artists of the second rank.

The best parts of 'Fra Lippo Lippi' are the most wavering, the most expressive of the ebb and flow of the speaker's consciousness, as it passes from joy to dejection, from the vision of what might have been to the sad reality of what is. After descending from a visionary plateau, Fra Lippo turns easily to conversation. But because he finds himself confronting disturbing limitations in his life and art, consolatory moods are hard to sustain. There is often a brusque grace to his idiom, and a fine dramatic pull between the monastery and the town, the ascetic and the sensualist, the votary of the spirit and the votary of the flesh. But no theory of art can be extracted from such a self-divided mind without doing damage to the speaker's subtle reservations, his weak and incessant rationalizations, and his introjections of a harsh censor figure in the Prior.

Fra Lippo is crippled by censorship: he is destroyed by the menacing figure of 'the good fat father' who offers him the mouthful of bread in exchange for renouncing the world, as he is destroyed later by the Prior. In the drama that Browning creates for the eye and ear, this censorship is felt most strongly in the rigidities of the blank-verse metre from which vagrant accents keep deviating.

> I did renounce the world, its pride and greed,
> Palace, farm, villa, shop and banking-house,
> Trash, such as these poor devils of Medici
> Have given their hearts to – all at eight years old.
>
> 'Fra Lippo Lippi,' 98–101

Like Pope, Browning can make poetry out of a laundry list. The ease with which an inventory of discordant items – 'Palace, farm, villa, shop and banking-house' – falls into an accentually irregular blank verse line, without violence to speech, is even more apparent on the printed page than in an oral reading of the lines.

Fra Lippo blames the monks for preventing him from achieving in practice what he knows he should achieve in theory. Either he paints a 'bowery flowery angel-brood' (349), levitating like disembodied spirits on the ceilings of baroque churches, where the absence of physical constraint is mocked by the billowing feminine rhymes at the centre of the line, or else he revels in a riot of sensuality, as caught by surprise in a corner of his own painting he plays hot cockles 'Under the cover of a hundred wings' (379).

The monk is embarrassed by his sensuality: in the projected painting he shuffles sideways with his blushing face, and is equally uneasy in his role as the over-sexed rat, nipping 'each softling of a wee white mouse' (10). He jokes about embarrassments that are also a source of pain to him. Or perhaps it is truer to say that the pain of having squandered his artistic talent is deflected to a more superficial anxiety, his pretence of being embarrassed by a *joie de vivre* of which he is secretly proud.

Like Fra Lippo Lippi, Andrea del Sarto and Caliban are dramatis personae turned inside out: because they are regions of Browning's own mental landscape, we and the poet feel shockingly close to them. In his introspection and his speculative reach, Caliban is less a triumph of Browning's negative capability than a triumph of the poet's ventriloquism: his ability to hear internal voices and project them. Similarly, Fra Lippo's hunger for experience and Andrea's conviction that a man's reach should exceed his grasp are memorable credal statements: the voice that comes forth at such moments is Browning's voice, uttering part of God's 'everlasting soliloquy.' And just as Browning has turned the longings of such speakers into a geography of his own mind, so Caliban, Fra Lippo Lippi, and Andrea have internalized such menacing figures as the godlike Prospero, the ascetic Prior, and the censorious Lucrezia.

The sudden volley of short questions at the end of 'Andrea del Sarto' – 'Must you go? / That Cousin here again? he waits outside?' (219–20) – is like the volley of questions fired off by Gloucester at the beginning of *King Lear*. Andrea is breathless, panting to keep up with yesterday's news. Events are overtaking him. Eight staccato questions in five lines are a record, even for Browning. And their nervous agitation is in sharp contrast with the leisurely, appositional style of Andrea's twilight piece, as he grows peaceful as old age, relaxing into a mood of serene acceptance and passivity. The accents of an aggrieved and troubled soul keep challenging and displacing the casuist's over-easy complacency and bad faith. Though putting on a Stoic's armour keeps Andrea from being hurt, it also keeps him from growing. If you expect life to be fair, the Stoic counsels, your heart will be broken by injustice. But by lowering his expectations in marriage and art to avoid the pain of disappointment, Andrea forfeits part of God's image in himself. Though he knows his reach should exceed his grasp, he settles for commercial success when he loses his power to dream of something noble enough to be worth failing at. Like Karshish and Cleon, Andrea is a soul in the vestibule of Dante's hell, tormented by his great refusal to reach gloriously high and fall short. Once again, we feel surprisingly intimate with a speaker whom we know from inside, someone who is resigned, tender, self-satisfied; yet with all this, agitated, stretching out his arms for something more.

Not only does Browning use his painters as dummies through whom to ventriloquize, annexing them to himself only to expel them violently, but also, by a species of double ventriloquism, Andrea and Fra Lippo turn a censorious third person into a geography of their minds. This introjection takes place even when the persona half fears as well as half desires the assimilated censor, and is as eager as Fra Lippo, Andrea del Sarto, or Caliban to expel as well as absorb such a menacing critic as the Prior, Lucrezia, or Prospero.

By double ventriloquism I mean the process by which Browning's speakers perform operations on other characters that replicate the operations Browning himself is performing on the speakers. We become strangely intimate with the characters on whom such operations are performed, because we seem to have met them, not just once, but two or three times. As in any experience of *déjà vu*, we know more about Caliban and Browning's modern Bryon than we consciously know we know. The introjection and doubling are especially evident in the vistas of infinite regress that recede before our eye in 'Le Byron de Nos Jours,' where Browning's female speaker displays the same privileged knowledge of her lover *manqué* as the savage in 'Caliban upon Setebos' displays of everyone else. He knows that his domination of the crabs mirrors Prospero's similar assumption of authority to subjugate Caliban, and that the god Setebos abuses his own despotic power when he enslaves everyone to himself except the Quiet, the god beyond god, into whom Setebos as the lesser deity may some day evolve.

Paradoxes of Role-Playing: Browning and Pound

Precariously balanced between intimacies of empathy and free projection, Pound's prostitute in 'Portrait d'une Femme' performs the same demanding high-wire act of the mind as W.J. Fox's poet. On the one hand, her personality must be 'modified' and even changed by the men she is intimate with. On the other hand, her own personality should never be wholly 'absorbed,' as Fox insists of his transmigrating Vishnu.

Total absorption leads to promiscuity or death. As an alternative to the categorical living of a shore-dweller, the prostitute has chosen a life of risk and high adventure. Instead of chaining herself to the repetitive routine of 'One dull man, dulling and uxorious, / One average mind – with one thought less, each year' (9–10), whose dullness extends to the dull shape of the lines, she chooses to collect a sea-hoard of exotic wares and shipwrecked treasures. Though she revels in her freedom, the prostitute also discovers she has a price to pay for being promiscuous:

> In the slow float of differing light and deep,
> No! there is nothing! In the whole and all,
> Nothing that's quite your own.
>   Yet this is you.
>
>   'Portrait d'une Femme,' 27–30

Unless Fox's artist remains firmly in control of the licentious process of casting her spirit 'into any living thing, real or imaginary,' she degenerates into a moral cipher. No impersonation can lack the authority of a presiding personality who 'gives' generously of herself even while taking back from others. When such authority is lacking, the role-player becomes a mere 'poetic harlequin,'[14] a chameleon like Pound's prostitute or Keats's poet of negative capability who, in trying to be everyone, retains no residual qualities of her own.

Pound uses an equally intimate metaphor in 'Tenzone' to describe the plight of a lyric poet who has not yet found in a monologue's silent auditor the necessary 'stand-in' or surrogate for an appreciative public. As stupid virgins, his verses, he fears, are still too chaste and reclusive to be mated with an audience. Though he warns friendly critics against 'procuring' (9) him readers to whom his virgin verses may be forced to surrender their chastity, his sexual word-play cannot disguise the seriousness of his joke. Unless his lyrics, in becoming more dramatic, can be 'touched with the verisimilitudes' (16), they will remain as stupidly chaste as the 'timorous wench' (3) who takes flight from the centaur.

A dramatic mask becomes deceptive, an instrument of either hypocrisy or irony, whenever it tries to hide disparities between appearance and reality. In Pound's 'The Temperaments' the hypocrite who has committed 'nine adulteries, 12 liaisons, 64 fornications and something approaching a rape' (1) assumes the incognito of a reserved monk, who seems 'both bloodless and sexless' (4). By contrast, the ironist who is the married 'father of twins' (6) and whose wife has been unfaithful to him four times assumes the incognito of a lewd sensualist, who 'both talks and writes of nothing save copulation' (5).

Pound offers a subtler exploration of the paradoxes of the mask in 'The Flame,' where the poet is thought at first to be identical with the characters he has impersonated. If he has merged his soul with 'aught here on earth, / There canst thou find [him].' But just as the verb 'slipped' slips the grasp of the strongly end-stopped lines, so the impersonator slips the reader's grasp, too.

> If thou hast seen my shade sans character,
> If thou hast seen that mirror of all moments,
> That glass to all things that o'ershadow it,
> Call not that mirror me, for I have slipped
> Your grasp, I have eluded.
>
> 'The Flame,' 39–43

At the very moment we think we have captured the poet's 'shade sans character,' we are reminded that as a god of many masks he is as evasive as a butterfly and as hard to catch as a bird. Even in taking the 'senses, feelings, nerves, and brain' of the people he impersonates, Pound's poet is still 'himself in them.' Like Fox's Vishnu, he is 'modified but not absorbed by their peculiar constitution and mode of being.'[15]

Anticipating Pound's playful poems on role-playing and masks, Browning's lyric 'The Boy and the Angel' invites us to ponder the critical difference between Christian Incarnation and mere Gnostic tricks of impersonation, which assume that flesh is only an optical illusion and the body a mere disguise or garment that a masked god can remove at will. When the devout monk, Theocrite, a humble craftsman, dies in his cell, the angel Gabriel, another of Fox's 'transmigrating Vishnus,' uses tricks of ventriloquism and switched identities to impersonate him. But his ventriloquism is unpleasing to God, who quickly penetrates the deception of his angel's singing through the dead monk as a ventriloquist might intone through a puppet. Instead of assuming mere 'flesh-disguise' as a 'transmigrating Vishnu,' the true poet of negative capability must authentically become what he impersonates, just as God became flesh through the mystery of *kenosis* that emptied the Father's godhead into his Son.[16]

The politically liberal Fox creates the masked God of his review essay

on Tennyson in his own Unitarian image. Working against this democratic tradition is the High Church typology of John Keble and his
Tractarian heirs, who feel impelled to rescue God from a slightly vulgar
habit of impersonating everyone. The classical posturing of Matthew
Arnold, who as Keble's godson is a High Church agnostic who admires
everything about Catholicism except its Christianity, provides a stage
prop for a more epic and cosmopolitan culture than any Browning had
envisaged. Even the esoteric typologies of Keble's *The Christian Year* and
the oblique biblical allusions in T.S. Eliot's monologues 'Journey of the
Magi' and 'A Song for Simeon' preserve intact the serene High English-
ness of a God whose Archbishop of Canterbury is a kind of British
Minister for Divine Affairs. It is important that Eliot should regard the
Incarnation as a mere fugitive 'hint half guessed,' a 'gift half understood'
(*Dry Salvages*, 5.32). Otherwise, the more humanized Christ of the Broad
Church Browning and the Unitarian Fox might have represented an
excess of condescension and proletarian zeal on the deity's part.

As a proprietary tyrant who chooses 'never to stoop,' Browning's
Duke of Ferrara parodies the democratic God of Fox, the Unitarians, and
Evangelical Anglicans, who always 'stoops to rise.' Like many tyrants
and despots in Browning's monologues, he dramatizes the disastrous
implications of taking the metaphor of a mystical incorporation into
Christ's body too literally. In the monologues Browning celebrates the
democracy of a masked God who opposes the totalitarian politics of
swallowing up or annexing alien bodies. In the Incarnational theology of
'Saul' and 'A Death in the Desert' he shows how the metaphor of inte-
gration can be reversed into a wholly decentralized or democratic one, in
which, as Northrop Frye explains, 'the total body is complete within
each individual.'[17]

As a metaphysical adventure story, Browning's *Fifine at the Fair* poses
a dilemma confronting every writer of dramatic monologues. In proliferating a host of self-created identities, the role-player may lose his own
identity in the people he impersonates. When he removes the last dramatic mask, what does he confront: a subtler, more nuanced version of
himself (as in Keble's and Dobell's hermeneutical theories of the mask),
or a mere emptiness and void (as in the agnostic theories of Sir William
Hamilton and H.L. Mansel)?[18]

In section 120, as edifice dies into edifice, the shadow that sucks the
whole façade into itself is in danger of turning into the night in which all
cows are black, as Hegel says of Schelling's Absolute. In Oscar Wilde's

phrase, 'the truths of metaphysics are the truths of masks.'[19] The hope is that Browning will present the spectacle of a finely nuanced whole. But what kind of unity do the merging forms consent to?

'What common shape was that wherein they mutely merged
Likes and dislikes of form, so plain before?'

Fifine at the Fair, 2040–1

Because the poet fears that the last mask conceals a void, he is as reluctant as Carlyle's Teufelsdröckh in 'Natural Supernaturalism' to confront the Victorian equivalent of the Titan's 'Three-formed Fate' (2226) in Aeschylus's *Prometheus Bound* by removing the last remaining garment from the body of God.

Shelley's teaching that sympathetic imagination is the indispensable agent of moral growth finds a theological counterpart in the divine condescension of St John's God, who 'stoops' to 'rise' in Browning's monologue 'A Death in the Desert' (134). One theological model of Keats's poet of negative capability is the hidden god of the agnostics, the elusive 'Fate beyond the Fates' in 'Demeter and Persephone' (128) or the 'something over Setebos / That made Him' in 'Caliban upon Setebos' (129–30). Another prototype is the hidden god of the early Greek Christians, who sometimes call Christ the *prosopon* (πρόσωπον) or mask of God, who may conceal as much as he reveals.

In choosing not to choose a single identity for himself, the Keatsian impersonator may be created in the image of two different gods. To the degree that differences between the poet and the speakers he impersonates can be honoured and maintained by gifts of sympathetic identification and empathy, the poet of 'Fra Lippo Lippi' and 'Saul' is fashioned in the image of the Hebraic-Christian God of Love and Relationship. But to the degree that the Browning of *Fifine at the Fair* blends the carnival's diversely coloured masks into pure white light, he is created in the image of a God who is masked and nameless. Sustaining a world which would otherwise vanish like a shadow in the dark, such a master of negative capability gives everything away to his personae: he has no qualities he can properly call his own. 'Unshadowable in words,' which are 'Themselves but shadows of a shadow-world,' this God of many masks, Tennyson's 'Nameless of the hundred names' ('The Ancient Sage,' 238–9, 49), is too lonely and remote to have anything particular to do with the universe. Like the Zeus whom Tennyson arraigns behind the mask of Demeter in the classical monologue of his old age, the God of many masks is no more personal, moral, beautiful, or true than Spinoza's austere God. He resembles the Brahm of Indian theology, or that Mystery beyond Knowledge that F.H. Bradley calls the Absolute, a being in whom justice and personality can no longer be preserved as ultimate attributes of deity.

5

The Agnostic Legacy:
Ghosts of Departed Faith

Just as Sir William Hamilton's and H.L. Mansel's negative theology culminates in an agnostic theory of masks, so another turning point in post-Romantic culture takes place when the deconstruction of the Platonic thought studied in chapter 2 culminates in the nominalism of Walter Pater and in the mere surface masks of poets like William Morris and D.G. Rossetti. By Pater's nominalism I mean his notion that words no longer refer to Platonic universals. They do not even denote an abiding sensory referent. They evoke at best a surface pattern of sounds, a self-contained verbal music. To blur Plato's distinction between an archetype and its replica, purists like Swinburne and Morris either thicken the verbal medium or so attentuate its content that reading their verse is like the experience of proof-reading. I mean that the reader is forced to pay such exclusive attention to the details of spacing, typography, punctuation, and syntax that the meaning itself starts to disappear. The purist side of Platonism resides in Plato's teaching that truth itself is a formal principle. The purist side of deconstruction lies in Pater's art in *Plato and Platonism* of stripping the philosopher of any metaphysical illusions. Pater dismantles Plato's doctrine of being while retaining in Plato's pleasing aesthetic masks a poetry of pure surface over void.

But to empty a poem of spiritual content is more difficult than most reductionists imply. As Swinburne shows in his monologue 'Hymn to Proserpine,' any act of burying the gods carries the seeds of its own destruction. As long as change persists, Persephone cannot die, because she is the genius of change itself. To predict that even the newly triumphant Christ will die is to forget that no gods will die as long as there are worshippers to extol them or infidels to write their epitaph: 'Yet thy kingdom shall pass, Galilean, thy dead shall go down to thee dead' (74). A phrase like 'All delicate days and pleasant' (47) creates a hole at its centre. Like Milton's locution, 'in this dark world and wide,' where the blind poet seems to lose his way in a world too spacious for him, the use of a correlative conjunction that is not required by the meaning mocks the emptiness of a soft pastoral world soon to be 'cast / Far out with the foam,' like Tennyson's lotos-eaters as they sweep 'to the surf of the past' (47–8). But even as Swinburne's sceptic relishes the death of a slave morality in which the sheep conspire to persuade the wolves that it is sinful to be strong, he cannot ironically reconcile his elegiac prophecy about the death of Christianity with his other resounding axiom about the eternity of consciousness: 'Fate is a sea without shore, and the soul is a rock that abides' (41).

Wallace Stevens's 'Sunday Morning,' a miniature narrative poem which modulates by way of free indirect discourse into the dramatic mono-logue of the central verse paragraphs, brings Swinburne's sceptic into the boudoir. The more self-consciously the speaker tries to banish God from her private devotions, the more persistently the ghost of this dead god returns to haunt her. 'Old' is a repeated impression in the poem: 'that old catastrophe' (1.7), 'any old chimera of the grave' (4.7), 'an old chaos of the sun' (8.5). As superannuated fictions, are the catastrophe and chimera 'old' in the sense of obsolete? Or are they 'old' because venerable? 'How cold the vacancy,' as Stevens says in 'Esthétique du Mal,' 'When the phantoms are gone and the shaken realist / First sees reality' (8.14–16). Even as the speaker tries to supplant these fictions with her hedonistic rites, they rise from their grave to disturb as well as console her.

The hendiadys that pries 'green' loose from its home in 'cockatoo' to give it a new dwelling place in 'freedom' mingles with other vagrant impressions.

> Complacencies of the peignoir, and late
> Coffee and oranges in a sunny chair,
> And the green freedom of a cockatoo
> Upon a rug mingle to dissipate
> The holy hush of ancient sacrifice.
>
> 'Sunday Morning,' 1.1–5

But even as a liberated imagination exorcises the ghosts of otherworldly theology, it involuntarily endows these ghosts with life. Composing an elegy for a bloodless paradise beyond the misty fields and wakened birds, the celebrant tries to negate the beautiful but obsolete fictions that increasingly beguile her – fictions of a Homeric underworld or a Christian paradise of resurrected souls.

Even in reversing the substance of Milton's cosmology, the Miltonic placement of a noun between two framing adjectives – 'cloudy palm / Remote' (4.10–11) – lends a 'haunt of prophecy' to the speaker's vaunted exorcism of ghosts.

> There is not any haunt of prophecy,
> ...
> Nor visionary south, nor cloudy palm
> Remote on heaven's hill, that has endured
> As April's green endures; or will endure
> Like her remembrance of awakened birds,
> Or her desire for June and evening, tipped
> By the consummation of the swallow's wings.
>
> 'Sunday Morning,' 4.6–15

Like the verb 'endure,' which survives in its past, present, and future forms, remembrance is a triumph of the power of memories to inspire prophecies, in defiance of the opening prophecy about the death of prophecy. Instead of exorcising such impulses, the speaker's memory allows the banished ghosts to enjoy a resilient posthumous life in tropes that are self-enfolding and reflexive. Such is the power of the swallow's wings, whose power to tip to perfection or to 'consummate' is transferred from the birds themselves to the speaker's 'desire for June and evening,' a longing and remembrance that bind her to the world with obligation and affection. Because a desire so exquisite and multiple in its capacity both to mirror and be mirrored is as ubiquitous as air, it can never be wholly banished from our minds.

Stevens's speaker keeps conferring life on the gods she hopes to exorcise. When she tries to bury the ghost of a resurrected Jesus in the final stanza, she does so by raising another ghost in the voice that cries out 'upon that water without sound':

> 'The tomb in Palestine
> Is not the porch of spirits lingering.
> It is the grave of Jesus where he lay.'
>
> 'Sunday Morning,' 8.2–4

To announce the death of God is to resurrect God in the form of a silent-speaking voice that is just as ubiquitous and just as spectral as the spirits it tries to banish.

Equally precarious is Ezra Pound's art of self-voiding in 'The Garden,' a satire on a refined young woman 'dying piece-meal / of a sort of emotional anæmia' (3–4). Refined beyond the point of being civilized, her 'exquisite and excessive' (9) boredom is a result of shrinking from an act she secretly longs to perform: an act so natural and spontaneous as talking to Pound. It is impossible to banish from the line 'In her is the end of breeding' (8) the ghost of a faintly ironic phantom-meaning. For behind the refinement of her breeding there flickers the impossiblity of any further procreation of her type. Ironically, she is not only the termination or end-point of all breeding but also its apogee or goal, the condition to which breeding suicidally aspires.

Arthurian Ghosts: The Phantom Art of 'The Defence of Guenevere'

In describing her dead husband as a medium through whom historical and legendary voices once spoke, Jane Morris in Richard Howard's monologue 'A Pre-Raphaelite Ending' offers an important insight into William Morris's achievement in *The Defence of Guenevere and Other Poems* (1858). 'It was, through him,' Jane Morris muses,

'an ancient voice speaking, or a voice from
          a previous life
          jerking the words out
    of a body which it had
    nothing to do with.'

'A Pre-Raphaelite Ending,' 166–70

As Howard's persona suggests, Morris writes as a kind of medium: in conjuring legendary Arthurian ghosts he combines the seer's gift for hearing voices with the ventriloquist's gift for projecting them. In this chapter I want to examine three devices Morris uses to make his medieval conjurings more ghostly than Browning's art of resurrecting ferociously alive and energetic historical ghosts in *Dramatic Lyrics* (1842) and *Men and Women* (1855).

Morris's first and most important means of ghostly conjuring is to turn his words into soulless bodies, as if language itself had contracted Alzheimer's disease. When Guenevere uses words like 'gracious' and 'verily,' she seems to have lost all memory of what they traditionally mean. The material survival of words whose conceptual meaning has departed might seem at first to produce a merely materialist or fleshly art, as critics from Robert Buchanan to Jerome McGann have in fact argued.[1] But in practice, except for moments of tactile drubbing and brute sensory horror in 'Sir Peter Harpedon's End' and 'The Haystack in the Floods,' the effect of Morris's hollowing out the referential soul of words is usually the opposite of tactile. In trying to bury the concepts that words normally signify, Morris confers on the corpses of these concepts the posthumous life of ghosts. To banish a phantom by first evoking it is already to endow that phantom with spectral life.

A second way of making the Arthurian poems ghostly is to perform deathlike operations on their syntax and diction. In 'King Arthur's Tomb,' for example, the hyphenated oxymoron of a living that is 'half-sleep, half-strife' (16) compacts the death-in-life status of Morris's own ghostly conjurings. The phantom art of 'The Chapel in Lyoness' is also made spectral by the use of archaisms. Several words at the ends of quatrains – 'a-near,' 'a-pace,' 'is writ' (4, 12, 78) – are intelligible to the eye and ear but are no longer found on any reader's tongue. They are ghostlike, because they share the life-in-death of an obsolete idiom.

Equally spectral is Morris's use of a third device, the trap or double bind. To expose Guenevere's rhetorical sleight of hand in the title poem is to reveal that to fall in love with words and visual surfaces is to fall in love with pictures. But because it is impossible to read a poem as if it were a gallery of pictures, the reader who interprets the poetry sooner or later has to conjure from its visual surfaces the ghosts of its departed moral and religious meanings. And to do so is to fall into the very trap that Guenevere has set for her victims. She hopes that readers will bestow upon the ghosts of meanings she has banished from her speech a resilient posthumous life. So to resist Guenevere's seduction is to make the poetry impossible to read. And to make the poetry intelligible is to perpetuate her error. The art of William Morris is a phantom art, because it is self-voiding and spectral, an art that demonstrates its own impossibility. In order to understand the poetry the reader must first commit a version of the errors that the poet behind the mask implicitly repudiates and condemns.

The Language of William Morris: A Soulless Body

In speaking of Morris's materialist aesthetic, Jerome McGann is only the most recent critic to repeat Robert Buchanan's charge that the Pre-Raphaelites are a fleshly school of artists. But Morris's retention of the mere material husks of language, signs over which the ghosts of dead or departed referents keep hovering, usually produces poetry that is the opposite of materialist. Its indeterminate syntax, contradictory clues, and self-voiding narratives produce instead a phantom art through which Arthurian characters keep flitting like ghosts in a seance or disturbing memories in a dream. The detached 'hair,' 'head,' and 'wandering... mouths,' which leave the 'hands' far behind them in 'The Defence of Guenevere' (128, 131, 136, 138), levitate like bodies on the ceilings of baroque churches, or – if that seems too ecclesiastical – like the exuberant play of released skeletal parts in Tennyson's *danse macabre*, 'The Vision of Sin.'

Even as the sensory husks of language are being made ghostlike by the transformation of Guenevere's rising 'breast' into 'waves of purple sea' (226–7) and the sound waves in her throat into the sensory marvel of rising ripples, Guenevere's persuasive redefinition of key words like 'wonderful,' 'gracious,' and 'true' is causing morality itself to undergo a sea change. One of the most seductive and phantomlike features of the poem is its redefinitions, which allow moral ideas to survive as beautiful aesthetic ghosts. Though the words 'gracious' and 'true' retain their favourable emotive meanings, their descriptive meanings are altered beyond recognition.

<blockquote>
will you dare,
When you have looked a little on my brow,

'To say this thing is vile?   236–8

am I not a gracious proof –

...

also well I love to see
That gracious smile light up your face, and hear
Your wonderful words, that all mean verily

'"The thing they seem to mean

'The Defence of Guenevere,' 241–50
</blockquote>

As 'grace' declines from the favour of a gracious God or virtuous knight to mere grace of manner or bearing, virtue and vice become matters of good or bad taste. Words mean 'verily,' Guenevere insists, if they are 'the thing they seem to mean.' But if appearance is the only reality and words are mere sensory marvels, like the ripples of sound that rise in Guenevere's throat, they cannot be what they seem to be. If truth has any referential meaning, Launcelot cannot be true. And if he is true, the word 'truth' has to be redefined as a pure intuition of moral values. Since a perception of good and evil is as immediate as a sensory presentation of blue or red, moral judgments are assimilated, as in the ethical theories of G.E. Moore, to the perception of a colour. For Morris, the poet behind the mask, Guenevere's understanding of truth is a self-voiding concept, made obsolete as a ghost at the very moment a correspondence theory of truth is invoked to reaffirm the traditional distinction between what a thing is and what it refers to or means.

As if to alert us to the scene-stealing theatricality of Guenevere's performance, Morris allows the auxiliary verb of illusion to multiply at an alarming rate: 'making his commands / *Seem* to be God's commands' (31–2); 'She stood, and *seemed* to think' (58); '*seemed* to chime' (64, all italics mine). As form supplants content, even the act of never shrinking is registered as a metrical expansion, swelling out the hypermetric second line with an extra syllable: 'Though still she stood right up, and never shrunk, / But spoke on bravely, glorious lady fair!' (55–6). Despite the Miltonic syntax, which frames the noun between two adjectives, the 'lady' is glorious and brave, not because she is one of Milton's moral heroines, but because she is a dazzling actress. The musical dynamics of her voice – its crescendo and fall – are more potent than any libretto she is called upon to render.

More enamoured of the sound of words than of their sense, she discovers that the 'little change of rhyme' (66) is as much a feature of her own frugal *terza rima*s as of the chimes that keep ringing out the name of King Ban's son. Even the *terza rima*'s two enclosing rhymes are ghostlike echoes of the contained rhymes in each preceding tercet (*a b a, b c b, c d c*), which enjoy a kind of phantom life in the rhymes that survive them.

'Listen, suppose your time were come to die,
And you were quite alone and very weak;
Yea, laid a dying while very mightily

'The wind was ruffling up the narrow streak
Of river through your broad lands running well
'The Defence of Guenevere,' 16–20

The evocation of 'the narrow streak / Of river through your broad lands running well' (19–20) is less a description of the landscape than of the visual surface of the tercets, with their thin middle line of verse 'running well' between the broad enclosing outer rhymes, and surfacing like ghosts as the dominant rhymes of the next tercets. Sometimes the end-words create a phantom rhyme for the eye alone. The rhyme survives, like the poem's moral values, only as part of an intricate visual pattern. 'Blow' replicates 'brow' visually, but fails to create a rhyme for the ear. Because the same is true of 'die' and 'mightily' and 'commands' and 'wands' (2, 4, 16, 18, 31, 33), the drama for the eye is not always a drama that the ear can share.

Lethal Words in Morris's Arthurian Monologues

Without disturbing the surface perfection of the *terza rimas*, which seem calm and unruffled to the eye, the ellipses and two-way meanings in 'The Defence of Guenevere' convey to the ear an indeterminacy that begins to unravel the syntax, even disintegrating at moments into break-downs and stammers: 'Ah Christ! if only I had known, known, known' (41). As a dramatic monologue, 'The Defence of Guenevere' owes the formal arrangements of its fluent iambics and tercets to William Morris, the poet behind the mask. But to its dramatic speaker the monologue owes the flashes of feeling in its indeterminate syntax and short swoops of phrasing.

> then I could tell,
>
> Like wisest man how all things would be, moan,
> And roll and hurt myself, and long to die,
>
> 'The Defence of Guenevere,' 42–4

Is 'moan' a noun or a verb? Will nature make a universal moan, or are we to understand an ellipsis of the human subject that aligns Guenevere's 'moan' with the succession of verbs – 'roll and hurt myself, and long to die' – in the next line?

Equally ghostlike is the way Morris's Arthurian characters declaim into the void. Even when Launcelot and Guenevere are in each other's presence in 'King Arthur's Tomb,' they talk past each other with the result that two monologues seem to be in progress. The silence at the end of 'The Defence of Guenevere,' when the queen refuses to speak another word but turns sideways to listen for Launcelot, is truly a void. The absence of any answer is as audible as a gong.

Six times in 'The Blue Closet,' another poem on Arthur's death, the italicized refrain can be heard tolling toward the grave. Shadowing the ultimate ellipsis of death is the blankness of the fourth refrain, where death is precisely the absence of sound, signalling both the wind's death and Arthur's. Most affecting, however, are the blank intervals and losses of sound in the last refrain, where only the tumbling sea is left to toll the death of the king, the sisters, and the wind, and finally the slow expiry of language itself.

Another surreal, potentially lethal operation that Morris performs on words is his oddly liberated use of the trope metonymy. Set free from the body, the lovers' mouths and hands are allowed to kiss or roam at will.

> '... – In that garden fair

> 'Came Launcelot walking; this is true, the kiss
> Wherewith we kissed in meeting that spring day,
> I scarce dare talk of the remember'd bliss,'

> 'When both our mouths went wandering in one way,
> And aching sorely, met among the leaves;
> Our hands being left behind strained far away. ...'
> > 'The Defence of Guenevere,' 132–8

The lines betray a strong weakness for oxymoron, for the intense pleasure of what is painful, and for the sure accuracy of moving in unison by committing what is also an act of moral vagrancy or wandering off course. There is even an inspired economy in the tight tautology of 'this is true, the kiss / Wherewith we kissed in meeting' (133–4), which uses cognate forms – 'the kiss ... we kissed' – to mirror the death-dealing tautologies that every worshipper of sense in Morris's Arthurian poems seems greedy to embrace.

As Christopher Ricks observes in *Beckett's Dying Words*, language becomes deathlike when it acquires the power to mean its own opposite.[2]

> Why did your long lips cleave
> In such strange way unto my fingers then?
> So eagerly glad to kiss, so loath to leave
> When you rose up?
> > 'King Arthur's Tomb,' 249–52

There is a lethal aliveness in the verb 'cleave,' which can mean 'cut asunder' as well as 'cling to.' Usually, words are tipped with arrows: when Tennyson's Ancient Sage exhorts the sceptic to 'cleave … to the sunnier side of doubt' (68), he uses 'cleave' to point in one direction only. But Morris gives us the axis without the arrow: even as Launcelot's 'long lips' 'cleave … unto' the fingers, they also seem to 'cleave … in two,' mutilating what they kiss. We catch the flicker of an 'anti-pun' in the archaic preposition 'unto,' which is alive only on Ruskin's tongue in *Unto This Last*, though even there it has an archaic biblical feel to it. The phantom meaning of 'in two,' which is mordantly alive in the preposition 'unto,' cannot be wholly banished from the mind once it is raised. As in dreams, where there are no contraries, the paralysing possibility that Launcelot's lips are long because they tarry long, to immobilize and kill as well as kiss and revive, makes the language deathlike. We feel what Ricks calls 'the torpedo-touch'[3] in a verb like 'cleave,' whose antithetical senses give the kiss a sinister glow. Like Tennyson's Maud, whose ghastly glimmer has the luminous appearance of a ghost, Launcelot, for all his ardour and lust, has the emotional vigour of a vampire.

If Guenevere moves her auditors, it is not by her arguments, but by the inspired simplicity of her language.

'Do I not see how God's dear pity creeps
All through your frame, and trembles in your mouth?
Remember in what grave your mother sleeps …'
'The Defence of Guenevere,' 151–3

By rotating the simple sounds – 'creeps,' 'tremble,' 'Remember' – she imagines what is otherwise beyond imagining, the 'dear pity' of 'God' and the severed head of her accuser's brutally murdered mother. The 'awful drouth / Of pity' which 'drew' that 'blow' is not so much a trope as a rotation of sounds that turn the speaker slowly toward the darkness of death (156–57).

What Morris tries to capture in the unheard words that are forever rising to the surface of his Arthurian poems is death the void, the absence of consciousness. When Galahad hovers on the edge of oblivion, the poetry's imperfect rhymes – 'weary,' 'Miserere' – and strong seventh-syllable caesuras drift into easeful death with him.

> Right so they went away, and I, being weary,
> Slept long and dream'd of Heaven: the bell comes near,
> I doubt it grows to morning. Miserere!
>> 'Sir Galahad: A Christmas Mystery,' 150–2

The words are what they say, a drift into oblivion, and as such mimetic. But they are also antimimetic, a presentational assault on mimesis, since the subsiding cadences are also the unspoken subject, which keeps rising to the surface of the poem, becoming indistinguishable from the flagging metrical pulse which all but stops at the late-breaking caesura, barely able to sustain its beat to the end of the line.

Morris's renovation of clichés also makes dying forms of language curiously alive.

> And you were quite alone and very weak;
> Yea, laid a dying
>> 'The Defence of Guenevere,' 17–18

Though 'lay a dying' is a commonplace, Guenevere imagines someone who is not merely lying or reposing in a near-death state. She is 'laid' or placed somewhere, as one is said to be 'laid' in a grave. To be 'laid a dying' is to be interred in a grave while one is still in the act of dying but not yet dead. Like a cliché's power to mingle life and death, there is an unimaginable horror in the Poe-like fantasy of burying someone who is · still half alive.

Morris uses clichés and puns to bury the living and quicken the dead. Even his narrator's cliché, 'The tears dried quick' (10), is animated by antithetical energies in the pun on 'quick' and in the moist eyes and 'cheek of flame' (9). As two physical forces contend against each other, the 'quick' or fast drying of the eyes buries the shame that the burning cheeks ought to keep alive in a revival of 'quick''s forgotten etymology.

Aestheticism and the Monologue: Surface Masks

A purely presentational art is self-voiding: it drains its representations of any stable meaning. Morris voids Guenevere's fictions by subverting their authenticating mechanism: the beauty and nobility of her physical gestures. The 'passionate twisting of her body' (60), which bears a 'trace' of the very 'shame' it is said to efface (59), alerts us to several other contradictions in her story. Her tacit admission of guilt in line 13, 'God wot I ought to say, I have done ill,' contradicts her several protestations of innocence in defiance of Gauwaine: 'God knows I speak truth, saying that you lie' (48, 144, 285). One and the same event, Guenevere's adulterous love for Launcelot, is presented in several conflicting versions that allow her simultaneously to affirm and deny that it ever took place.

The same two-way pull can be felt in the migration of a word like 'slip' through several stanzas. The slippage is partly a matter of slipping gracefully across the breaks between tercets. Morris's enchanting confusion of moral and aesthetic slippages is also captured in a series of lovely 'cadences' or falls.

> '... as if one should

> 'Slip slowly down some path worn smooth and even,
> Down to a cool sea on a summer day;
> Yet still in slipping was there some small leaven

> 'Of stretched hands catching small stones by the way
> ...
> No minute of that wild day ever slips

> 'From out my memory'; ...
>
> 'The Defence of Guenevere,' 93–106

The moral slippage of the word 'slip' is beautifully disguised as a refreshing slip down a seaside path on a summer day. The cord that binds Guenevere to Launcelot, and which is her only tie to God, prevents her slipping on the stones. If the past is dreadful only to those who lose all memory of it, as Tennyson's lotos-eaters maintain, then this slipping down the path is also the opposite of slippage, for it continues to bind that day to memory with gratitude and affection. By comparison with such graces, Arthur's virtue is appalling: it lacks a single vice to redeem it.

Even repetitions have a morally numbing effect: Arthur's 'little love' hollows out the queen's marriage vow, turning it into a 'little word,' which is further diminished by a third use of 'little,' the power of Launcelot's love to make Guenevere 'love God ... a little' (83, 86, 90). Such repetitions are valued, not for their meaning, which is hollowed out by casuistry and special pleading, but for their enigmatic formal qualities, like a refrain in a ballad or a recurrent cadence in music, whose 'fall' resonates more seductively each time it is heard.

The kind of purely presentational text that Morris tries to write, a text with musical or vocal 'falls' but no moral ones, demonstrates its own impossibility. This is because a dramatic monologue like Guenevere's, or an interior monologue like Launcelot's in 'King Arthur's Tomb,' Galahad's in 'A Christmas Mystery,' or the sisters' in 'The Blue Closet,' always requires a performative speech act: an act of ghostly conjuring or summoning. To the extent that ghostly conjuring evokes something new, like God's performative decree 'Let there be light,' it can sustain Morris's new presentational aesthetic. But to the extent that ghostly conjuring is still a grounded act, an act of hearing voices that antecedently exist and then finding an art form to project them, the dramatic or interior monologue is not a genre that allows Morris, like the 'idle singer of an empty day,' to bracket either legend or history. In *The Defence of Guenevere and Other Poems* Morris cannot create an earthly paradise of heroes and heroines who, because they never lived, 'can ne'er be dead' ('Apology,' *The Earthly Paradise*, 7, 19). On the contrary, Morris's Arthurian poems conjure the shades of heroes and heroines who are very dead indeed. Because they return like the ghost of Arthur, 'stiff with frozen rime' in 'The Blue Closet' (68), to accompany the sisters across the bridge of death, they are consigned to a vigorous half-life as mere ghouls or vampires.

The Void behind the Mask: Richard Howard's 'A Pre-Raphaelite Ending'

The void behind the masks of Morris's Arthurian monologues is nowhere better intimated than in Richard Howard's monologue on William Morris, '1915: A Pre-Raphaelite Ending,' the last poem in his volume *Untitled Subjects*. In asking her daughter May to breathe life into the words that Gabriel Rossetti has inscribed on paper, William Morris's wife, Janey, is inviting May to do what every reader of a monologue must do in raising ghosts from the grave of history.

> 'Absence can never make me
> so far from you [Janey] again as your presence did
> for years. Yet no one seems alive now—
> the places empty of you are empty
>   of all life.'
>
> 'A Pre-Raphaelite Ending,' 37–41

To bring to life Gabriel's paradox of intimacy at a distance, the monologue allows the pronouns 'me' and 'you' to share a physical proximity on the printed page that they do not share in the proximities of real life. Transcribing words from Rossetti's letters of 30 July 1869 and 4 February 1870,[4] Howard uses the slight pause at the end of the penultimate line to magnify the emptiness. As we round the corner of the line, we discover that what is withheld is nothing less than life itself. The past lives on in Janey Morris's memory. But once she is dead, to what court of memory will the Pre-Raphaelites be summoned?

At times William's self-doubts, including the fear that he is a mere craftsman, obsessed with time-pieces, transfer themselves to his widow, who shows occasional traces of mental wandering and dotage. Unable to remember whether William said he was a mere tinkerer of locks or clocks, Janey allows the rhymes to linger on after their sense has gone, like the ghost of some departed meaning in one of Morris's strangely beautiful Arthurian monologues.

> 'Is it
> nothing but make-believe, and I no more
> than Louis xvi
> tinkering with locks?'
> You know what his rages were –
> I saw him drive his head against that wall,
> making a dent in the plaster. 'With locks,'
> he said, 'tinkering with locks, and too late ... '
> With locks, did he say,
> or clocks? Clocks, I think.
>
> 'A Pre-Raphaelite Ending,' 51–60

In an oral recitation the symmetrical placement of 'locks' and 'clocks' in successive lines counterfeits the harmony of two perfect end-rhymes. Only on the printed page can the written words deftly mute, masquerade, or even mock that harmony by burying the rhymes in the middle of successive lines. Since Louis xvi was a keen amateur locksmith, William probably uses the phrase 'tinkering with locks' to comment on his own waste of talent. Speaking in the twilight of an era, Janey is also afflicted with a panic-stricken awareness of the transience and hence the seriousness of beautiful objects and people. More obsessed with 'clocks' than 'locks,' she has a crazed sense of the paradise that became a domestic hell when love leaked away and no finish proved worthy of its start.

Like Morris's Guenevere, Howard's Janey has the courage of her features, if not the steadfast allegiance of her heart. In typographical imitation of her struggle for survival, the one word that literally survives successive lines of print is 'life' itself.

> What survives is the resistance we bring
> to life, the courage of our features, not
> the strain life brings to us.
>
> 'A Pre-Raphaelite Ending,' 68–70

Despite her tenacity, however, the verse form introduces moments of sudden contraction, when deeply indented words retreat to the extreme right-hand margin of the page and life itself shrinks to the vanishing point.

> Each doctor says
> a different thing
> when I awaken
> gasping in the night.
>
> 'A Pre-Raphaelite Ending,' 70–3

Like the truncated feet, which unexpectedly ebb away, Janey's life threatens to end during the night when she wakes up gasping for breath.

The ménage in which Jane Morris lived was a nightmare. On the printed page the tapering line-lengths create the visual emblem of the abyss in which, beneath the surface harmonies, reciprocity is swallowed up in schism.

> It was an abyss then, an imbroglio
> then and after. The reciprocal
> life of 'well persons'
> grew impossible.
>
> 'A Pre-Raphaelite Ending,' 141–4

The monologue moves toward a discovery of withheld illumination in which the pattern of the imperfect and quotidian 'is laid before us, plain.'

> And so begins
> a long decay – we die from day to dream,
> and common speech we answer with a scream.
>
> 'A Pre-Raphaelite Ending,' 152–4

One 'plain' pattern is the discovery that the monologue's only chiming couplet is a nightmarish rhyme of 'dream' with 'scream.' The 'long decay' sets in with the revelation that the only appropriate response to the unrelenting boredom and horror of waking experience is a stricken cry. The only harmony is a disharmony.

As the visual arts move in to occupy the place vacated by the sacred, William is said to exist for a moment in a world of white bodies, moving and crowned with gold, set apart from the workaday world in a kind of aesthete's paradise.

> Then he saw white bodies
> moving, crowned and bound with gold. That faded.
> I went for the post, and when I returned
> he stifled the blood
> streaming from his mouth
> and held fast to my gown ...
>
> 'A Pre-Raphaelite Ending,' 200–5

The rare use of two internal rhymes – 'crowned and bound' – offers a counter-principle, a momentary stay against oblivion. We can see as well as hear how the sudden contraction of sounds at the centre of the second line opposes the centrifugal, dissipating force of the participles 'moving' and 'streaming.' Not even the sudden contraction of stresses in the phrase 'held fast' can oppose the run of unstressed syllables in the words that keep haemorrhaging, streaming away like blood from the dying man's mouth. As the body's disappearance conjures up pictures of both a wasted beauty and a ghost, nothing can allay the horror of William's seeing his wife propped up grotesquely as richly draped but empty clothes.

> 'The clothes are well enough,' were his last words,
> 'but where has the body gone?'
>
> 'A Pre-Raphaelite Ending,' 207–8

The etymological word-play that allows William's inventive Gothicism to decline from the genuinely 'medieval' to the merely 'middle-aged' brings the final disenchantment. As long as Janey can cross line-breaks and continue to speak, she is saved from oblivion. But as her language winds down and the hope of saving anything permanent begins to die, her fractured lines occupy shorter and shorter grammatical units on the page. Even the parity of its most exiguous forms – 'Save them,' 'save them' – masks a profound disparity of meaning.

> Will you
>   do as I say, save it all –
> the rest of the things are mere images,
> not medieval – only middle-aged:
> lifelike but lifeless, wonderful but dead.
>   These are mine. Save them.
>   I have nothing save them.
>
> 'A Pre-Raphaelite Ending,' 210–16

With the desperate play on 'save,' and the shrinkage of the last two lines to three short sentences, even the words on the printed page are allowed to imitate the shape of the speaker's life by declining from the modest to the minimal.

The Oddity of Morris's Achievement

As Cecil Lang observes, Morris's Arthurian poems are 'like no others in the language, before or since, even in his own works.'[5] The sheer oddity of these beautiful poems, which trace 'the drift of ghosts through a nightmare of passion,' in J.H. Buckley's haunting phrase,[6] is even stranger when we remember that Morris believed 'it is not possible to dissociate art from morality, politics, and religion.'[7]

Morris is what A. Dwight Culler calls an 'Alexandrian poet.'[8] In love with the obscure corners and byways of legend, and seeking out neglected aspects of the Arthurian stories in order to retell them from unfamiliar angles, he is literally eccentric in his off-centre efforts to reach the centre. Intrigued like Ovid by female points of view that male writers had tried to marginalize, Morris exercises his fastidious imagination on the most unfamiliar narratives. As in 'Concerning Geffray Teste Noire,' where the true subject is a mere increment or gloss to a Froissart chronicle, the marginalia and the text have a way of switching position, just as they do in Jacques Derrida's glosses, which exceed in importance the texts they are glossing. Incidents that are merely peripheral or off-stage in Malory – Launcelot's visit to King Arthur's tomb or Guenevere's defence before her judges – move to centre stage in Morris.

Though few of Morris's Arthurian characters are as holy as Galahad, they are all secular equivalents of the holy, because they inhabit a spiritual territory of chapels, palaces, and tombs that Morris rigorously segregates from the workaday world. Guenevere's forensic rhetoric is purist art in disguise, because like purist art (as opposed to a craft like bookbinding or an art like architecture) it is conspicuously useless and impractical. Because nothing Guenevere says is likely to convince a jury not already converted to her cause, the gratuitousness of her performance turns into a sustained travesty of the aesthetic ideal Morris formulates in his mature prose criticism. Far from throwing over art's absence of point the halo of the sacred, Morris like Ruskin defends in his criticism a theory of art for work's sake, not art for art's sake. Declaring that 'art is man's expression of his joy in labor,'[9] Morris opposes any purist separation of art or craft from the everyday world.

Like Matthew Arnold, however, who embraces neoclassicism as a critic but practises Romanticism as a poet, Morris's poetic theory and practice radically diverge. In Morris's most beautiful early poems the absence of moral or rhetorical ends is shown to possess inherent value. The tenderly darkened fingers, the shadow in the hand that looks like wine inside a gold-coloured cup, the breast rising like waves of purple sea, are enough to make Guenevere a heroine, not because all things are equally heroic or beautiful to Morris, but because they are all equally indifferent. A 'terrible beauty' attaches to Launcelot and Guenevere, not because they represent a class of special people, but because they present the special class of love's martyrs and aesthetes. Their purity would be less inviolable if it were not so arbitrary.

In Morris's purist poetry severe abstention from all practical habits of perception that would associate blue with fidelity, for example, or green with amorous passion requires a medieval scholar like Johan Huizinga heroically to suppress his understanding. Readers must see with Ruskin's 'innocent eye' what a child might see, or what the retina of the eye might register if it could be cut off painlessly from the brain. To renounce representation by offering immediate presentations of tear-filled voices or rippling words rising in the throat is to emancipate the sensory medium.

Nothing is more eloquent in such poetry than an abstract posture like Guenevere's leaning eagerly in an immovable gesture, tense with expectation, as she strains like a leashed greyhound to catch sounds of her deliverer's voice. In abandoning the representation of outcomes, such poetry ends at the penultimate moment, offering mere hints and indications. If Launcelot is coming to save her, he comes as a mere wraith or phantom, like Ulysses at the end of Wallace Stevens's monodrama 'The World as Meditation.' Morris perfects a ghostly art in which the portraits are a caricature, the narratives a phantom, and the medieval past a mere dissolving fantasy.

In stripping away the pompous drapery of convention, Morris even reduces his speakers to cartoonlike travesties.

> 'Christ! my hot lips are very near his brow,
>   Help me to save his soul! – Yea, verily,
>
> Across my husband's head, fair Launcelot!
>   Fair serpent mark'd with V upon the head!
> This thing we did while yet he was alive,
>   Why not, O twisting knight, now he is dead?
>
> 'King Arthur's Tomb,' 207–12

Strip away the rhetoric, and what we find is the twisting serpent body of the knight seduced by the queen over the head of her husband's corpse. Salvation lies in a caricature of Launcelot, the branded snake, a Cain among outcasts. Because one form of caricature is to be brutal or vulgar, Morris occasionally flaunts what is out of place in a picture, spoiling the composition. After praising Guenevere as glorious and fair, for example, the narrator in 'The Defence of Guenevere' scorns the picture he has just painted of her by exposing in the 'passionate twisting of her body' (60), a gesture that is ugly and deformed. Even the pictures of Galahad and Sir Ozana expiring on their deathbeds are stunted and pathetic caricatures: we seem to be looking at corpses 'laid out,' as George Santayana says, 'in pontifical vestments.'[10]

Often, as in 'Concerning Geffray Teste Noire,' Morris is most faithful to a medieval chronicler like Froissart when he omits all psychological speculation and allows a pictorial description of outward circumstance to acquire tragic force on its own. As Huizinga says, 'Froissart's soul was a photographic plate.'[11] After boasting that such a soul knew nothing of the tale he has imaginatively reconstructed from a pile of bones, Morris's narrator decides to imitate Froissart's more objective methods by forgoing introspection and speaking simply as a connoisseur of art, like Browning's Duke at the end of 'My Last Duchess.'

> Notice Neptune, though,
> Taming a sea-horse, thought a rarity,
> Which Claus of Innsbruck cast in bronze for me!
>
> 'My Last Duchess,' 54–6

This Jacques Picard, known through many lands,
Wrought cunningly; he's dead now – I am old.

'Concerning Geffray Teste Noire,' 199–200

Praising the effigy of stone-white hands and bright gold hair commissioned by him for the slain lovers, Morris's speaker finds that in order to chart the undertow of oblivion and come at last to the abyss in things he must remain wholly on the surface.

To interpret Morris's Arthurian poetry is to re-present it in the language of critical discourse. If all critical commentary is allegory (an assignment of conceptual meaning – or lack of meaning – to poetic signifiers), then every critic of these poems is committing a version of the representational error Morris's necessarily unsuccessful attempt to void language of concepts is designed to expose. So to interpret Morris's early poetry by reducing it to allegory is necessarily to misinterpret it, and to interpret it correctly is to defeat the critical intelligence by not talking about it at all. Strictly speaking, interpreters are reduced to either silence or misreading. This perhaps explains why it is hard to write well about Morris's early poetry, which, like much analysis of prosody, tends to produce either readable commentary that is inaccurate or accurate commentary that is unreadable.

We can formulate this conclusion another way by saying that to fall in love with Guenevere's pagan beauty is presumably to love less well the ghosts of such departed mediations of her value as her virtue and her goodness. Johan Huizinga cites numerous examples in the late Middle Ages of the mindless multiplication of such moral ghosts. For Olivier de la Marche, to use one of Huizinga's examples, each article of female costume symbolizes a virtue: 'the shoes mean care and diligence, stockings perseverance, the garter resolution.'[12] It is not merely that each thing means something, but that each thing means almost anything. It is clear that like the symbolic meanings of the blue and red wands in 'The Defence of Guenevere,' such virtues as diligence, perseverance, and resolution survive only as ghosts of their original moral meanings, and that the search for these virtues in shoes, stockings, and garters has become a meaningless intellectual pastime.

Whereas T.S. Eliot's 'blue' in 'Ash Wednesday' has an assigned connotation, 'blue of larkspur, blue of Mary's colour' (4.10), Morris's 'blue' is an unconsummated symbol. Its meaning exhausts the freakishness of arbitrary caprice.

'And one of these strange choosing cloths was blue,
Wavy and long, and one cut short and red;
No man could tell the better of the two.

'After a shivering half-hour you said:
"God help! heaven's colour, the blue:" and he said, "hell." ...'

'The Defence of Guenevere,' 34–8

It is possible, of course, that the use of 'blue' as a floating signifier is historically grounded. Morris may expect us to know that blue, originally a symbol of fidelity in love, came in the Middle Ages to represent its own opposite. As Huizinga explains, 'by a very curious transition, blue, instead of being the color of faithful love, came to mean infidelity, too, and next, beside the faithless wife, marked the dupe. In Holland the blue cloak designated an adulterous woman, in France the "cote bleue" denotes a cuckold. At last blue was the color of fools in general.'[13]

Morris has a way of predicting events, of creating dramas in his monologues and then repeating them in real life. As life overtakes the fictional love triangle in 'The Defence of Guenevere,' William Morris might reasonably construe as acts of betrayal or infidelity Jane's gifts of blue gowns and cloaks to Gabriel Rossetti. In a letter dated Saturday, December 1880,[14] she writes to Gabriel as a self-appointed wardrobe mistress. And in an earlier letter she tells Gabriel that she ritually dresses and undresses in blue gowns in front of his drawings, which she arranges over her bed so that she will 'always have the pleasure of feeling them near me.'[15] In celebrating the power of eros to bind her more closely to her absent Launcelot than to the partner of her marriage bed, Jane half justifies William's odd use of blue to signify hell instead of heaven in 'The Defence of Guenevere.' Though Jane, like William's own Guenevere, at once intensifies and refines erotic experience by turning it into an aesthetic devotion, William himself never forgets that there are urgencies of moral witness as well as urgencies of erotic pleasure and delight. When Rossetti dies, Morris is the first to concede that his going 'has left a hole in the world.' But he cannot refrain from attacking Rossetti's 'arrogant misanthropy,'[16] which has always made him an aloof absence rather than a living presence. Like Guenevere's deliverer in Morris's monologue, Rossetti is experienced as a negation. His intimacy is always a product of love or genius in some middle distance.

Though it is historically accurate to say that Morris dramatizes the phase of culture that Huizinga analyses in *The Waning of the Middle Ages*, a historian of ideas would be equally justified in arguing that Morris is not merely re-presenting medieval symbolism in its decline but also exploring the nature and function of the presentational forms that his Victorian contemporary, H.L. Mansel, analyses in *Prolegomena Logica* (1851).[17] Unlike a conceptual representation, Mansel says, the poet's presentational images can be immediately 'depicted to sense or imagination.' Whereas representative or discursive signs 'fix the concept in understanding, freeing its attributes from the condition of locality, and hence from all resemblance to an object of sense,'[18] the poet's presentational images are examples of representative ghosts, or what Susanne Langer calls 'unconsummated symbols.'

As in music, to which Pater says all art aspires, the presentational language of Mansel's poet possesses, in Langer's words, all 'the earmarks of a true symbolism except one: the existence of an assigned connotation.'[19] Because Morris's Arthurian monologues abound in presentational language that possesses the outward form or the ghost of a representational sign without its conventionally assigned significance, the lovely cadences or 'falls' in his verse, which are vocal but not moral 'falls,' approximate music's 'unconsummated' form of symbolism. In short-circuiting the process of using a word to represent a concept that is then denoted by a sensory object, Mansel's presentational forms play an increasingly important role in late-Victorian aesthetics. They influence the poetic theories and practice of such Victorians as Arthur Hallam, David Masson, Walter Pater, and A.C. Swinburne, who often use images to project meanings too elusive for conceptual language to express. By analysing the intuitional theory of logic and knowledge that informs such images, Mansel's *Prolegomena Logica* offers an explanation of purist poetry's antimimetic mimesis, or what I prefer to call its 'representational ghosts.' The *Prolegomena* is a work we know Pater admired, since he praises its 'acute' philosophy in his essay on 'Style.' Mansel's treatise almost certainly influences Pater's own purist criticism, including the well-known analysis of Morris's verse in Pater's 1868 essay on 'Aesthetic Poetry.'

Paradoxically, the harder Morris's Guenevere tries to bury the ghosts of moral judgment, the more these phantoms survive their burial by returning to haunt her. To opt for the flesh rather than the spirit is not, as we might first think, merely to slay the latter in the act of giving life to the former. Rather it is to fall victim to a phantom art, to an art that conjures shades from the gloom. These are shades that, as F.H. Bradley says of 'the ghosts of Metaphysics,' never 'speak without blood ... and accept no substitute.'[20]

In hovering resourcefully between a historical re-presentation of late-medieval symbolism in its decline and a pure presentation of sensory forms, Morris produces a phantom art that is neither one nor the other. The historical ghosts that Morris conjures in his Arthurian monologues are mere ghosts of ghosts, mere phantoms of the departed representations that Huizinga identifies in the decline of late-medieval symbolism. And the purist forms that these poems cultivate are never entirely pure, because the theological and moral ghosts they try to exorcise refuse to die. Like phantoms, they enjoy a resilient posthumous life.

To conjure ghosts and converse with shadows the poet must first become a shade. Morris apparently thought of his own early poetry as a penitential exercise, a rite of exorcism to which he must first submit, before producing the kind of 'mighty art' he extols in 'The Prospects of Architecture in Civilization.' Though his Arthurian monologues are, in his own words, the mere 'reflection and feeble ghost of that glorious autumn which ended the good days of the mighty art of the Middle Ages,'[21] they remain the strangest and most beautiful poems he ever wrote, poems to which generations of readers keep returning with enduring satisfaction.

Brides of Darkness: The Ghostly Monologues of Robert Lowell

Despite his Roman Catholicism, Robert Lowell's best monologues often substitute a pagan underworld for hell or purgatory. And they are usually just as spectral as the phantom monologues of William Morris. Nowhere are the ghostly allusions to a bride of darkness more powerful or harrowing than in Lowell's 'The Mills of the Kavanaughs,' which is spoken by a New England Persephone to her dead Pluto. Even as the husband's silent-speaking words continue to haunt Anne, to most modern readers their appeal is also as tender and plaintive as the plea of Matthew Arnold's agnostic lover to his bride in 'Dover Beach' – 'Ah, love, let us be true / To one another!' (29–30) – which Lowell quotes in his epigraph.

When the dispersion of rhymes transports Anne back in time, the separation of the rhyme words 'blue' and 'true' allows the young Anne and Harry, 'A boy and girl a-Maying in the blue,' to echo at a distance of four lines the corresponding petition of the young lover, who cries out with wayward innocence, like Arnold's young bridegroom: 'O dandelion, wish my wish, be true.' The words' carefree straying across the formal divide between successive verse paragraphs combines impressions of Anne's husband as the ravaged veteran with memories of him as the boy Harry and the young lover. Even the four-line separation of the rhyme words 'comb' and 'home' acts out the free vagrancy of Anne's will.

> Her husband's thumbnail scratches on her comb.
> A boy is pointing at the sun. He cries:
> *O dandelion, wish my wish, be true,*
> And blows the callow pollen in her eyes.
> 'Harry,' she whispers, 'we are far from home –
> A boy and girl a-Maying in the blue
>
> Of March or April.
>
> > 'The Mills of the Kavanaughs,' 75–81

The children 'are far from home,' as Anne says, partly because the line in which she makes the observation literally removes its rhyme word 'home' from its phonetic 'home' in 'comb,' a rhyme which appears four lines earlier. Reaching back in memory and forward in hope, the dispersed rhymes help Anne build a bridge into her uncertain future by arriving at a better understanding of her past.

We are most intimate with the speaker when she violates taboos. Anne's half-incestuous sexual initiation with Harry, her husband-brother, takes the form of a wrestling match under the 'sea-green smother' of a whirlpool. Held down by her assailant, Styx, this New England Persephone is 'smashed to plaster,' 'balled' sexually 'Into the whirlpool's boil' (134–5). Echoes of dying and moving down momentarily converge in the word

> deadfall, while the torrent pours
> Down, down, down, down – and she, a crested bird,
> Or rainbow, hovers, lest the thunder-word
>
> Deluge her playmate in Jehovah's beard
> Of waterfalls.
>
> > 'The Mills of the Kavanaughs,' 142–6

Amid the turbulent churning the reader 'hovers' for a moment, like

Anne, waiting at the climax for the grammatical completion of the potent 'thunder-word,' which spans the divide between lines and paragraphs by pouring over the white spaces in a playful display of power.

Immediately, however, the self-love implicit in this lavish romp is shown to be narcissistic, a marriage to an echo of oneself. Narcissus's error of falling in love with his own reflection in a mirror generates a series of self-reflexive images, some increasingly malignant and perverse.

> 'I am married to myself,'
> She hears him shout ...
>
> '... They called me Cinderella, but I said:
> "Prince Charming is my shadow in the glass."'
>
> '"Who are you keeping, Anne?" you mocked me, "Anne,
> You want yourself."'
>
> 'The Mills of the Kavanaughs,' 150–1, 245–6, 372–3

Anne's fantasy lover, a young boy whom she substitutes in her erotic dream for the war-ravaged Harry, is not a flesh and blood lover but a mere self-reflexive 'shadow in the glass' (246). The more energetically she affirms her self-reflexive trope, using tautology to declaim to the youth that 'You are you; not black / Like Harry' (356–7), the more the merely hollow or sinister echoes begin to spread.

> '... "I will shake you dead
> As earth," you chattered, "you, you, you, you, you. ...
> Who are you keeping, Anne?" you mocked me, "Anne,
> You want yourself." ...'
>
> 'The Mills of the Kavanaughs,' 370–3

As the hollow echo of 'you' sounds five times, the tautology 'You want yourself' combines with a delayed rhyme for 'you' and with the framing vise of the proper name – 'Anne,' 'you mocked me,' 'Anne' – to evoke a malignant solipsism, feeding incestuously off its own substance.

In early drafts of this monologue,[22] Harry's suspicions of his wife's betrayal are more than the ravings of a shell-shocked veteran. The genesis of his madness and horror is the well-kept secret of Anne's incest, a theme treated with less reserve in 'Her Dead Brother.' In the original manuscript the boy with bristling chin who gores Anne 'black and blue' is her sibling lover, Keith. And the grotesque ditching machine with flashing lights and 'thirty awkward feet,' 'crawling night and day / To get itself back home,' is a Mardi-Gras blow-up of their passion.

In a second, more sexually explicit draft, which turns the Ditcher's 'gangling feet of angled light' into a half-comic renegade from Ringling Brothers' Circus, Anne's words compact riot and madness in the blood with a sense of hot and heavy breathing.

> I, a girl of ten,
> I pushed you with my finger. Why not peep
> And spy it? I would wake you: Now was then:
> One child's bed held us. Sleep, sleep held us, sleep,
> (brother, brother!) My Brother! I caught you ...

Wild to the point of doubtful sanity, Anne dissolves at the end into aphasia. One remembers her expense of spirit in a waste of shame as a sort of taste in the blood or an agitation of the nerves.

In a third, more mythically allusive version, Lowell transforms the infernal Ditcher into Pluto's chariot, rising in the dark to avenge the even darker passion of his doomed bride.

> 'I know,' I said, 'The Black
> Knight, Love. Richard is on the Ditcher. Quick,
> Take me!' I ground my palm into your hand,
> Kissing and twisting and squeezing, till I lost
> All conscience, and the black night's shadow tossed
> Me Richard.

One may find the tone and temper of these cancelled lines distressing. But they reveal in a flash the illicit passion that the rest of the monologue tries hard to repress and keep subliminal. More important, the punning grammar that allows Anne to conjure out of 'black night' the Black Knight, Pluto, shows a poet working at the height of his imaginative power. The lines burst at the seams with a meaning that can be formulated only symbolically and that is intense to the point of being a myth.

The impotent rapist-husband, the dark knight whom Anne calls Richard, perfectly illustrates the type of 'cold' villain analysed by Lowell in his notes on the diabolical in literature. Just as 'the horror and the scandal of the Cross beguile modern intellectuals to read through the Sermon on the Mount,'[23] so modern readers, Lowell thinks, will accept his own mythic paradoxes once they are 'secure in the cool soothing arms' of his diabolical plots. Originally conceived as 'a hole without a doughnut' like George Eliot's Grandcourt, Anne's dark bridegroom is only a 'burnt-out place,' a void for his wife 'to fall into.'[24]

The same deathlike quality casts a pall over the coda. In the penultimate verse paragraph, the repetition without change of the end-word 'mill' unlocks the adjective 'ill.' And 'failing' discloses in 'ailing' a pervasive sickness about the heart. In context, even the trite phrase 'Time out of mind' acquires a spectral half-life.

> Now we near the sluice
> And burial ground above the burlap mill;
> I see you swing a string of yellow perch
> About your head to fan off gnats that mill
> And wail, as your disheartened shadow tries
> The burial bedstead, where your body lies –
> Time out of mind – a failing stand of spruce.
>
> 'The Mills of the Kavanaughs,' 586–92

Harry's body is an 'out-of-mind' body, because its great disheartened spirit has been wandering like a ghost until Anne's monologue summons it back to life.

Though Anne's marriage to Pluto was as imperfect as her marriage of 'harm' to 'warm,' which offers a rhyme for the eye but not the ear, her elegy on a failing family, 'Who learning and forgetting nothing, knew / Nothing but ruin' (596–7), is not without its own sombre consolations.

> And yet we think the virgin took no harm:
> She gave herself because her blood was warm –
> And for no other reason, Love, I gave
> Whatever brought me gladness to the grave.
>
> 'The Mills of the Kavanaughs,' 605–8

Have words betrayed Anne, with the result that she carries to her own grave the grounds of the deep joy Pluto once gave her? Or has the giving all been on her side? Has she willingly fed her warm blood to a vampire? The alliterating consonance of her final couplet seems to dramatize harmonies between them. Like Persephone and Pluto, Anne and Harry have known their own beautiful and moving continuities. Whatever the toll of suppressing incestuous fantasies, their love has been reciprocal.[25]

In Lowell's monologue 'Her Dead Brother,' the young speaker suddenly trespasses on our intimacy by breaking taboos against the incest and suicide themes that 'The Mills of the Kavanaughs' manages to repress. As a dark pendant to T.S. Eliot's monologue 'Marina,' Lowell's two-part fragment uses the ellipses of its broken narrative and trancelike reveries to evoke the silences of secrecy, shame, and unvoiced prayer.

> My mind holds you as I would have you live,
> A wintering dragon.
>
> 'Her Dead Brother,' 11–12

To rouse the hibernating brother, whom she has preserved from oblivion in 'the ice-house' of her 'mind,' the sister will have to join him in a late-winter death, once 'the ice is out' of the harbour where the motor-launches are moored. Her brother is her Troilus: the secrets of their incest are precisely what no one can perceive through the shade-drawn windows or hear in the sibilants her serpent brother hisses to her.

> No one could see us; no, nor catch your hissing word,
> As false as Cressid!
>
> 'Her Dead Brother,' 25–6

Only when the nautical language turns into metaphor, and Hope, the second of the three Christian virtues, comes to 'anchor in the narrows' of the brother's 'face' (29), do the hints of the speaker's unvoiced prayer promise an anchorage that is more secure.

Overcome by gas fumes in the monologue's second half, the delirious speaker relaxes all restraints. Lowell uses triple dots and dashes to intimate the drift into oblivion.

> *Quick, the ice is out...*
>
> ...
>
> Brother, my heart
> Races for sea-room – we are out of breath.
>
> 'Her Dead Brother,' 54, 59–60

The last line originally read: 'Races your stop-watch – they are running dead.'[26] Not only does 'breath' provide a rhyme for 'death' in line 57, but it also confirms Randall Jarrell's insight about Lowell's search for the grace of open spaces. Doomed speakers in Lowell's monologues are always racing for 'sea-room.'

The phrase 'we are out of breath' coincides with the last exhalation of the reader's breath, as the speaker's life expires and her monologue exhausts itself in a final gasp. Will the dying sister join her brother's squadron by the Stygian landing, or will she be joined in death to God, the forgiver of all sins, including incest and suicide?

> The Lord is dark, and holy is His name;
> By my own hands, into His hands!
>
> 'Her Dead Brother,' 46–7

In an oral reading, there is no means of vocalizing the capitalized possessive pronoun. And even when the printed page discloses that the sister is commending herself into God's hands rather than her brother's, the many silences and elisions withhold an answer to the monologue's most puzzling question. Is the sister's suicide a way of extending her incest into eternity? Or does she take her life by her own hand in order to deliver herself into hands less feeble?

Lowell gives potent expression to suicidal and incestuous impulses, though as a Catholic poet it must have wrenched his soul to do so. To be intimate with Anne and her deranged Pluto, Lowell must not only give away part of himself to these underworld figures. He must also be willing to take their underworld back into himself. Such readiness and vulnerability on Lowell's part, such openness to pain, are also essential features of the dramatic poet's art. They are part of his negative capability, of that dangerous versatility which at once entranced and frightened Keats.[27]

Since many of our most cherished projects sink into oblivion, we tend to be intimate with such endearing anomalies as Robert Lowell's ghostly Mother Therese or Robert Browning's spectral grammarian, whose life is spent in chasing phantoms. The Renaissance humanism of patience and delay encourages the grammarian to defer present satisfactions in favour of future attainments. But his incapacity to achieve his chosen goals also demonstrates his unsuitability for his role.

The dead Mother Therese in Lowell's monologue establishes an intimate rapport not only with her partisan supporter, the New Brunswick nun who commemorates her, but also with the reader. As a French-Canadian version of Chaucer's Prioress, the aristocratically born Mother

Therese is as pagan as she is Christian: the paradox of a hunting nun and an indulgent spiritual leader dramatizes her unsuitability for her vocation. She is imaginatively subversive, operating like her protégée from a different centre. But because the garden of Epicurus is closer to many readers' hearts and minds than the garden of Gethsemane, the nun's incongruous *détente* of paganism and Christianity makes sympathetic strangers more intimate with her than they realize. Although she recognizes that her religious vocation is partially a Fall, like Persephone's, her relaxed and spontaneous enjoyment of Rabelais does nothing to diminish her love affair with the shy Bridegroom who years ago ravished her soul and stole away her heart.

Like his dramatic monologues, Lowell's literary sketches of New England writers[28] rivet attention on some paradox or contradiction. According to Lowell, Thoreau was the epitome of 'disciplined negligence,' an ascetic loafer: and Stevens was the quintessential New Englander who never wrote about New England. As a possible model for Mother Marie Therese, Santayana is described by Lowell as 'a Roman Catholic by birth and tastes, an absolute agnostic by faith.' New England fashions 'were too hateful, and in a way too cherished, for him to quite deny their existence.' 'A fantastically displaced person; pure Spanish by blood, pure New England in upbringing and education,' Santayana is the Mother Superior's perfect prototype. Perpetually displaced as 'an émigrée in this world and the next' (66), the Mother Superior can only half renounce 'her flowers and fowling pieces for the Church' (49). And just as Santayana quips that his monastery in Rome 'is the next best thing to an English pub,'[29] so Lowell's Mother Superior, 'a lordly child' (44) who wears fleur-de-lis and whips her hounds, can boast that her convent has all the amenities of a royal hunting lodge, suitably appointed with the king's 'standards' and 'Damascus shot-guns' (57–8).

In penetrating a moral labyrinth, Lowell's 'Mother Marie Therese' shows the same power of revealing secret relations and unguided wanderings as a character in a Browning monologue. Like the superstitious atheist who bewitches Browning's Gigadibs, the Mother Superior is an oxymoron – a worldly ascetic, a self-indulgent nun. Though the male hierarchy of Pope, King, and Father Turbot sets limits to her enjoyments, she is an aristocratic scion of the old regime. Entranced like her mentor by the dream of lost French empire, the Mother Superior's protégée blends history and eschatology in a vision of 'Monsieur de Montcalm,' chevalier and knight of faith 'asleep ... on Abraham's bosom' beneath the plains that bear his name.

In shocking contrast to the Mother Superior's relaxed and easy faith is the horror of her death by drowning. Her descent from her well-appointed hunting lodge to a convent made of fossils evokes impressions of the corpse engulfed by 'roaring wells' in *In Memoriam*.

> I hear the noise about thy keel;
>
> ...
>
>   O to us,
> The fools of habit, sweeter seems
>
> To rest beneath the clover sod,
>   That takes the sunshine and the rains,
>   Or where the kneeling hamlet drains
> The chalice of the grapes of God;
>
> Than if with thee the roaring wells
>   Should gulf him fathom-deep in brine;
>   And hands so often clasped in mine,
> Should toss with tangle and with shells.
>
> *In Memoriam*, 10.1, 11–20

Like the lyric's bland beginning, the overwrought periphrasis of the 'kneeling hamlet' draining 'The chalice of the grapes of God' cloaks the truth in a pall. But as the hands that used to clasp Tennyson's are imagined to 'toss with tangle and with shells,' fathom-deep in brine like the corpse of the drowned Lycidas, honesty impels the elegist to reinvent and amend his deceptively soothing first impressions.

Similarly in Lowell's monologue the picture of Persephone's flowering in hell (46–7) corrects the unreal romantic picture of the Mother Superior's love affair with her 'shy Bridegroom' (56). We are gently reminded that the nun's ardour for Christ's 'wedding ring' (55) has never matched the love she squanders on her royal guns. Under the monologue's unsparing review the whole disturbing truth about drowned corpses and ruined hopes comes slowly into focus for the reader.

>   We are ruinous;
> God's Providence through time has mastered us:
> Now all the bells are tongueless, now we freeze,
> A later Advent, pruner of warped trees,
> Whistles about our nunnery slabs, and yells,
> And water oozes from us into wells;
>
> ...

> We cannot say
> Christ even sees us, when the ice floes toss
>
> His statue, made by Hurons, on the cross,
> That Father Turbot sank on Mother's mound –
>
> 'Mother Marie Therese,' 108–18

Ironically, every separation is also a bond. The more relentlessly the nun's submarine sockets fill with tears, the more intimately she and the speaker are bound together by invisible ties of memory and affection. These bonds are most fully acknowledged at the end of the monologue when, energizing the stasis of the convent hearth, the Mother Superior who has been dead for sixty years can be heard breathing in the nun's ear, in the most intimate and moving lines of the poem.

> Tonight, while I am piling on more driftwood,
> And stooping with the poker, you are here,
> Telling your beads; and breathing in my ear,
> You watch your orphan swording at her fears.
> I feel you twitch my shoulder. No one hears
> Us mock the sisters, as we used to, years
> And years behind us, when we heard the spheres
> Whirring *venite*; and we held our ears.
> My mother's hollow sockets fill with tears.
>
> 'Mother Marie Therese,' 121–9

We are stirred by the astonishingly expansive motion of the coda's run-ons, as we are moved by the nun's gallantry and grace, because we know that she, like the whirring spheres, is attuned to unheard words and mystery. For the first time the nun calls the dead 'Mother' 'My mother,' and commemorates her in a tribute that is – surprisingly – as apocalyptic as it is endearing and as fearful as it is heartfelt and tender.[30]

Most subtle is the monologue's flexible use of heroic couplets. Originally, the need to provide a rhyme for 'friend' had produced the grotesque conceit of the dead nun's 'shifting' at the bottom of the ocean 'like a fish, to know the end / Is nothing she could want.'[31] For a moment the Mother's shy Bridegroom seems to have less in common with Apollo than with the god of agnostic theology or some inscrutable deity of the underworld. It is as if the drowned Lycidas himself were suddenly to turn on God and lash out in anger. By contrast, the revised lines wonderfully enlarge the Mother Superior's narrow confines: 'Mother, there is room / Beyond our harbor.' Now it is no longer the soul of the drowned nun herself that has to 'come to terms / With the Atlantic,' but only a fragile edifice of fossils and decaying bones.

In 'After the Surprising Conversions,' another monologue written in heroic couplets, the use of 'friend' as a half-rhyme for 'whined' had originally produced the worst lines in the poem.

> as though some peddler whined
> At it in its familiar twang: 'My friend,
> Come, come, my generous friend, cut your throat. Now;
> 'Tis a good opportunity. Now! Now! ...'

Jarrell's negative reaction to these lines is devastating: 'The idea of having it just like the peddler's invitation is good, but I don't think you've really made a good peddler's invitation, either in rhythm or words. If a peddler went around saying *'Tis a good opportunity* he would starve to death – that isn't nearly as urgent and impressing as he'd make his sales-talk. And though the *Now! Now!* might work ... if you fixed up the rest of the speech, I think that the rhythmical effect of "my generous friend, cut your throat" hurts particularly.'[32]

In turning Spenser's giant Despair from *The Faerie Queene* into a New England peddler, Lowell had gained in sly civility what he had lost in rhythmic drive and convincing conversation. His revision abandons the near-rhymes in favour of a double use of phrases within a single line: 'Cut your own throat. Cut your own throat. Now! Now!' (43). Since the injunction to commit suicide is figuratively a loss of rhyme and reason, it is appropriate that Lowell's revised version should contain the only pair of lines in the monologue whose dissonant end words ('groaned' and 'friend') literally fail to rhyme.

In the Ovidian tradition of the betrayed woman, Lowell's monologue 'Bathsheba's Lament in the Garden' conflates two time frames: the deserted wife's current conversation with her child, Solomon, and the happier sequence from the past, when she and David swam together in the same pool.

> You nod and babble. But, you are a child;
> At last, a child – what we were playing, when
> We blew our bubbles at the moon, and fought
> Like brothers, and the lion caught
> The moonbeams in its jaws.
>
> 'Bathsheba's Lament in the Garden,' 24–8

The pivot on the hinge word 'child' turns the sportive play of the two lovers in the pool into a romp that sounds fraternal. It confers in retrospect a childlike innocence upon the great love affair that led to King David's betrayal of Bathsheba's husband, Uriah.

But the doomed Uriah, Bathsheba now feels, is not mocked. As a bride of darkness, a kind of Old Testament Persephone, Bathsheba's own powers of judgment assimilate her to Uriah, the 'unreconciled / Master of darkness' who will 'sit / And judge' (22–4) her, just as she now sits in judgment of David, her enigmatic lover, the stranger who has broken his vows by marrying another woman.

Comparable to the pivotal use of 'child' in Bathsheba's monologue is Marie de Medici's deft use of 'cry' in 'The Banker's Daughter.' Catching the cruel decisiveness of her 'brutal girlish mood-swings' in the swoops of the falling trochees and final spondee, Marie de Medici mocks the sordid anticlimax of her husband's end.

> He feared the fate of kings who died in sport ...
> Murder cut him short –
> a kitchen-knife honed on a carriage wheel.
>
> 'The Banker's Daughter,' 17–19

Cut as short as the poetic line in which his murder is announced, the king's life is suddenly as emptied of his vaunted political prowess as it is of his sexual powers: 'Your great nerve gone, Sire, sleep without a care' (20).

Though the wronged queen can master the dead king, she is still a victim of her own children. The jaunty couplet of her funeral benediction for Henry cuts two ways:

> Ring, ring, tired bells, the King of France is dead,
> who'll give the lover of the land a bed?
>
> 'The Banker's Daughter,' 31–2

However shrewd and remorseless, Marie de Medici is also an isolated figure, baffled and defeated at the height of her powers. Since her husband has passed from his deathbed to his grave, who will provide a bed for his adulterous queen? Clearly not her Orestes-like son. Modulating from satire into nightmarish prophecy, the formidable queen becomes the subject of her own choral commentary.

Sing lullaby, my Son, sing lullaby.
I rock my nightmare son, and hear him cry
for ball and sceptre; he asks the queen to die.

'The Banker's Daughter,' 35–7

The son whom she rocked in his cradle will live to rock the state and rout his mother. The pivotal verb is 'cry,' which turns without warning from the infant's cry of vexation, as he tries in vain to snatch a toy ball, to the despot's cry for the ball and sceptre of empire and his vow to avenge a faithless bride of darkness. Behind the 'scything' children we can hear the blows of the great reaper, death himself, lying in wait not just for Henry, king of the underworld, but for his queen as well. Compared with the turbulent Marie de Medici, the complaints of the betrayed Bathsheba are a lacework of frail and tentative questionings. Marie owes something, I think, to Lowell's interpretation of Dido, who shatters Virgil's great pattern of justice at the very moment she makes it vivid and fully real.[33]

Ghostly conjuring may resurrect not only a host of obscure historical speakers but also a society of dead precursor poets. In Lowell's 'Colloquy in Black Rock' the sudden descent of the bird stirs the same awe as the buckling of Hopkins's falcon in 'The Windhover' or the glancing of light off the kingfisher's wing in 'Burnt Norton.'

I hear him, *Stupor Mundi*, and the mud
Flies from his hunching wings and beak – my heart,
The blue kingfisher dives on you in fire.

'Colloquy in Black Rock,' 24–6

As the bird falls to the heart like darting light, dispelling the crust and mud as leaven works through dough, echoes of Hopkins and Eliot[34] lift Lowell into what one critic calls 'the realm of freedom, of the Grace that has replaced the Law, of the perfect liberator whom the poet calls Christ.'[35]

But lines of inheritance are most haunting and memorable, I think, when echoes of poetic ghosts are less audible and when even an attentive reader is in danger of missing them. In Lowell's epistolary monologue 'After the Surprising Conversions,' God's withdrawal is experienced as a new form of pressure: not as the pressure of grace, opening outward to salvation, but as the crowding together of two injunctions to cut one's throat, which are made more insidious by the imperious and rash 'Now! Now!'

> 'My friend,
> Cut your own throat. Cut your own throat. Now! Now!'
> September twenty-second, Sir, the bough
> Cracks with the unpicked apples, and at dawn
> The small-mouth bass breaks water, gorged with spawn.
> 'After the Surprising Conversions,' 42–6

The substitution of 'unpicked apples' for 'yellow' ones[36] appropriately clogs the motion of the lines by piling up alliterating consonants the way the boughs pile up fruit. Nothing at the end is 'enlarged, idealized, or simplified.' The concluding observation seems 'to avoid poetic conventions,' as Lowell says of Dante, and has 'the seriousness, unexpectedness and humility of a scientific discovery.'[37]

In imitating the kind of hysteria that Spenser's giant Despair tries to induce in *The Faerie Queene*, the jostling nouns and full assonances reach a climax in the final line, where the religious force dies of its own incipient life, like fish gorged with spawn. The sensory glut is part of the 'Green-dense ... dim-delicious' world of Browning's 'Caliban upon Setebos' (40). One thinks less of the 'Meshes of fire, some great fish breaks at times' (14) than of 'the toothsome apples' left to 'rot on tree' (273) and of the blasphemous prediction that God himself will 'doze, doze, as good as die' (283).

All but one of the words in the fully packed last line of Lowell's monologue are monosyllables: 'The small-mouth bass breaks water, gorged with spawn.' Swollen but inert, the long vowels and spondees recall the plenitude of stacked nouns that all but choke off life in the crowded final line of Hopkins's elegy, *The Wreck of the Deutschland*: 'Our heart's charity's hearth's fire, our thoughts' chivalry's throng's Lord' (35.8). God reenters the world only through 'the uttermost mark,' which is not (as in stanza 33) a dash, but literally the last word of the poem. Lowell's echo of Hopkins is all the more disturbing, I find, for being remote, and for using the same tortuous coil of open vowels to contrast God's slow removal from Lowell's monologue with his long delayed entry into Hopkins's elegy.

The poetic ghosts whom Lowell conjures most effectively are seldom directly named. I am thinking of such poets as Hopkins and Milton, who hover over Lowell's monologue 'Mother Marie Therese' without gaining entry through direct quotation. Phantomlike echoes of Edward King's death by drowning in 'Lycidas' or of the nuns' fatal shipwreck in *The Wreck of the Deutschland* are all the more spectral for being subliminal. Just as Childe Roland at the moment of his death hears the names of dead companions, 'lost adventurers' of old, ringing in his ears, so Lowell in 'The Mills of the Kavanaughs' discovers that all a writer of dramatic monologues may be capable of eliciting from history are the eerie voicings of poetic ghosts. I have suggested that for Lowell these poets may consist of such father figures as Browning in 'Caliban upon Setebos,' T.S. Eliot in 'Marina,' and Tennyson in *In Memoriam*. In the dramatic monologues explored in this section the ghosts of such fathers are as ubiquitous as Pluto's bride of darkness, the resilient Persephone: they are also as remorseless, importunate, and hard to ignore as a conscience.

6

The Legacy of the Unconscious: Bad Faith and Casuistry

One theory of the unconscious, associated in the Victorian age with Carlyle and Keble, assumes that what is out of consciousness is in principle recoverable: it resembles the pit at the centre of a fruit. Influenced by Friedrich Schiller's teaching that man's health originally consisted in a 'naïve' state of unconsciousness, Carlyle argues in his essay 'Characteristics' (1831) that since 'the sign of health is Unconsciousness,' all 'Inquiry is Disease.' 'Had Adam remained in Paradise, there had been no Anatomy and no Metaphysics.'[1] And applying Tractarian doctrines of reserve to poetics, John Keble argues that all epic and dramatic genres are displacements of the poet's repressed or unconscious lyric impulse.[2] In striking contrast, an alternative Victorian theory enunciated by E.S. Dallas assumes that the unconscious may merely signify the involuntary manner of a speaker's presentation. According to Dallas the imagination is not, strictly speaking, a faculty at all, but any mental operation that is performed unconsciously. The imagination, he contends, is 'but another name' for 'the automatic action of the mind or any of its faculties.'[3] Many dramatic monologues appear to be influenced by this second theory of the unconscious: their speakers' unconscious self-deceptions appear to be no more separable from their total mode of presenting information than a pattern of braided hair is separable from the hair that is braided.

Since the essence of a deception is to mask the truth, a liar has to possess the truth he is hiding before he can lie. By contrast, in bad faith (or unconscious deception) the truth is hidden from the liar himself: his deception is no longer grounded in a consciously embraced truth. The anguish of Browning's Andrea del Sarto or his austere Victorian Prufrock in 'A Toccata of Galuppi's' may merely be a mask of anguish. In order to escape the genuine anguish of acknowledging his guilt for crimes against King Francis and his parents, Andrea may only pretend to be disturbed by Lucrezia's refusal to stay at home with him. And in order to avoid the despair of facing his own mortality, the chilly moralist in 'A Toccata of Galuppi's' may merely pretend to be distressed by Galuppi's failure to commemorate a less frivolous beauty in his music. In each case bad faith takes the form of unconsciously lying to oneself. Though a lie posits the duality of deceiver and deceived, bad faith implies the unity of a single consciousness. Whereas the priest lies to the woman in Browning's monologue 'The Confessional,' Andrea del Sarto lies to himself. In bad faith the deceiver and the dupe are one and the same person.

As Jean-Paul Sartre explains, to be in bad faith I 'must know in my capacity as deceiver the truth which is hidden from me in my capacity as the one deceived ... Better yet I must know the truth very exactly in order to conceal it more carefully.'[4] Chaucer's Pardoner, Andrea del Sarto, and many of Browning's casuists both know and do not know they are liars. As self-deceivers they are more dangerous than a simple liar like the priest in Browning's 'Confessional,' because if they deliberately and cynically try to lie to themselves, they will fail completely in their attempt to deceive their auditors.

Sartre's analysis of bad faith provides a new model of single and double irony. As Adena Rosmarin has argued, a dramatic monologue invites its readers to see that a characterized speaker's meaning is different from the poem's meaning: it is an instance of single or double irony.[5] In single irony, the poet as ventriloquist, momentarily entering into the consciousness of Porphyria's lover, functions as a censor. But if the censor himself becomes an object of censorship, like the moral critic of the life-loving Venetians in 'A Toccata of Galuppi's,' and if it seems possible to make a case for the dear dead women with the golden hair, whom the speaker censures, then the result may be double rather than single irony. The monologue is then inviting us to endorse simultaneously two apparently contradictory codes. Examples include 'The Grammarian's Funeral' and 'Bishop Blougram's Apology,' where Browning invites us to side with both the scholar and his satiric detractors, with both the pragmatic theologian and his sceptical critic, the journalist Gigadibs. If there is no discernible trace of irony (either double or single), then the monologue is probably what Ralph Rader calls a 'mask lyric'[6] rather than a full-fledged dramatic monologue: it is a mere mouthpiece for the poet rather than a genuine species of ventriloquized verse.

Sartre offers an intriguing model of both single and double irony.[7] If

another person is looking at me and I am too ashamed or guilty to return
her look, then she reduces me to an object both censored and censured.

> And Lancelot knew the little clinking sound;
> And she by tact of love was well aware
> That Lancelot knew that she was looking at him.
>
> 'Lancelot and Elaine,' 976–8

If Lancelot can return the censor's look, then he may disarm her censure
by making her an object of his own power to censure. If a Third comes
on the scene in the person of a censor who looks at the speaker, he may
align himself with the Other to form a pair of censors. In 'Andrea del
Sarto,' for example, the God who 'compensates, punishes' seems to join
the Parisian lords in looking down on Andrea: 'The best is when they
pass and look aside; / But they speak sometimes; I must bear it all' (141,
147–8). If, however, the Third casts a critical look at the censors who are
looking down on the speaker, the result is more complex: 'God is just. /
King Francis may forgive me,' Andrea half persuades himself (213–14).
Andrea can summon up the courage to look at anybody as long as he is
convinced that he and the Third are now in league: 'God and the glory!
never care for gain' (128). But when Andrea subsides into a weak fatal-
ism that lowers his expectations of life to avoid the pain of disappointment ('Love, we are in God's hand,' 'All is as God over-rules,' 49, 133),
he is betraying God's image in himself by turning God into another
object he can control and blame like Lucrezia.

   This last scenario allows for complicated double ironies. If a speaker
aligns himself with the Third against the Other, as the voice that speaks
to Karshish through the thunder aligns the Arab physician against his
mentor, Abib, or as the Christ who sees only scandals 'After the passion
of a thousand years' (157) seems to align Fra Lippo Lippi against the
censorious Prior and other monks, single irony may still prevail. But
what happens when the process is destabilized? If I subdue the Third
who subdues the Other, does the Other still subdue me or do I subdue
the Other? Can the god Setebos whom the Quiet overthrows still subdue
Browning's Caliban, or is Caliban now able to subdue Setebos and other
authority figures like Prospero?

   For most Victorians humanity is no longer 'the eye with which the
Universe' of Shelley's 'Hymn of Apollo' 'Beholds itself and knows itself
divine' (31–2). Oscar Wilde would say that Browning's dislike of such
Promethean theology is the rage of Caliban seeing his own face in the

glass. Browning's God, like St Paul's, is seen 'through a glass, darkly.' He is an incomprehensible Certainty who validates the otherwise interesting uncertainties and risks of those experiments in self-making which often end in separation or brokenness: 'Already how am I so far / Out of that minute?' Browning's thwarted lover protests in 'Two in the Campagna' (51–2). Because wholly human efforts to achieve fulfilment in that monologue are endlessly thwarted, they seem always to result in irony: 'Only I discern – / Infinite passion, and the pain / Of finite hearts that yearn' (58–60).

The only ironist who cannot himself become an object of irony, and for whom the exercise of irony is never simply the wielding of a two-edged sword, is the unapproachable Third, the God whom Browning associates with the iceberg 'Hungry with huge teeth of splintered crystals' in 'One Word More' (171). Precisely because God's passion is 'infinite,' it alone can withstand the two-edged blade of double irony. The God that Moses saw 'Stand upon the paved work of a sapphire,' the 'very God, the Highest' ('One Word More,' 175–6), is the limiting concept of humanity's ironies. The double-irony concept of humanity and the limiting single-irony concept of God imply one another and are correlative. Browning's Saul and his reformed Paracelsus believe that we experience God at humanity's boundary point or limit. Like the enabling medium of light, the Author of their good moments is a spectator who is not himself visible, even though he is the source of vision in all who look.

Browning and Donne: Unconscious Deceptions

M.H. Abrams identifies an important feature of the dramatic monologue when he points out that speakers in monologues are generally unconscious of their deepest truths. They are less likely to be self-conscious casuists than unconscious self-deceivers. Like Yeats, they can embody or live their truths but never speak them. Whereas the metaphysical Don Juans in Donne's 'The Ecstasy' and 'The Canonization' are highly self-conscious casuists, the seducer in Browning's 'Two in the Campagna' is a self-deceiver: he acts in bad faith because, until he unsuccessfully launches his plea for free love, he cannot identify his deepest feelings. He is not so much lying to the woman he is trying to seduce as lying to himself.

Abrams calls 'The Canonization' and 'The Flea' dramatic lyrics rather than dramatic monologues since they lack the essential feature of unconscious revelation. 'The focus of interest' in Donne's dramatic lyrics 'is primarily ... the speaker's elaborately ingenious argument, rather than ... the character he inadvertently reveals in the course of arguing.' In a dramatic monologue the speaker's revelation of his or her temperament must be 'unintentional.'[8] If the speaker in a monologue is a liar, he must be an unconscious liar, a practitioner of bad faith rather than a simple casuist. In 'The Ecstasy,' for example, Donne's lover, a metaphysical Don Juan, rehearses his argument carefully and proceeds logically to his foreseen conclusion. More characteristic of the genre is Browning's monologue of failed seduction, 'Two in the Campagna,' whose most revealing meanings are not rehearsed or prescribed but disclosed inadvertently or unconsciously as the monologue unfolds.

Even when Donne's seducers are themselves momentarily seduced by a metaphysical conceit or metaphor, the anticipated conclusion of their arguments, though temporarily delayed, is never in doubt. Quite different are monologues like 'Two in the Campagana' or 'Love among the Ruins,' in which Browning's speakers assimilate new insights as they proceed. 'The Ecstasy' turns into a full-fledged monologue (or 'dialogue of one,' to use Donne's own phrase) only halfway through the poem. Having praised the way in which love, though rooted in sex, rises to a point where sex is forgotten, the speaker tries to stage-manage an important transition. Turning to address his silent auditor directly, he tries to persuade her to pass at once from one-sided conversation about Platonic love to love's carnal enjoyment.

> But O alas, so long, so far
>   Our bodies why do we forbear?
>
> 'The Ecstasy,' 49–50

As the reverberation of open vowels passes like a wail – or stricken cry – down these short tetrameter lines, the three caesural breaks make it impossible to speak the words quickly. Though the final appeal to the silent auditor to descend to the body is never in question, the speaker's elaborate analogies also postpone that moment. Even as Donne's lover creates the heart-wrenching effect of an unnatural postponement or deferral, he may still prefer talking about sex than having it.

In a sense the lover is less in love with lovemaking than with his ingenious reversal of the Platonist's traditional metaphor of the body as the soul's prison. The body is love's book, the seducer argues, and just as medieval astrology holds that the stars' influence has to be transmuted to humanity through the air, so Donne's seducer thinks of the body as providing a similar connecting medium between the two lovers. Taking his cue from the address of Milton's archangel Raphael to Adam in *Paradise Lost* (5.571–6), Donne's seducer is himself seduced by the great doctrine of accommodation: the principle that like the souls of angels, 'pure lovers' souls' must

> descend
> T' affections, and to faculties,
> Which sense may reach and apprehend,
> Else a great Prince in prison lies.
>
> 'The Ecstasy,' 65–8

Even as the alignment of analogies in tetrameter quatrains is deploying a disciplined *a b a b* rhyme scheme to carry the speaker to a foreseen outcome, the lover is continually being sidetracked by his rhetoric and conceits. If the woman finds his blend of passionate feeling and paradoxical argument less ingenious than absurd, then the seducer's analogies and conceits may be the fatal temptress for whose sake he is still willing to defer, and even risk losing his paradise.

Though any 'dialogue of one' may reveal more about the speaker than he is aware, in Browning's monologues the accidental nature of the revelation is a far more prominent and defining feature of the genre. Perhaps the importance of unconscious disclosures in Victorian monologues owes something to Thomas Carlyle, who was one of Browning's first mentors, and who as early as 1831 in his essay 'Characteristics'[9] developed a theory of the unconscious. Though only the unconscious is healthy, once the fall into self-consciousness occurs the exile's memory of Eden may partly be restored by his demon of self-conscious response, which resembles a serpent with two natures, able to heal as well as wound.

One can read 'The Ecstasy' without registering the irony that the speaker is inadvertently postponing his avowed goal. But since Browning's Don Juan in 'Two in the Campagna' cannot satisfactorily conclude his argument for free love, his unconscious disclosure that he is an unsuccessful seducer becomes, not just a diverting irony, but the principal meaning of a monologue that seems to hold some secret truth – or some ultimate absence of truth – in reserve.

Browning's seducer unconsciously betrays his own misgivings about free love by allowing a tentative wavering tone to enter his opening lines: 'I wonder do you feel today / As I have felt?' (1–2). As in 'By the

Fire-Side,' the lingering uncertainty is made more acute by the tentative force of the *a b a b a* rhyme scheme, in which the final *a* rhyme abides like an unsettling echo, just when we assume we have heard the last of it.

Even when the aspiring lover adapts Renan's argument that nature knows nothing of chastity, the ugly mounting of the small orange cup by five groping beetles is not reassuring. The speaker exhorts his silent auditor to help him hold his ideas fast. But his proliferating thought branches out in directions he cannot control, like the obliterating weed and floating weft that tumble over the break between stanzas 3 and 4 in the only such crossover in the poem.

> yonder weed
> Took up the floating weft,
>
> Where one small orange cup amassed
> Five beetles, –
>
> 'Two in the Campagna,' 14–17

When the lover moves hesitatingly toward a seductive climax, the falling trochaic pattern of the words 'primal,' 'naked,' and 'flowers' establishes a sombre counter-movement of diminution and decline within the dominant rising rhythm of the iambic pentameter.

> Such life here, through such lengths of hours,
> Such miracles performed in play,
> Such primal naked forms of flowers,
> Such letting nature have her way
> While heaven looks from its towers!
>
> 'Two in the Campagna,' 26–30

What should be the culminating appeal to the auditor ('How is it under our control / To love or not to love?', 34–5) becomes a turning point instead. Browning's self-critical Don Juan starts out to say, 'how can I help loving you?' but ends by confessing, 'How can I help not loving you, you who are just so much to me, no more?' No sooner has the speaker experienced a pang of the soul's incurable loneliness than he protects himself against loss by teaching himself not to care too much. Afraid of declining into a predictable Don Juan, who wants one thing an infinite number of times, the thwarted lover prefers to be an unsatisfied Faust, who is denied an infinite number of things all at one time.

Already how am I so far
  Out of that minute? Must I go
Still like the thistle-ball, no bar,
  Onward, whenever light winds blow,
Fixed by no friendly star?

'Two in the Campagna,' 51–5

In resisting idolatry, is the reluctant lover protecting himself against illusion? Or in looking for intimacy without risk, is he losing part of his soul? Because the heavy caesuras match the lover's halting heart, they contradict his boast of confronting no obstacles or barriers. Since the words that appear to lurch forward over the line-endings are brought short by early-breaking caesuras, they also inadvertently disclose to the attentive reader far more than the lover intends to say.

In striking contrast is Donne's monologue 'The Canonization,' where the lover's lucid, self-confident defence of his love is designed to control a scoffing male critic. Unless we imagine the implied criticisms of this actively silent auditor, we shall have difficulty explaining the monologue's swift progression in tones, as the lover passes from brusque and familiar jesting to an energetic defence of his ennoblement through love. To the extent that 'The Canonization' avoids static discursive statements and consists instead of situationally motivated speech acts, it is a dramatic monologue. But to the extent that its refutation of an opponent's implied arguments is coherent and self-aware, its speech acts are too controlled to trace the ambiguous swerves and curves of human response in Browning's speaker. Even when Donne's witty ironist passes swiftly through the whole gamut of drowned merchant ships, tear-flooded ground, and lovesick fevers, he deftly converts his contradictory rejection of Petrarchan hyperbole into a rhetorical trope, *paralipsis*, over which he continues to exercise full and self-conscious control.

For examples of double irony, in which a poet whose own allegiances are divided appears to endorse two contradictory codes simultaneously, we have to examine the conflict between political acumen and serving one's own interests in an unconscious liar like Browning's Prince Hohenstiel-Schwangau, or between religious pragmatism and worldliness in his cleric Bishop Blougram, who 'said true things, but called them by wrong names' (996). Like Blougram, Browning's Mr Sludge is both a casuist and an unconscious self-deceiver. He wants to tell the truth for the first time not only to his dupe, Hiram Horsefall, but also to himself. The double ironies in his monologue make it hard to separate

the student of human nature and the artist of fictions from the liar.
Sludge knows that a cynic like Horsefall makes the best victim: believing
nothing, he ends by believing anything. In one critic's words, Sludge
also 'excuses himself for the earlier stage of the trickster's life by a
survey of the border-land between truth and fiction.'[10] Like Chaucer's
Pardoner, he even exposes traits more difficult to confess than fraud: for
instance, effeminacy. His real confession is that he is a thief, an adventurer, a deceiver of mankind, but not a disbeliever in spiritualism.

The best comment on the double ironies of such casuists comes from
G.K. Chesterton: 'With Browning's knaves we have always this eternal
interest, that they are real somewhere, and may at any moment begin to
speak poetry. We are talking to a peevish and garrulous sneak; we are
watching the play of his paltry features, his evasive eyes, and babbling
lips. And suddenly the face begins to change and harden, the eyes glare
like the eyes of a mask, the whole face of clay becomes a common
mouthpiece, and the voice that comes forth is the voice of God, uttering
His everlasting soliloquy.'[11]

Persuasive Definitions and Casuistry: The Earl of Rochester

One of Browning's neglected precursors is John Wilmot, Earl of Rochester,
whose monologues are often high-spirited exercises in bad faith and
casuistry. Sometimes it is hard to tell whether Rochester's speaker is an
unconscious deceiver – a liar even to himself – or a coldly calculating
seducer of the women he addresses. In the monologue 'Upon Leaving
His Mistress,' for example, he declares that, far from justifying his own
infidelity, he allows his mistress to be true to her promiscuous nature.

'Tis not that I am weary grown
Of being yours, and yours alone;
But with what face can I incline
To damn you to be only mine?
  You, whom some kinder power did fashion,
  By merit and by inclination,
  The joy at least of one whole nation.

'Upon Leaving His Mistress,' 1–7

In an extraordinary feat of moral acrobatics, the casuist redefines fidelity
as damnation, and the freedom to be a whore to a whole nation a form of
salvation by preelection. Redefining monogamy as the satisfaction of

'meaner spirits' (8), the speaker celebrates promiscuity as the perfect expression of a more 'impartial sense' (12), one that dispenses its bounty more judiciously. Not only is immorality made to sound disinterested and moral but the unfaithful speaker also makes a whore of Demeter, the great earth-mother, whose 'kind seed-receiving earth' (15) affords every grain a birth.

A masterpiece of casuistry and single irony, Rochester's 'Very Heroical Epistle in Answer to Ephelia' mocks the self-centred complacencies of his enemy, the Earl of Mulgrave. Responding arrogantly to an earlier verse epistle by George Etherege, in which 'Ephelia' reproaches 'Bajazet' for his infidelity, Rochester's Mulgrave protests that his inconstancy has always been self-evident: he has never set out to deceive anyone. In his persuasive redefinition of the word 'infidelity,' he tries to give inconstancy a favourable emotional meaning while retaining its standard descriptive meaning.

> If you're deceived, it is not by my cheat,
> For all disguises are below the great.
> What man or woman upon earth can say
> I ever used 'em well above a day?
> How is it, then, that I inconstant am?
> He changes not who always is the same.
>
> 'A Very Heroical Epistle in Answer to Ephelia,' 1–6

Boasting about the infidelity that most moralists would condemn, Mulgrave spins a web of transparent casuistries. Since he is constant in his inconstancy, how can anyone say he is truly inconstant?

In straining to make his own absurdities heroic, Mulgrave uses the formality of the heroic couplet to turn himself into a surrogate god, like Browning's Duke of Ferrara, who also speaks in couplets. An amoral hedonist whose 'maxim' is 'to avoid all pain,' this British Count Guido is also a seventeenth-century Bentham without any of the Utilitarian's vaunted altruism. As glorious as the sun, but also as fickle and mobile, Mulgrave is a shameless self-promoter. Boasting that his blazing sexual potency portends many a woman's 'death,' he even debases his sexual conquests into hungry beggars, haunting the door where once his charities were dispensed.

If we listen carefully, we can sometimes hear Rochester, the ventriloquist behind the mask, detonating a land mine in enemy terrain. Sometimes a single damaging phrase may acquire explosive force: 'Secure in solid sloth,' for example, blows up Mulgrave's whole mindless edifice of gloating and self-praise.

> Thy crouching slaves all silent as the night,
> But, at thy nod, all active as the light!
> Secure in solid sloth thou there dost reign,
> And feel'st the joys of love without the pain.
>   'A Very Heroical Epistle in Answer to Ephelia,' 39–42

In conjunction with 'sacred,' the word 'grace' even transfers to the speaker the sultan's despotism, as Mulgrave continues to address himself as a god.

> Then from thy bed submissive she retires,
> And thankful for the grace, no more requires.
>   No loud reproach nor fond unwelcome sound
> Of women's tongues thy sacred ear dares wound.
> If any do, a nimble mute straight ties
> The true love knot, and stops her foolish cries.
>   'A Very Heroical Epistle in Answer to Ephelia,' 47–52

The sultan's 'barbarism,' initially presented as a neutral synonym for 'foreign' – 'O happy sultan, whom we barbarous call' (32) – comes disconcertingly to life by the end of the monologue. Like Browning's brutal but godlike Duke of Ferrara, Mulgrave sounds most repulsive when voicing his approval of the slave's skill in turning his master's 'true love knot' into a death knot dextrously slipped as a noose over his mistress's neck.

The void behind Rochester's dramatic masks is chillingly evoked in his superb meditation on the nothingness out of which God has paradoxically fashioned the universe. Like oblivion itself, the fools who populate his monologues are masked in 'grave disguise,' a lethal pun strangely at odds with the quirky life conferred on the phrase by its two-way meanings.

> Nothing! who dwellst with fools in grave disguise,
> …
> The great man's gratitude to his best friend,
> Kings' promises, whores' vows – towards thee they bend,
> Flow swiftly into thee, and in thee ever end.
>   'Upon Nothing,' 43, 49–51

As the 'Great Negative' (28) swallows up the faithless whores and lying profligates who abound in Rochester's monologues, a universal darkness descends upon the scene, like the curtain that Pope's 'great Anarch' lets fall at the end of *The Dunciad* (4.655–6).

Lying to Oneself in Browning and Chaucer

Browning's best-sustained and subtlest study of bad faith and casuistry is 'Andrea del Sarto.' Inadvertently and half consciously, the speaker who tries to persuade his wife to stay at home with him also contrives to drive her into the hands of her seducer, the amorous 'Cousin.' He acts in bad faith because he is an unconscious deceiver whose most important victim is himself. At the end of the monologue Lucrezia's beautiful gold hair is transformed into a terrifying hallucination of gold bricks stolen from the French king, each fierce and fiery, branding into Andrea's mind the horror of his guilt. Ironically, the fantasies that were designed to allay his anxiety by turning Lucrezia into a scapegoat have the opposite effect. Instead they perpetuate anxiety by turning Lucrezia into Andrea's super-ego and conscience, privy to his most private shames.

In contrast to the casual opening, the ending of the monologue is an attempt to impose the speaker's will on Lucrezia. But his illusion of control is deceptive. Though he wants to seem in charge, Andrea is merely commanding Lucrezia to do what she is going to do anyway. Even when Andrea dramatizes the end of strenuous illusion by pretending to know the worst about himself and his art, he still acts in bad faith. For he keeps acting out fantasies of ascribing his failures to the inattentive but often censorious Lucrezia. Worst of all, the scapegoat who should ease his guilt makes it more intense, since she is painted onto his soulless canvases, which stare back at him in silent admonition and rebuke.

As a master of bad faith and casuistry, Andrea is the target of Browning's sustained double irony. As a weak pleader, contriving to hold his wife's hand by pressing money into it, he is a figure of some pathos if not much dignity. But as an off-stage actor, who is continually inventing fictitious roles for himself (first as an unappreciated genius, then as the faithful husband who places perfection of his domestic life with Lucrezia above perfection of his work and loyalty to his patron, and finally as the thrifty son whose hard work excuses hardness of heart toward improvident parents), he is also an unconscious liar. In shifting blame from himself to God and Lucrezia, Andrea is acting in bad faith: the person he tries hardest to deceive is himself.

Yet, oddly enough, his moments of self-dissolution, when he swoons away in a peculiar atmosphere of mixed grey and silver lights, sinking into the precise and grave mystery of 'autumn in everything' (45), are also our moments of greatest intimacy with him. In his solitary cultivation of beautiful things, Andrea seems weak as always with some inexplicable weakness. But because he is tortured at the centre of his faith, which conjures into being a palpable illusion of beauty on the darkening air, his justly famous gesture of reaching out for something intangible, for something more than he can ever grasp (else 'what's a heaven for?' 97–8), is one of the most surprising and haunting gestures in all of Browning.

Andrea and his wife are simultaneously close to each other and remote. The parenthetical aside, 'forgive now' (13), framed by dashes, sets the weakly conciliatory but intimate domestic tone. The illusion of intimacy is shattered, however, by the chain of friends and lovers that intrude between them. Andrea is forced to please, not just his wife's friend, but her 'friend's friend,' in a vista of receding obligations (5). Smooth run-ons mime the ease and quietude of their married life. But that complacency is disturbed by another trick of Andrea's voice, his habit of speaking in edgy triads.

My face, my moon, my everybody's moon

My youth, my hope, my art, being all toned down

'Andrea del Sarto,' 29, 39

Each successive item in these triads becomes more alien, as Andrea's love and youth are placed at a greater and more desolating distance from him.

The puns play the same role in 'Andrea del Sarto' that the muted couplets play in 'My Last Duchess': they alert us to the subterranean motives, to the artifice behind the offhand tone, and to the bad faith of a seductive speaker. Aware that the wife he cherishes has been bought at a high price, he jokes that she is 'very dear, no less' (32), smugly confident that the punning rebuke will fail to register. Though Andrea is the admiring celebrant of his own Madonna, the architect of his own triumphalism,

– It is the thing, Love! so such things should be –
Behold Madonna! – I am bold to say.

'Andrea del Sarto,' 58–9

he is also his own harshest censor: 'All is silver-grey / Placid and perfect with my art: the worse!' (98–9). Even his two-way meanings are less an evasion of self-criticism than an acknowledgment of losses that cut two ways at once.

> This chamber for example – turn your head –
> All that's behind us!
>
> 'Andrea del Sarto,' 53–4

Does the preposition 'behind' have a spatial or a temporal meaning? Is Andrea referring to the great canvases that are literally 'behind' them, lining the walls of his studio, and which Lucrezia could see if she bothered to turn her head? Or is he alluding to the more intimate pleasures of the marriage bed, which appear to have receded into a lost paradise for both of them?

The bad faith and casuistry that abound in many Victorian and modern monologues, which tend to be difficult because of their psychological complexity, are easier to understand if we study a simpler version of them in Chaucer's monologues. The Wife of Bath, for example, seems at first to be a mere comic butt of Chaucer's single irony. She offends against dramatic propriety by talking too long and citing only those authorities that support her feminist cause. But single irony deepens into double irony as soon as we realize that, though the Wife is an overbearing zealot, so, too, are her male adversaries. And what we first mistake for her intimidation of all suitors is also an appeal in disguise for reciprocity between the sexes, especially in marriage.

In the *General Prologue*, where the wife of Bath is said to be partially deaf, the wry parenthesis – 'that was scathe' (446) – seems to harbour an understated irony at her expense: it is a pity she could not have heard better, because then she might have been a better listener. Deaf to the wisdom of her adversaries, she is a verbal despot, sworn to hold centre stage in a 'dialogue of one' by intimidating any male critics into silence. Energetic in pursuit of her own self-interest, she will brook no rivals in either speech or business. She has had five husbands, to say nothing of many youthful lovers. But as far as the narrator in the *General Prologue* is concerned, the less said about them the better. He pretends to pass over them in decent silence and reserve.

The Wife's subversive love of contradictions and antinomies already identifies her as a practitioner of double irony. She quotes scripture to prove that the married state is as blessed as celibacy. In principle, she is not a zealous partisan but a fair-minded and judicious double ironist, who believes that something cogent can always be said on both sides of an issue. Though she admits she is bewildered by Christ's reproof of the Samaritan woman for having five husbands, she has no difficulty quoting a cogent counter-authority: 'God bad us for to wexe and multiplye' (*The Wife of Bath's Prologue*, 28). When texts contradict each other, she opts for the gentler, more humane injunctions she can apply most readily. An apostle of experience rather than of learned authority, the Wife of Bath has the longest prologue in *The Canterbury Tales*, partly because she loves to hold centre stage and talk directly about herself, but also because she possesses the double ironist's refined sense of how multifaceted the truth can be.

Although the Wife of Bath is herself a practitioner of double irony who argues that one must be disengaged and sceptical, and a free interpreter of many contradictory texts about marriage and chastity, she is also an object of Chaucer's own double ironies. Are we meant to laugh at the Wife of Bath's theological conceits or approve them? Though we may admire her rhetorical cunning, we may disallow her use of *petitio principii*. In baking barley bread herself, which is of a coarser grain than the pure white seed of Jerome and the virgins, the domesticated Wife of Bath is assuming in her premise what she purports to discover only in her conclusion: namely, the suitability of all women for procreation. Since procreation is presumably the final cause of all seeds, which (if left unsown) would defeat their natural purpose of propagating the species, the Wife's chosen analogy imposes a mask of intellectual cogency on a mode of reasoning that is wholly circular.

The Wife of Bath's word play alerts us both to the double worlds she inhabits and to the double irony of Chaucer's complex treatment of her. 'If I be daungerous, god yeve me sorwe!' (151), she swears, signalling that she is quite prepared to turn her pilgrimage into a medieval version of the modern love boat. In promising not to be 'daungerous' to any man who is brave enough to propose marriage to her, the Wife seems to be addressing medieval and modern audiences simultaneously. She will not endanger her wooer's manhood by playing the Amazon. But 'daungerous' means more than just perilous, in the modern sense. It means fastidious, hard to please, and, by extension, sexually withholding and frigid. As if addressing an appreciative audience of future readers as well as her immediate medieval companions, the Wife of Bath tries to be encouraging: she will be forthcoming without endangering any future lover's manhood. As an inhabitant of double worlds, the Wife of Bath also addresses a double audience. She combines coded cues to a special male admirer with a spellbinding public demonstration of the art of *paralipsis*, the denial of being reserved or restrained in the very act of perfecting those qualities.

The complex truth about marriage entails a double ironist's capacity to acknowledge the dignity and rights of each partner. The Wife practises such irony when, begging one last kiss from Jankyn before she dies, she slaps the clerk's face as he bends over her. 'You deserve to be rebuked for pushing me into the fire,' she appears to be saying, 'but don't take my rebuke too seriously: I'm not too hurt to play a joke on you.' And so she extracts promises of submission from Jankyn before pretending to expire. Having achieved sovereignty in marriage, she can then afford to be generous. Though marriage ought to be a democracy, for women it is usually an autocracy: only strong-willed feminists can establish the desired and necessary balance. Solicitous of Jankyn, the Wife takes care that she and her favourite husband will serve each other's needs. Though she never grieves unduly over the death of her fourth husband, her grief for Jankyn is genuine and goes quite deep.[12]

The most complex word in the Wife of Bath's prologue is the noun 'daungeresse,' which is the equivalent of the equally complex 'gentylesse' in her tale. The speaker in a monologue is 'daungerous' if she has wit and craft enough to find in language the rhetorical equivalent of the subtle interplay of aggression and restraint, giving and withholding, that delights the Wife in her sexual encounters. To promise a revelation that is then deferred is to whet the audience's appetite for further disclosures. By dallying with her auditors as she dallies with her lovers, she performs a kind of narrative striptease. Like her handling of Jankyn, the Wife of Bath's monologue perfects the art of feigning. She baits the marriage trap by inventing a delightfully erotic dream, which is explicit enough to leave no doubt of her sexual wants but also veiled enough as a dream to permit contradictory interpretations that preserve intact some vestige of female 'daungeresse' (575–84). Ironically, the embattled feminist who poses the most peril to a possible male admirer, who is most 'dangerous' in the modern sense, is also the most coy and withholding, the most 'daungerous' in the medieval sense as well.

Single and Double Irony: Tennyson, Dickens, Landor and Arnold

The bad faith of Tennyson's St Simeon takes the form of lying to himself. Though his lofty pillar discredits his fantasy of being low and abased, his deception is not to be confused with lying in general. He is not a master of deception like Chaucer's Pardoner, who tries to sell worthless relics to the pilgrims. Because the Pardoner's lies mask the truth, he has first to possess the truth he is hiding. By contrast, Simeon's bad faith hides the truth from himself. The deception of the proud hedonist masquerading as an abased saint is an irony of which Simeon himself is only subliminally aware. For Simeon the great enemy of truth is not the lie – deliberate and contrived – but the bad faith of a would-be martyr who enjoys all the comfort of ascetic posturing without any of the challenge of self-critical thought.

Paris deliberately deceives Tennyson's Oenone, and Guinevere deceives Arthur. Even Aurora lies to Tithonus about the nature of the immortality she agrees to confer on him. Like the speakers in 'Locksley Hall' and *Maud*, however, Tennyson's Lucretius and his lotos-eaters lie only to themselves. We recall that in 'bad faith,' as Sartre defines and then develops the term,[13] the deceiver and the dupe are one and the same person. The lotos-eaters try to trick themselves into believing that life in lotos-land is worthy of them. Tennyson's Lucretius, face to face with nothingness, possesses in his capacity as a poet and cosmologist the truths which are hidden from him in his official capacity as a materialist philosopher and atheist. For Tennyson, the poet behind the mask, Lucretius the disenchanted unbeliever – the unraveller of other people's deceptions – is himself self-deceived. As John Keble explains in his *Oxford Lectures on Poetry*, which Tennyson owned, Lucretius was a believer without knowing he believed.[14]

If the lover in *Maud* is to conceal from himself the truth that he is already in love with Maud, he must know this truth very exactly himself in order to maintain the protective fiction that he hates her. The anguish of Tennyson's dying Lucretius seems genuine. But the despair of the jilted lovers in *Maud* and 'Locksley Hall,' like the anguish of St Simeon, decaying by slow degrees on his pillar, is a mere pretence. Such speakers act out a fantasy of anguish in order to escape genuine despair.

Despite the energy with which the angry young men in 'Locksley Hall' and *Maud* play their roles of outcast and victim, the near-hysteria of their rhetoric keeps betraying them, even to themselves. They both know and don't know they are liars. Dickens's Pip observes that the greatest of swindlers is the self-swindler. Certainly, self-deceivers like the lotos-eaters or the Byronic heroes in 'Locksley Hall' and *Maud* are more dangerous than simple liars like Chaucer's Pardoner or Browning's Mr Sludge. The essence of bad faith is that the person who lies to himself is honest and sincere. Such a speaker's project would fail completely if he were deliberately and cynically to lie to himself.

A complex example of lying to oneself can be found in Dickens's prose monologue 'George Silverman's Explanation.' The silences and ellipses imply that George leaves more unsaid than said. Why does he open his discourse with two false starts? He seems to have trouble with the concept of explanation itself, as if he is unsure what has to be explained. Perhaps he has to explain why he accepted bribes from his friend and pupil Granville to help seduce the young woman he is hired to teach. Or has he truly loved Adelina himself, and brought George and her together out of generous good will? He may have been unfairly abused for his benevolence. Or he may have unconsciously shaped his life in the mould of Brother Hawkyard, the Evangelical hypocrite who has raised him.

There are insistent suggestions that in discharging the will of George's dead grandfather, Hawkyard has retained more of the inheritance for himself and his Evangelical brethren than he bestowed on the indigent heir. Imperceptibily, George assumes the parenthetical speech mannerisms that he professes to despise in the Evangelicals, a mark – he says – of their self-divided minds.[15] He is of two minds himself, uncertain whether his life repeats the hypocrisy of his Evangelical guardian or whether both he and Hawkyard (despite their compromising names) are models of benevolence. Interesting tricks of language can be found in the speaker's use of self-affirming parentheses and in his self-censoring reinventions of meaning that still allow corrected first impressions to stand.

Both Browning and Walter Savage Landor engage the immortal dead in conversation that explores the boundaries of our own imagination. They are interested in philosophical encounters rather than historical exhumations. But they also value a capacity for entering sympathetically into the minds of speakers whom they come to know, not the way a chemist knows the content of a test tube, but the way a parent knows the character of a daughter or a son. Instead of treating ideas as symbols in a scientific equation whose truth is timeless, without either a past or a future, Browning and Landor both assume that ideas have a history and that this history is capable of illuminating the ideas. The single and double ironies of such historical understanding are the most obvious influence of Landor's *Imaginary Conversations* on similar qualities in Browning's monologues.

In the preface to his *Conversations* Landor says that all his discourses are meant to tilt in the direction of one privileged speaker. Scaliger is introduced to 'show better the proportions of the great' Montaigne, and the obscure Home, an Evangelical playwright, is allowed to speak as a foil for his famous kinsman, the sceptical philosopher and historian. But the Evangelical Home is not just 'a beggar under a triumphal arch.' Nor is he 'a camel against a pyramid' (1, frontispiece). The conversation between Home and Hume is not so much a lecture by the philosopher as a two-way dialogue between equals in which the religious apologist and the sceptic learn from each other.

Like Browning's casuists, Landor's Hume is a cultural relativist. In a different age he would have studied theology in a monastery. Meaning depends on cultural context, and truth is so provisional that it varies unpredictably from the unconscious lies of one generation to the cherished fictions of the next. Welcoming the risks of unprotected living, Browning and Landor both abandon the search for categorical definitions in an effort to cultivate more flexible habits of mind. Substituting conversations for proofs, and open dialogue for closed system-building and the construction of *summae*, both writers practise forms of double irony that embrace multiple values simultaneously.

Like the monologues by Browning in which Cleon confronts St Paul or Karshish encounters the biblical Lazarus, Landor's conversation between the free-thinking David Hume and his religiously orthodox kinsman, John Home, sets two habits of mind against each other. One is evangelistic, assertive, homiletic – Hebraic, if you will, deploying powerful single ironies; the other is amused, 'cool,' analytic, lightened by a Hellenistic preference for seeing all round an issue instead of choosing sides. When the earnestly Hebraic Home redefines Parisian tolerance as a deficiency of zeal, his sceptical adversary contrasts the intellectual despotism of many theologians with the free play of mind that a healthy secular culture ought to value. Like Browning's Bishop Blougram, who believes that only the intellectual élite can discuss theology without risk to their souls, Hume keeps joking about his kinsman's incapacity for eating cherries. Home is made timid by the intellectual equivalent of a scarecrow, by a fear of authority and dogma that prevents the frank exchange of opinion about religion and ethics.

Knowing that it is hard to refute a joke, Hume attacks his kinsman's Calvinist belief in a devil, which is too Manichean for his more indulgent Pelagian tastes, by blithely announcing that the 'the evil principle ... was ... hardly worth the expense of his voyage from Persia.'[16] If gratitude for such consoling fictions as causality or God is a civilizing goddess, as Hume believes, then the philosopher has no desire to ring her death knell. But the modest Hume is under no delusion that his philosophical essays will be widely influential. And since he knows that no refutation of causality or necessity will make him a sceptic when he leaves his library for the idols of the marketplace, Hume also denies (in the spirit of a self-deprecating ironist) that his writings will make people less happy or civilized. Blessed with a keen eye for the humanizing power of social customs, Hume ironically redefines 'Wisdom' as the intellectual animus that divides people whom 'a few paces, a glass of wine, a cup of tea,' would otherwise be perfectly effective in reconciling (4, 9, p. 18).

The cultivated relativism of a double ironist like Landor's Montaigne is strengthened by the fact that there are some people like his guest, Scaliger, who are not polite relativists and sceptics. If everyone were a sceptic, then the skeptics who embrace a double vision of the world (in which there are always counter-arguments to be made) would be forced to abandon their antinomianism for the tediously predictable single ironies of a dogmatist like Calvin. Landor's Montaigne would feel imprisoned in Zion, and he uses every stick at hand to beat a dogma. In particular, he detests Calvin, whose voluntarist theology is a target of Browning's own irony in 'Johannes Agricola in Meditation.' Though a lavishly annotated copy of the second edition of Montaigne's *Essais* (Lyon, 1593) finds a place of honour in Browning's library,[17] *The Apology of Raymond Sebond* would not be found in Calvin's library, nor would Calvin's *Institutes* be found in Montaigne's.

Landor's dialogues between Diogenes and Plato[18] have been criticized for the cynic's petty fault-finding. But in theory the exchange is designed to be faithful to the Socratic spirit. The Plato of the liberal Anglicans is being challenged by a sceptic who tries to represent the Socrates of George Grote and his fellow Utilitarians. For Landor's powerful single ironies at Diogenes' expense, Browning in 'Bishop Blougram's Apology' substitutes a more complicated double irony which allows him to say 'true things, but [call] them by wrong names' (996). The pragmatism of Diogenes-Gigadibs is less a caricature of a cynical auditor than a pretext for the speaker's energetic and sometimes cogent defence of a pragmatic theory of faith.

Equally resourceful uses of single and double irony can be found in Matthew Arnold's masterpiece, *Friendship's Garland*, a series of epistolary prose monologues. Who is the true target of Arnold's censure? Is he poking fun at Arminius, the German critic of English culture, or at its

complacent advocate? When the Anglophile used by Arnold as his letter-writer makes a commonplace book out of articles from *The Times*,
which is the organ of atheism and *laissez-faire* liberalism in *Culture and
Anarchy*, Arnold is clearly mocking him. But no sooner has the correspondent made a secular scripture out of Satanic verses than the focus of
censure starts to shift. Instead of mocking the letter-writer for defending
an indefensible social system against Arminius's witty criticisms, Arnold
allows his persona to piece together some fragmentary truths about the
organic quality of a healthy culture: 'In England we like our improve-
ments to *grow*, not to be manufactured.'[19]

Torn between admiration and criticism, the letter-writer's ambivalence toward German culture is characteristic of the self-divided sensibilities explored in the best dramatic monologues, which are the genre
par excellence of a culture in crisis. Like a latter-day Carlyle, the letter-
writer has been assiduously studying German philosophy under
Arminius's guidance. At the same time he is just as critical of Arminius,
whom he calls 'a bureaucracy-ridden Prussian' (5, 6, p. 66), as Carlyle is
of Teufelsdröckh in *Sartor Resartus*. The letter-writer's own vulnerability
tends to increase in proportion to his personal display of ill temper and
sarcasm. When he claims that Arminius's contempt for British education
is 'beneath [his] notice,' his dismissal of well-founded criticism as an
'ebullition of spite' (5, 6, p. 68) is a sure sign that the Prussian critic has
touched a raw English nerve.

More complex are the many passages in which it is hard to decide
which side of the cultural debate Arnold endorses. When Arminius
presses the letter-writer about the education of aristocrats at Eton, is
Arnold supporting or mocking the Englishman's defence of 'the grand,
old, fortifying, classical curriculum'? If 'the most astonishing feats of
mental gymnastics' (5, 6, p. 70) at Oxford are feats of not sleeping for
four nights and consuming incredible quantities of 'wet towels, strong
cigars, and brandy-and-water' (5, 6, p. 70), then Arminius would seem to
be vindicated. Because the abuse of a classical education is no argument
against its right use, however, it is equally clear that the Oxford Professor of Poetry is also endorsing his speaker's eloquent praise of liberal
education for 'training and bracing the mind for future acquisition' (5, 6,
p. 70).

For the double ironies of letter 6, *Friendship's Garland*'s seventh letter
substitutes powerful single ironies. When Arminius contemptuously
dismisses the latest triumph of scientific engineering, the Atlantic tel-
egraph, as a Victorian version of the Internet – a 'great rope, with a

Philistine at each end of it talking inutilities' (5, 7, p. 73), we can hear in the voice behind the mask a satiric animus that is radioactive with wit, energizing and sometimes detonating the language. Equally destructive is the ironic praise of Lumpington, Hittall, and Bottles, whom Arnold secretly despises, and the use of phrases like 'great' and 'pitch of splendour,' which bristle with irony by looking two ways at once: 'Be great, O working class, for the middle and upper classes are great!'; 'I see the unexampled pitch of splendour and security to which these have conducted us' (5, 7, p. 76).

Double irony is also a feature of many of the best classical monologues in post-Romantic poetry. The casuistry and bad faith that abound in Tennyson's monologue 'Tithonus,' for example, allow the poet to maintain an ironic distance from his speaker. Tithonus tries to model his passing into easeful death upon a Keatsian ideal of ceasing upon the midnight with no pain. But even in paying his last meticulous courtesies to the radiant Aurora, returning daily on her silver wheels, he is made the target of a second cruel joke. Tennyson expects us to know that Tithonus will not end his life with as much relaxed dignity as he ends his beautifully composed monologue: he will be turned ignominiously into an insect instead.

The ironies are two-edged, however, for there is an urbanity, a tempered measure, in the coda that moderates the goddess's triumph even as it dooms the speaker. Tithonus expresses the eternity of his beloved in limited meteorological terms, as an everlasting brevity, an eternal dawn. The closing lines temper the triumph even further by granting the goddess the most tenuous of sanctuaries in the mind of a worshipper about to renounce memory altogether.

> Thou seëst all things, thou wilt see my grave:
> Thou wilt renew thy beauty morn by morn;
> I earth in earth forget these empty courts,
> And thee returning on thy silver wheels.
>
> 'Tithonus,' 73–6

While Aurora is renewing her beauty, her chief admirer will forget her. In the two entwined but contrasting cycles of 'morn by morn' and 'earth in earth' Tennyson has joined, in eternal paradox, the brevity of love and the fragile strength of beauty soon to be forgotten and dissolved.

In 'St. Simeon Stylites,' as in 'Tithonus,' Tennyson shows how a speaker, having announced a proper end for himself, succumbs to a different fate altogether. Prepared for his martyrdom, St Simeon is assured that every-thing will work out as exactly as an audit. Yet even in pronouncing that the end is at hand: 'The end! the end! / Surely the end!' (198–9), the word 'end' refuses to end. And neither does St Simeon's grotesque farce, which is protracted beyond the poem's anticipated limits. Tennyson parodies the last scene of *King Lear*, a play that refuses to end when it is expected to. Simeon's life, like Lear's, has been ready to end from the first verse paragraph, but it creeps on relentlessly in apparent defiance of the limits that are set for it. As minor masterpieces of double irony, equally suited to the conventions of elegy and Ovidian comedy and metamorphosis, 'St. Simeon Stylites' and 'Tithonus' deny their speakers the luxury of matching what finally happens with the anticipated heroic way of describing and responding to it.

7

Reading Monologues:
The Truth of Opposites

Most modern theories of the Victorian monologue are post-Nietzschean and relativistic: they assume that since every point of view is equally deficient, the monologues' 'truths' are best defined as fictions we choose to live by. By contrast, most Victorian approaches to the genre are perspectival: in positing two routes to truth (empathy and projection), Arthur Hallam and W.J. Fox[1] both assume that knowledge of the world is at least partially attainable. Does our understanding of the monologue depend on an arbitrary choice of one interpretive model? Or as in modern physics, where there seems to be a partial truth in both a wave and a particle theory of light, is there a portion of truth in each picture?

Whereas nineteenth-century culture favours an evolutionary model of continuous development, discontinuity is the favoured model of the twentieth century. As rifts begin to open between beliefs and their grounds, our so-called truths have a way of turning into preferred fictions or favoured models. The interpreter who peers into the mirror of history finds in the culture he is trying to interpret a tolerance for opposites that accurately reflects his own predilection for conflicting models. Has the cultural historian lost himself in a house of mirrors? Does the whole enterprise turn out to be a huge *petitio principii* in disguise? Or is the mirroring a necessary (even desirable) feature of hermeneutical inquiry?

I believe that the partial validity of both the Victorian model of continuity and the modern model of discontinuity, far from creating an impasse, reveals an important law about both cultural transition and the genius of the nineteenth-century dramatic monologue: namely, the capacity of each to cultivate the truth of opposites. The claim that A and not-A may each be valid encourages a tolerance for paradox that seems to me essential in a critic or historian who is trying to make sense of the conflicting claims and counter-claims of a culture in transition. It also helps explain the rise of the monologue in an age in which paralogisms and antinomies play an important role in Sir William Hamilton's Kantian 'Philosophy of the Unconditioned' (1829), in H.L. Mansel's *The Limits of Religious Thought* (1858), and in Oscar Wilde's claim in 'The Truth of Masks' (1885) that 'a Truth in art is that whose contradictory is also true.'[2] Not to be confused with George Orwell's 'doublethink' in *1984*, which sacrifices meaning to function by reforming language in predictably dishonest ways, the truth of opposites always assumes something beyond the antinomies. Its motive is Socratic, an attempt to upset thought and transform words in order to recover some lost wisdom or hidden truth incapable of being known or controlled in advance.

Fictions We Live By: The Post-Nietzschean Model

Like most of their contemporaries, W.J. Fox and Arthur Hallam, the most influential Victorian critics of the dramatic monologue, analyse the genre as a psychological form of poetry. As Ekbert Faas has shown, George Bernard Shaw's description of Browning's Caliban as 'a savage, with the introspective power of a Hamlet, and the theology of an evangelical Churchman,' merely reiterates 'a critical commonplace' of the Victorian period.[3] Though twentieth-century critics like Park Honan continue to be fascinated by the psychology of Browning's dramatic speakers, most modern critics of the monologue are also students of the genre's epistemological scepticism. Deploying modern, post-Nietzschean models of interpretation, and sometimes influenced by continental and North American methods of deconstruction, these critics are interested in charting the operation of bad faith or unconscious self-deception and of determining the limits of what can and cannot be known in a dramatic monologue.[4]

Though each influential critic has brought into focus some distinctive new feature, many of them are interested in deconstructing the genre by showing how in post-Romantic monologues the spontaneities and sincerities of Romantic lyric poetry are illusions which we have forgotten are illusions. The victim of bad faith has lost the power to decipher his lies. Like Browning's Andrea del Sarto, Tennyson's St Simeon Stylites has locked the door on his deceptions and thrown away the key. Nietzsche claims that nineteenth-century culture has removed from humanity the power to decipher the illusions it lives by. Modern post-Nietzschean critics try to expose these deceptions by showing that there is no such thing as a poetry of sincerity. Change the point of view by seeing Browning's de Lorge through the lady's eyes, or Count Gauthier through the accused's eyes, and everything, they point out, changes. All poetry consists of substitutions and inversions, what Nietzsche calls 'a movable host of metaphors, metonymies, and anthropomorphisms.'[5] Despite its sensory immediacy, the monologue is not a positivist but an interpretative genre. The positivist says there are only facts, but the writer of monologues affirms there are only interpretations: the only realities he can still call his own without illusion are the very illusions which have made up his interpretations. In the words of Browning's narrator in *The Ring and the Book*, 'Fancy with fact is just one fact the more' (1.453).

Like Nietzsche in his *Course on Rhetoric*,[6] Browning insists against Wordsworth that there is no 'natural' poetic language. The 'one lesson' to be learned, says Browning's narrator with manifest playfulness near the end of *The Ring and the Book*, is 'that our human speech is naught, / Our human testimony false, our fame / And human estimation words and wind' (12.834–6). If all discourse is figurative and potentially deceitful, however, then so is Nietzsche's own treatise 'On Truth and Lies in a Nonmoral Sense.' As in *The Ring and the Book*, any discourse on truth as a lie is drawn into the abyss of the liar: if what he says about lies is true, then it follows that his exposure of lies is also a lie.

The privileged seer of Romantic visionary poetry is to the writer of dramatic monologues what Descartes is to Nietzsche, the most privileged adversary of the *cogito*. For the post-Nietzschean critic the history of the monologue is the history of how far the Romantic *cogito* ('I feel, am what I feel, know what I feel') can be challenged and modified. Like Browning in 'Pauline,' who boasts that he has a 'most clear idea of consciousness, / Of self, distinct from all its qualities' (269–70), lyric poets believe they are autonomous. Monologues, by contrast, challenge this faith by showing how identity is bound up with the speaker's solicitude for an interlocutor and with justice for a neighbour. Whereas a lyric like Tennyson's 'Now sleeps the crimson petal' is private and self-enclosed, a monologue like 'Locksley Hall' or *Amours de Voyage* is open to censure: it is mocking, jaded, often self-critical. The disenchantment in these monologues may be just as sentimental as the rapture of Tennyson's lyric, which approximates in words a water-lily painting by Monet. But the pathos comes now from the gesture of breaking through the picture frame and suggesting that the whole performance is an exercise in play-acting, fantasy creation, and the loss of identity through self-deception or bad faith.

When we engage in transhistorical conversation with the immortal dead, we may find ourselves exploring the boundaries of our own understanding of such recently influential philosophers as Nietzsche and Wittgenstein. For a twentieth-century critic like Morse Peckham, 'reading Browning is not different from reading Wittgenstein.' He believes that 'their conclusions are remarkably similar, as are their methods.'[7] Perhaps Peckham means that analytic philosophy, having trained us to unmask verbal fictions, encourages us to see how dramatic monologues continue this sceptical enterprise by other means. To assume an agent behind every action or a ghost behind every mask may be only a grammatical habit, a 'bewitchment of our intelligence by means of language,' as Wittgenstein says.[8] Monologues like 'The Bishop Orders His Tomb,' 'Caliban upon Setebos,' and Lucky's meditation in *Waiting for Godot* ask us to imagine a world in which there are only surface masks, but no substratum of a subject in which perceptions and other acts of thought cohere or have their origin. The minds of such speakers are mere photographic plates on which sensory impressions have been etched.

Like the fiction of a unifying agent, Caliban's fiction of a ghost behind or beneath a two-dimensional surface may seriously confuse temporal priority (first Caliban is conscious of his godlike power and then of a world he tyrannizes) with priorities that are either logical (if X then Y) or causal (because X then Y). Too often natural theology posits a logical necessity between being good and prospering. But as Browning's Caliban (a kind of Wittgenstein in the swamp) discovers in his battle against mental bewitchment, prosperity may be a mere accident of spatial or temporal placement: 'Let twenty pass, and stone the twenty-first' ('Caliban upon Setebos,' 102). Even the fiction of a neutral God, the Quiet, installed behind a God of power called Setebos, may just be a trick of rhetoric, a deceptive *metalepsis* that reverses the true relation of cause and effect. Since the Quiet is invented to explain the cruel facts of nature in a God-created world, the cruelty is a cause rather than an effect. Natural calamity is not itself a direct result of the Quiet's neutrality or withdrawal; it is rather the reason for Caliban's positing a Quiet in the first place.

A Second Road to Truth: The Victorian Model

The most influential Victorian theories of the monologue posit two roads to truth: empathy and projection. In his theory of poetic empathy published in 1831 in the *Englishman's Magazine*, Arthur Hallam praises poets of sensation like Tennyson, Keats, and Shelley for their remarkable ability to find in the 'colours ... sounds, and movements' of external nature, 'unregarded by duller temperaments,' the signature of 'innumerable shades of fine emotion,' which are too subtle for conceptual language to express.[9] In a *Westminster Review* article published earlier in 1831 on Tennyson's *Poems, Chiefly Lyrical* (1830), W.J. Fox argues that the poet can best concentrate his energies by sketching his relation to a desolate landscape or to some ruined paradise, as in Tennyson's 'Mariana' or 'Oenone.' Tennyson, says Fox, 'seems to obtain entrance into a mind as he would make his way into a landscape; he climbs the pineal gland as if it were a hill in the centre of the scene.'[10] Every mood of the mind has its own outward world, or rather it fills the world with objects that the mind can inhabit. This insatiable Vishnu is a prodigal of versatility. In his incorporative fantasies, the subjects whom Vishnu impersonates are also his life-blood, victims he becomes as well as feeds off, like Dracula. The poet of theatrical impersonation is a versatile vampire, living off the dead selves he becomes.

The projections of such a Dracula cannot by themselves be a valid road to truth. Tempering the projector's biases, however, is the widespread deployment in Victorian culture of sympathetic imagination or empathy, the faculty that Vico calls 'fantasia.' Recommended by F.H. Bradley in *The Presuppositions of Critical History* (1874) and practised by such liberal Anglican historians as Julius Hare, Connop Thirlwall, Thomas Arnold, and A.P. Stanley, 'fantasia' allows the historians to re-experience the lives and thoughts of the people whose cultures they are trying to reconstruct. Not to be confused with the scientist's 'external' knowledge of physical nature, 'fantasia' resembles the 'internal' knowledge we have of Browning's Andrea del Sarto, whose curious blend of amorous melancholy and bad faith we know from inside.

Freely to project is to create a world *ex nihilo* out of one's imaginative substance. Empathy, by contrast, is the anchor that grounds the vagaries of free projection in subjects that exist already. Empathy is the faculty that turns Browning into an Elisha or Faust who, instead of projecting new universes like Blake or Shelley, resuscitates corpses or embodies historical ghosts.

As a male 'poetry of reflection' comes to assert its claims over Hallam's 'poetry of sensation,' the monologue turns into a species of Isobel Armstrong's 'double poem,' a Victorian mode in which subjective utterance and psychology become the focus of investigation.[11] This doubleness is nowhere more evident than in the self-divided minds of most speakers in dramatic monologues, who are pulled two ways at once. The lyric, visionary, and hermetic sides of the Victorian monologue are feminist and Coleridgean in inspiration: the rhetorical and argumentative sides are Benthamite and male. In the best monologues – Tennyson's 'Lucretius' or Browning's 'A Toccata of Galuppi's,' for example – the Benthamite and the Coleridgean traditions momentarily converge, balancing what Armstrong calls 'reserve and intensity, constraint and exposure'[12] as each tradition helps correct the excesses of the other.

The gendering of Victorian theories of projection and empathy may seem at first to tell us more about modern feminist critics than about the Victorian theorists themselves. But the human mind, though rich in its accidental varieties, is poor in its essential types: in the eighteenth and nineteenth centuries, critics regarded science and theory as male pursuits, while the writing of poetry and literary criticism were seen as feminine. As David Simpson has noted, 'the aftermath of the French Revolution saw in Britain both a reemphasis on the feminized identity of the literary and the aesthetic (of which the poetry of Keats was the prime example) and a corresponding remasculization of the vocabulary of theory and method.'[13]

J.S. Mill associates poetry with a female temperament: the poet's synchronous associations are intuitive and feminine, whereas the scientist's successive methods of associating ideas are masculine.[14] Mill's distinction between the male and female ways of compounding ideas is indebted to his father, James Mill, who contrasts the spatial and temporal association of ideas with their synchronous association. Mill is also influenced by James Martineau's articles on Joseph Priestley, which apply James Mill's distinction between two ways of associating ideas to the contrast between poetry and science. Mill anticipates, without influencing, Roman Jakobson's distinction between metonymic combinations of ideas (a masculine scientific mode of association) and metaphoric substitutions of ideas (a more feminine mode).[15]

As a genre of the soul, lyric is essentially a private and feminine genre, whereas the epic and the drama, the two 'greater genres' of Aristotle's classical world, are generally perceived to be public and masculine. These gendered differences are challenged and gradually broken down, however, in the dramatic monologue, where threats of undifferentiated sameness may pose a risk of sexual transgression or loss of self-identity.

Though the projection of subjectivity in most dramatic monologues is masculine, to the extent that the poet introjects what is alien to him by turning the world into a region of his psyche he develops a Christlike power of feminine empathy and compassion. His sympathetic identification with pain and suffering becomes a precondition of his art. The power to annex the outer world may assume a domineering male form of colonizing, which Alan Sinfield associates with an 'imperialism of the imagination.'[16] But at its best, annexation displays a power of gender-mingling that confers compassion and empathy on the aggressive male subject.

In Keats's analysis of Shakespeare's art, the dramatic objectivity that allows the whole personality of the playwright to be absorbed in a persona leads to a loss of self-identity. Such promiscuous absorption is androgynous, because the strong personality of the male playwright is lost in a host of incarnations (female as well as male) in which the poet of positive ethical identity may gain the whole world yet lose his own soul. Negotiating a complex adjustment of roles, the male subject of most dramatic monologues combines the feminine capacity for empathy and introjection praised by Arthur Hallam in his influential review essay of Tennyson's early poems with those male powers of projection that W.J. Fox compares to the incarnations of a transmigrating Vishnu.[17]

Whereas Victorian men launch outward or project, Victorian women are thought to be receptive; they incorporate or take in. Though modern feminist criticism rightly queries such stereotypes, negative capability and empathy are to female Victorian speakers like Tennyson's Mariana and Oenone what imaginations of power and projection are to male speakers like Ulysses. Christina Rossetti wants to be part of the universal glue: she wants Christ to drink her up or ravish her.[18] But like most male poets Tennyson and Hopkins have a horror of being absorbed in the General Soul of the Averroists or in Schelling's Absolute, the abyss in which all cows are black.

The power of self-effacement that Shakespeare possessed so prodigiously is a feminine capacity that allows a writer of dramatic monologues to encounter the objective world with awe. But unselfing oneself and speaking for those who cannot speak does not mean that Browning imitates Shakespeare in leaving hardly a trace of himself behind. Browning unites an intuitive feminine gift for impersonation with a powerful masculine gift for projection: Shakespeare's Caliban is irreplaceable and unique; he is always the inimitable monster of Shakespeare's play. But as the mouth of Browning's savage begins to change and soften, the voice that comes forth is the voice of an amateur scientist and theologian, a Victorian student of Darwin and Joseph Butler.

As the most assertively masculine writer of dramatic monologues and one of the most masculine love poets in English, Browning precipitates a crisis in post-Romantic culture by both perpetrating and wrestling with the problem of how to control destructive male projection. How can a male poetics escape the objectification of women, which is seen at its crudest (but also at its most self-critical) in monologues like 'My Last Duchess' and 'Porphyria's Lover'? One solution is to write a monologue spoken by a woman, as in 'Any Wife to Any Husband' or 'James Lee's Wife.' But too often the switch in genders restores conventional gender roles in a new form. Though 'Le Byron de Nos Jours' features a female speaker, as a woman she is unable to take the lead in a love affair, and so remains a victim of the obtuse Hamlet-like timidity of a lover who refuses to declare his love. She has to play Regina to a soulful Kierkegaard: the only solution would have been for the woman to take a male role in the courtship.

According to Isobel Armstrong, such nineteenth-century female poets as Felicia Hemans and L.E. Landon 'invent' the dramatic monologue as a way of opposing and controlling the poetic objectification of women.[19] Instead of merely adopting a mask to protect themselves from self-exposure, poets like Charlotte Brontë and Amy Levy write monologues by the wives of such celebrated men as Pontius Pilate and Socrates in order to forestall men's patronizing assumptions about them. Before Amy Levy can be caricatured as an intellectual oddity by her male oppressors, she seizes the initiative by assuming the mask of the infamous Xantippe, who inflicts as much anguish on her husband, Socrates, as he and his intellectual companions inflict on her.

As Dorothy Mermin wittily observes, an androgynous ideal 'generally turns out to mean appropriating almost all desirable qualities and powers to one's own gender, leaving very little for the other.'[20] Completely self-satisfied people of both sexes are narcissists. A measure of androgyny seems necessary to make soulful men love women and strong-spirited women love men. But often androgyny is allowable only without sex. Or when sex is the goal, as in *The Princess*, the androgynous language is clearly metaphorical. Tennyson has no use for effeminate men or masculine women. When androgyny is taken literally, it may produce the shudder and recoil of Ovid's tale of Hermaphroditus, who in trying to escape the nymph Salmacis is turned into a flowery fellow, a feminized man.

Taken to extremes, power-hungry speakers become homicidal, and any linking across boundaries in the intense kind of unity found in sexual union is parodied and profaned. As connecting becomes wholly imaginary, homicidal madmen like Porphyria's lover speak not in monologues but in soliloquies, which trap them in the prison of self-tortured minds. The powerful single ironies of monologues like 'The Confessional' and 'The Laboratory' place the reader in a role that is subtly or overtly sado-masochistic. Even when female speakers are impersonated, such ironies are generally the product of a decisive male imagination, while double ironies are the product of a more feminine capacity to empathize with more than one point of view at a time. If carried to extremes, however, a female predilection for double irony can produce the more cynical male irony of pure negativity and relativism. Such is the polite and cultured nihilism that Browning caricatures in 'Tertium Quid,' the male sceptic in *The Ring and the Book,* who holds that every truth is so true that any single truth must be false.

The Truth of Opposites: A Creative Scepticism

If there is a single axiom of knowing that accounts for the rise of the dramatic monologue in the Victorian and modern periods, it is a growing belief in the validity of antithetical beliefs. The monologue dramatizes the logically shocking axiom that the validity of both the merely fictive status of our points of view (as posited by modern deconstructive models of the monologue) and of the limited truth of each fiction (as posited by Victorian models of empathy and projection) enlarges the heart and strengthens the mind. The poet who writes monologues can function like Keats's poet of negative capability. He can be a thoroughfare for all thoughts and experiences, including the most painful – on the principle that only a wounded physician like Christ or Keats's Moneta can heal.

Browning knows that the moralism that defeats the lovers in 'The Statue and the Bust' and in 'Le Byron de Nos Jours' is a profane parody of ethics. Until we confront and recover the shadow of this moralism, which hides the soul in a sheath of conformity, we can never live ethically. To experience the sacredness of everyday life, nothing can be more helpful than the soul's recovery of its dark double. At a deep level, Tennyson's Persephone may love her dark bridegroom: she may be abducted from within. Working against the mother's plea for a return to more wholesome and familiar values, Tennyson's classical monologue allows us to feel the pull of the underworld, the land of soul, which, even in spoiling innocence, may deepen and transform it.

Blake says that if the fool could persist in his folly he would be wise. This aphorism even applies to Browning's Andrea del Sarto, whose soul apparently needs amorous sadness, a form of consciousness that may bring in the end its own unique wisdom. As the life-loving cleric Caponsacchi discovers, any genuine recovery of the soul is likely to involve a trespass of intimacy and a touch of the erotic. In Thomas Moore's phrase, 'every love involves a transgression. Soul is to be found in the vicinity of taboo.'[21] Even the quirks and deviances of Browning's Johannes Agricola or his Spanish monk may put us in touch with shadow tendencies of the soul – with its thirst for spiritual power or its desire for love.

Sceptics will argue, of course, that a predilection for shadow selves and for the truth of opposites is merely an idol of the modern scholar's cave. How shall we answer the critic who complains that a theory linking the post-Romantic monologue with double irony and dark doubles tell us more about the post-Jungian culture that is trying to interpret the Victorians than about the Victorians themselves?

Sooner or later we have to confront the fact that cultural history is always about the historian. Even when historians try to reconstruct a past horizon of understanding, they have to stand within their own. Though such considerations have led David Perkins to conclude that cultural history is both necessary and impossible,[22] it is useful to recall that the only faithful account of a past culture would be the culture itself, and that would not be history. Only the most naïve theorists have presumed to present a naked Clio.

Like the curators of a museum, historians have to identify what is still alive in the past. But unless history is used as a forum as well as preserved as a shrine, it will become a tomb of dead ideologies, a temple for embalming mummified ideas. Browning himself seems to have identified and successfully responded to this double challenge. On the one hand, no poet has ever tried harder to discover the truth about a past event than Browning in *The Ring and the Book*. Jowett is surely right in his essay *On the Interpretation of Scripture* (1860) to demand of the interpreter painstaking study and research. And yet Strauss, with his disquieting insights in *The Life of Jesus* about the freedom of poets and critics to impose a vocabulary of their own choosing, is right too. There is no way Browning can affirm Jowett's doctrine of the decidability of meaning without at the same time affirming Strauss's liberating counter-truth that the dead are dead, whereas every new interpreter is alive and owes something to himself.

To immunize themselves against the dead hand of the past as well as the dead hand of the present, historians of the nineteenth-century monologue may wish to profess both a historical and a saving faith in the value of learned ignorance or educated doubt. In delivering us from the undue influence of dogmatic scepticism, which is a legacy of our own culture, as well as from the undue influence of uncritical belief, which is a legacy of the earlier nineteenth century, contemporary historians should consider a third option. They may wish to entertain the theory I tend to favour: the thesis that, like the Socrates of Grote and Hegel, the major Victorians use the monologue to train their contemporaries in the skills of unprejudiced (and therefore uncommitted) thinking.

Exploring the shadowy spaces between categories, these undogmatic sceptics often locate themselves in the middle world of Thomas Hardy's Laodicean, the lovable but elusive Paula Power, who takes no sides in doctrinal conflicts and decides no great causes. Incapable like Browning's Karshish and Cleon of any decisive resolution, she is admired by Hardy for the sceptical reserve that draws her into the orbit of those lukewarm or Laodicean angels whose great refusal seems strangely heroic to uncommitted ironists as dissimilar as Clough, Pater, and Wilde, even though it leads Dante to consign them to the vestibule of Hell. In positing forms of Denis Donoghue's 'adversary knowledge,' which 'puts in parenthesis, for the duration of the reading, the claims that the world makes upon us,'[23] the best monologues perfect a 'rhetoric of pleasure, delay, leisure, and antinomian care' that Donoghue associates with the legacy of Walter Pater and of his intellectual heirs, Eliot, Joyce, and Yeats.

Secrecy and the Monologue: The Hidden God

Instead of fulfilling the promise of its title, J.H. Stirling's book *The Secret of Hegel* (1865) was accused of making Hegel's secret more impenetrable than ever. To reduce the risk of a similar fate I want in this final chapter to make as explicit as possible the important but neglected connection that exists between the rise of the dramatic monologue and the mysterious force exerted by one of its hidden causes: the masked God of nineteenth-century agnostic theology.

Cultural studies are possible only if we assume with Oswald Spengler that every historical phenomenon is an analogy or mirror of other phenomena that are roughly contemporary with it. I have examined the Victorian monologue as one part of an interlocking group of phenomena, all exhibiting what Foucault would call a common 'episteme' of learned ignorance or informed Socratic humility before the unknown.

The educated doubt and self-divisions in the monologue are a mirror of the paralogisms in Victorian agnostic theology and of the double ironist's capacity to perceive truth on both sides of an issue. These truths include the competing claims of Hebraism and Hellenism, of Utilitarian and Idealist thought, and (as Isobel Armstrong has shown) of a conservative Coleridgean tradition and a more radical Benthamite tradition in nineteenth-century poetics and psychology.

Sir William Hamilton and H.L. Mansel dissolve the stable God of Tractarian theology into an elusive Vishnu, the transmigrating God of many masks to whom W.J. Fox compares Tennyson. But if everything is sacred, then nothing is sacred. It is easy to see how Vishnu, the god of negative capability who is present indiscriminately in all his impersonations, may collapse into the masked god of the agnostics, who being truly present in nothing defeats the intelligence of his worshippers almost successfully. The masks of this second god are in slow but remorseless flux, like the hills and oceans in Tennyson's time-lapse photograph of the earth extending over billions of years.

> The hills are shadows, and they flow
>   From form to form, and nothing stands;
>   They melt like mist, the solid lands,
> Like clouds they shape themselves and go.

In Memoriam, 123.5–8

Despite the predictable alternation of solid and fluid elements, no chiasmus gathers in or rounds off the stark linearity of the syntax. Reminiscent of Carlyle's ghostly troops in 'Natural Supernaturalism,' the shadowy forms 'emerge from the Inane; haste stormfully across the astonished Earth; then plunge again into the Inane.'[24] In their unprotected vulnerability the simple repetitions have the finality and feel of death.

As contradictory, self-qualifying masks of the Unknowable, God's spectral attributes find a psychological equivalent in Claude's amorous self and its paralysed shadow (or anti-self) in A.H. Clough's *Amours de Voyage*. Torn like Socrates in his aporetic monologues between equally legitimate but conflicting demands – between claims of knowledge and action, the desire to contemplate and the desire to do – Claude is an object of Clough's unremitting double irony, which endorses opposite values and lines of action simultaneously. The multiple masks assumed by Claude function like the antinomies in Hamilton's and Mansel's agnostic theologies, or like the aporias in the 'Appearance' section of F.H. Bradley's *Appearance and Reality*. They tend to confirm Oscar Wilde's conclusion that the self, like God, is ultimately a mystery. Solving the mystery of the self, like piercing the mystery of the unknown Socrates, may move us toward the Unknown God, 'the father and maker of this universe.' But it can never bring us into his presence, because he 'is past finding out' (*Timaeus*, 28E) and is never ultimately knowable.

T.S. Eliot finds in M. Anesaki's *Buddhist Ethics and Morality* (a book that he bought and read as a graduate student at Harvard) the Oriental equivalent of Mansel's agnostic theory of God's attributes. To refine the rhetoric of 'neither this nor that' is Eliot's version of being in Hell. In his cruel certitude that those who hold themselves apart and aloof from choice are damned, Eliot is harsher in his judgment than even Dante, who confines such souls to the mere antechamber to Hell. Like the shades of those too immobilized to act, Eliot's Prufrock is a twentieth-century version of Clough's Claude, who comes as close to nothingness as it is possible to come and still exist. As his social rituals compose themselves into predictable triads – 'After the cups, the marmalade, the tea' (88), feminine rhymes like 'ices' and 'crisis' (79, 80) are used to mock the refined triviality of a life that has vaguely leaked away: 'I have measured out my life with coffee spoons' ('The Love Song of J. Alfred Prufrock,' 51). Sexual encounter is this Laodicean's great refusal, something he both deeply desires and deeply fears. As a parody of the *tathagata*, whom Eliot's teacher, Anesaki, defines as the 'one who has gone to the other shore,'[25] Prufrock is 'being in itself, unspecialized,' a paralysed figure of 'no actions, no changes,' in whom 'illusion and reality are only two different aspects' of the same mystery.[26]

In his 'Philosophy of the Unconditioned,' a principal source of Mansel's and T.H. Huxley's agnostic theologies, Hamilton distinguishes between two mutually exclusive realms:[27] the set of all things that are at present conceivable, whether real like quantum mechanics, quarks, and the concept of inconceivability itself, or merely imaginary like Tolkien's hobbits; and a second set that contains all things now inconceivable and beyond the reach of human understanding. Though much that is now inconceivable will become comprehensible in the course of time, it is presumptuous to assume that the unfamiliar second set, consisting of all inconceivable things, will someday become as intelligible to the human mind as the world of quantum mechanics is now to an atomic physicist. Hamilton argues that any attempt to understand God generates antinomies that are intrinsically unresolvable. A philosophy of religion must

operate from – and demonstrate – the proposition that God exists and
has certain properties: Hamilton thinks that God must be either absolute
or infinite. But to say God is both absolute and infinite is like a quantum
physicist's saying that matter is at once atomic and infinitely divisible.
Only a fool or an idolator would presume to say that a subject possess-
ing such contradictory predicates is truly understood or known.

The Victorian crisis of religious intellectualism reaches a climax in
Mansel's Bampton lectures for 1858, *The Limits of Religious Thought Examined in Eight Lectures*. A lecturer on Kant and the Dean of St Paul's,
Mansel contends that the divine nature can never be logically grasped
by the mind's mutually exclusive concepts of a being that is at once
absolute, infinite, and a First Cause. An absolute God is the negation of
all relation, but the concept of a First Cause is the absolute affirmation of
a particular relation. If we try to peer behind these contradictory masks
of God by introducing the idea of succession in time, Mansel finds that
we are checked by a third conception, the idea that God is infinite and
therefore outside time altogether. Any attempt to know a God whose
inexhaustible dynamic life cannot be enclosed within any logical scheme
turns every definition of God into a profane caricature or distortion.

Like the cultural historian's knowledge of the Victorian age itself, each
dramatic monologue is analogous to the masks of God in Mansel's
Bampton Lectures, in Hamilton's philosophy of the unconditioned, or in
the curiously masked God of *In Memoriam*. Both a 'He' and a 'They,' a
'One' and an 'All,' Tennyson's God is simultaneously personal and
impersonal, singular and plural, both 'within' and 'without' the human
mind.

> That which we dare invoke to bless;
> > Our dearest faith; our ghastliest doubt;
> > He, They, One, All; within, without;
> The Power in darkness whom we guess: –

> *In Memoriam*, 124.1–4

God's masks create a crisis for understanding because, being multiple
and contradictory, they are not strictly conceivable.

In his pendant poems 'All Things Will Die' and 'Nothing Will Die,'
Tennyson is able to speak with equal authority and firmness on both
sides of an issue. In 'The Lotos-Eaters' and 'Ulysses' he does something
more remarkable: he presents pictures of elegiac repose and strenuous
heroic effort within single monologues. Instead of allowing one of these

pictures to displace the other, he keeps both in suspension. The edgy rhythm of 'Come, my friends, / ... Push off' arrests the expansive repose of 'The long day wanes: the slow moon climbs: the deep / Moans round with many voices' ('Ulysses,' 55–8). But unlike an underpainting that is painted over, Ulysses' call to action never completely obliterates his picture of decline, which survives in his vision of being washed down by the gulfs and his glimpse of 'the great Achilles' in the underworld (62, 64). Double irony, which is the capacity to endorse opposite positions simultaneously, is less the conscious aim of the dramatic monologue than the result of the genre's recognition that apparent oppositions between a heroic adventurer like Ulysses and an elegist like Tithonus may signify less opposition than a common search for an unknown truth. As a long agnostic tradition assures us, Socrates' God is a 'father and maker' who, though 'past finding out' (*Timaeus*, 28A), stands like Sir William Hamilton's God beyond all the mind's dichotomies at the furthest bound of human thought.

As Carlyle's early faith in a noumenal world is replaced by the agnosticism of H.L. Mansel and Sir William Hamilton, it is possible to trace a line of Victorian descent from Kant's God to Hamlet's ghost. In the mystery behind knowledge, which is shadow but not darkness, the British Kantians explore the theological equivalent of the self-doubt that paralyses Clough's Claude, Pater's Marius, and the lover in *Maud*, which Tennyson calls his little *Hamlet*. Immobilized as ever by the pale cast of thought, these heirs of Hamlet may choose *not* to choose when learned ignorance teaches them the truth of opposites. According to Goethe, men of action are usually devoid of scruples. The counter-truth is that conscience is a product of Hamlet-like caution and reflection. Like the ghost of Hamlet's father, who is himself the bearer of ambiguous tidings, Tennyson's Ulysses and Tithonus may be oracles of truth. But they are also highly speculative ghosts, analytic and self-critical.

From Hamilton's God to Hamlet's Ghost: The Truth of Masks

So far I have concentrated on Tennyson and Clough. But the line of descent from Hamilton's God to Hamlet's ghost applies with equal force to Browning, who combines the scruples of his Victorian Prufrock in 'A Toccata of Galuppi's' with the Jamesian will to believe of the agnostic Cleon. Elizabeth Hardwick claims that 'the enchantment of [William James's] *The Varieties of Religious Experience* comes from its being a kind of race with James running on both teams – here he is the cleverest sceptic and there the wildest man in a state of religious enthusiasm.'[28] Browning's monologues are also a race in which the poet runs for both sides. Mr Sludge can be a spiritual con man; but if, as G.B. Shaw maintains, a miracle is an event which creates faith, Sludge is also a miracle-worker. Through hospitable openings in Sludge's psychical experiments, dead spirits can be conjured – in spite of the vulgarity of Sludge's cult and the dinginess of his seances.

Like the self-concealing God of Hamilton's agnostic theology, the Browning of *Men and Women* creates fictional masks for himself to counter the falsehoods invented about him by unfriendly critics like the young J.S. Mill. Ridiculed in his first published poem for failing to fall in love with a real Pauline, Browning learns to play God by inventing masks that hide a secret self. But in 'One Word More,' the lyric poem in which *Men and Women* is dedicated to Elizabeth, Robert Browning discovers that to be believed in, like God, the poet of masks must also believe in someone else. If Browning is a ghost, he is at least a married ghost who holds private conversations with his wife.

At the climax of 'Cleon' the ghost's lips start to move and words of a much greater ghost can be heard speaking through the mask. Torn between the polarities of knowledge and ignorance, pride and anxiety, confidence and fear, Browning's pagan philosopher resolves the paradox that 'Most progress is most failure' ('Cleon,' 272) into the raw, heart-taking pathos of his unforgettable 'double exposure' of both his present self – the 'feeling, thinking, acting man' – and his future self, the 'man who loved his life so over-much' (321–2) asleep now in his urn. In a desperate effort to retrieve belief in human dignity, Cleon suddenly discerns in the unknown God of the Christians, in a Zeus who is 'latent everywhere' (126), a secret that is undisclosed to the pagan philosopher and his fellow Greeks. Cleon has such an exalted idea of man's soul that he cannot bear to think that the barbarian Jew's idea of it can be wrong. The whole of Cleon's happiness lies in his esteem for this supreme fiction. Though he protests that such a 'doctrine could be held by no sane man' (353), Browning invites us to see that men like Cleon are so unavoidably mad in exposing as insane the enhancing fictions they ought to live by that, in Pascal's phrase, 'it would be another twist of madness not to be mad.'[29]

As trickster writers who honour hidden gods, masters of masks like Browning and Kierkegaard often do the opposite of what we think they are doing. Preferable perhaps to Browning's Guido, an unethical amoralist who turns blasphemy into a heroic enterprise, is an unethical moralist like the chilly censor in 'A Toccata of Galuppi's,' who feels proudly superior to the Venetians. But paradoxically superior to both is Caponsacchi, the ethical amoralist who, in breaking the moral law in order to be ethical, validates the most heroic but subversive act of Robert Browning's own life: his elopement with Elizabeth Barrett. It may be better to be a saint like Pompilia than a Satanic overreacher like Guido. But Guido finds his wife's virtue appalling, without a single vice to redeem it. Pompilia is not just 'holy still and stupid ever': like Tennyson's King Arthur or Virgil's Aeneas she is also a very sad heroine. Compared to Pompilia with her oppressive load of virtue, Guenevere with her burden of sin is a light traveller: as Arnold says of Socrates, she would be remarkably at ease in Zion.

Browning often plays cat-and-mouse games with his readers, the same game that Kierkegaard plays with Regina or that God plays with Abraham in *Fear and Trembling*. Even in separating aesthetic, ethical, and religious experiences, Kierkegaard also obliterates their boundaries by disclosing behind the masks of Don Juan or Socrates the face of Kierkegaard himself, who turns out to be a knight of faith in hiding. Similarly, the most moral of Victorian poets, Browning, is also the most subversive. In allowing 'Agonies, masks and resurrections' to 'weave and unweave [his] fate,' in Jorge Luis Borges's phrase, Browning consents to abase himself, to become Caliban in the mud as well as the exalted David. In impersonating 'the friend who hates [him]' and the villain 'who accepts / the blessed destiny of being a traitor' (Borges, 'Browning Resolves to be a Poet,' 25–6, 32, 34–5), Browning is willing like Socrates to cross any cultural boundary if the transgression allows him to proclaim and honour some neglected virtue or hidden god.

In *The Ring and the Book* a whole coiling cluster of monologues has to circle and recircle the enigma at their heart without ever penetrating it. Like Kant, Hamilton, and Mansel, Browning discovers that the most enlightened truths are often fictions we should live by, 'noble lies,' or what Kant would call 'regulative' rather than 'constitutive' truths. Ironically, all the contradictions which are used to keep rationalists like Guido, Karshish, and Cleon away from the knowledge of God are what lead Browning to it. What gives authority to Browning's theological monologues and edge to their magnificently balanced paradoxes and dilemmas is the skill with which Browning dramatizes a quester's encounter with a hidden God.

The same masked God hovers in the background of Browning's most Darwinian monologue, 'Caliban upon Setebos.' Both Setebos (the vengeful world-builder of the Gnostics) and the passive Quiet appear to be contradictory masks of an inscrutable God beyond God, an unknown deity superior to any of the masks he may assume. As in the critical philosophies of Kant and his British disciples Hamilton and Mansel, a merely equivocal knowledge of God supplants any sane or serious attempt to understand God analogically. Just as Joseph Butler finds a corresponding anomaly in nature for every anomaly in revealed religion, so Caliban – a kind of Butler in reverse – finds a corresponding contradiction in religion for every contradiction in the order of nature. Creating the world out of hate instead of love, and using the island and its inhabitants to remedy defects in himself, Caliban's god is a grotesque parody of the God described by Butler in his *Analogy of Religion*. For if the analogies between revealed religion and natural theology are valid, then (as Caliban also shows) any contradiction in either area of inquiry has two foreseeable consequences. A thinker is free to accept both natural theology and revealed religion, as Bishop Butler intends. Or he is equally free to reject them both.

As Caliban turns into a vengeful David Hume, he teaches lesser forms of life that causality is one of natural philosophy's obsolete fictions – a mere psychological feeling rather than a logical necessity.

> 'So must he do henceforth and always.' – Ay?
> Would teach the reasoning couple what 'must' means!
> 'Doth as he likes, or wherefore Lord? So He.
>
> 'Caliban upon Setebos,' 238–40

In a bold redefinition of deity, Caliban asserts that to be a divine First Cause is to dispense altogether with the hypothesis of causality. In exhausting the freakishness of arbitrary caprice, Caliban's anthropomorphic God falls as far below a reasonable understanding of deity as the sublime God of the psalmist rises loftily above it. As Benjamin Jowett wryly observes of the logical paradoxes in Plato's *Parmenides*, 'every possible conception which we can form of [God] is limited by the human faculties. We cannot by any effort of thought or exertion of faith be in and out of our minds at the same instant.'[30] Caliban's attempt to understand God as both Setebos and the Quiet generates contradictions that are just as unresolvable as the antinomies in Plato's most paradoxical dialogue.

'Caliban upon Setebos' is as stunning an image of human tragedy as

Tennyson's picture of man the cosmic accident, a lonely and self-blinded Oedipus stumbling on stairs that slope down to darkness even as they rise up to God (*In Memoriam*, 55.15–16). Both proudly omniscient and doubting everything, Browning is as contemptuous but self-abasing as his paragon of monsters, the ignorant yet precocious Caliban. Despite his exuberance and bravado, there is a deep sadness about Browning. A disciple of Shelley in pursuit of the master's 'pure white light,' he devotes his vast resources of mind and will to a lifelong denial of the contradictions that keep splitting his world into fragments. Like his autistic Spanish monk or the monster who initiates his monologue as a stammer from the mud, Browning gives the impression of stepping out of a Slough of Despond to cheer himself up with boisterous swearing-songs. But if *to be* is *to speak*, what will happen to the ventriloquist when his loquacious puppet stops talking and returns to the swamp? One sometimes fears Browning will sink into a depression as deep as King Saul's the moment he suspends his incessant chatter or even pauses an instant for breath.

The secret of the monologue's self-critical quest, like the secret of Socrates in his dialogues of search, is a respect for what Nicholas of Cusa calls 'learned ignorance.'[31] A constant and resourceful restoration of such ignorance has important affinities with Socratic irony and with the theory of ignorance that the Victorian philosopher J.F. Ferrier calls 'agnoiology.' A friend of Tennyson and a kind of Victorian Bishop Berkeley who insists that the minimal unit of cognition is the world in union with a perceiving subject, Ferrier distinguishes total nescience from the defective knowledge of mere ignorance,[32] which can be partially remedied (at least in principle). As Edward Harrison explains, 'the greater the knowledge, the greater the doubt, and hence the greater the urge of many members of society to banish doubt by the attainment of more reliable knowledge.'[33] Like T.H. Huxley, Clough, and other Victorian agnostics, the monologue's best practitioners are willing to concede that bewilderment is 'the family secret of ... science, and of ... arts and letters as well ... The more we learn, the more we are – or ought to be – dumbfounded.'[34]

As an ascendant genre in a sceptical age of dissociated sensibility, whose paralogisms and antinomies pull the mind two ways at once, the dramatic monologue portrays the quest of ethical immoralists like Browning's Caponsacchi and Grote's Socrates for a new morality that can subvert the authority of unreflective custom and received opinion. Like Socrates' *agnostos theos* or Hopkins's deity, who is 'past all / Grasp God'

(*The Wreck of the Deutschland*, 32.6–7), this new genre confirms the truth of Sir William Hamilton's austere but liberating idea of a masked God. It also explores two of Oscar Wilde's most tantalizing axioms: his claim that 'the truths of metaphysics are the truths of masks,' and that 'a Truth in art is that whose contradictory is also true.'[35]

Sceptics may detect a recurrent flaw in my argument. In making a case for the truth of opposites, for the partial and the contradictory, am I not at the same time making a nonpartial and noncontradictory set of claims about the dramatic monologue? Am I not looking back at the monologue and affirming confidently that the genre grows out of a culture that is partial and contradictory? Am I not in effect claiming to *know* the Victorians?

My reply is that the knowledge each generation of cultural historians and critics has about the past is the knowledge that they as living interpreters can find in the past, including the very idea of contradiction and partialness. The apparent contradiction in my argument shows that I am alive (at least) and that as an interpreter I owe something to myself and to the sceptical understanding of my own generation. Only a pedantry of dates can obscure the fact that the age of Mill and Browning is no less past than the age of Shakespeare. There is only one possible place to meet the great Victorians, and that is the forum of the present. Moreover, if my scepticism is relative instead of absolute, can I not be sceptical about the Victorians' capacity to overcome self-division and doubt without being sceptical about my reasons for being sceptical? Before my interpretation is swallowed up and lost in the flood of future scholarship, I hope that a few of the facts I have recovered will seem to accord reasonably well with important features of nineteenth-century scepticism and that these may prove serviceable to future students of the subject.

Though no critic or historian can step outside his own shadow, I like to think that the line of intellectual descent I have traced from Hamilton's God to Hamlet's ghost accurately reflects the uncertainties and doubts of a culture caught between two worlds, 'one dead,' as Matthew Arnold says, 'the other powerless to be born' ('Stanzas from the Grande Chartreuse,' 85–6). The dramatic monologue's antithesis or tension of opposites imparts a keen sense of absent or hidden gods and of the mystery behind knowledge that eludes Andrea's grasp. The old faith has grown intolerable; it is undermined and doomed; but the hunger for something new is a genuine *cri de coeur*. Like the Virgilian dead whom Charon refuses to ferry to their final abode, Browning's Andrea del Sarto and Tennyson's Ulysses are haunted by the ghost of that most Hamlet-like of pagans, Marcus Aurelius, 'wise, just, self-governed,' in Arnold's words, 'yet, with all this, agitated, stretching out his arms for something beyond.'[36]

By the same paradox of history that affirms each generation is converted by the saint or hero who contradicts it most, political reformers from Carlyle to Morris discover in the mysteries of the Middle Ages their cultural anti-mask or double. The politically radical Ruskin is as beguiled by the strange infinitude of Browning's Italian monologues as he is by the hidden inwardness of Abbot Samson. And the socialist Morris, himself a master of illusion in his ghostly Arthurian monologues, models his ideal community in *News from Nowhere* on a medieval dream vision stripped of its theology and presented as a kind of communist Utopia.

The great rift in nineteenth-century culture between natural theology and natural selection, God and his creation, runs deepest in *In Memoriam*. Indeed nothing can quite explain away the sense of comprehensive human wrongness in that poem, the most representative testament of its great but troubled age. Many of Tennyson's most stirring monologues – 'Ulysses,' 'Tithonus,' 'Demeter and Persephone' – are filled with the sorrow of that elegy's large unanswered questions. Tennyson never got over the impermanence of everything he saw, the fragility of his love for Hallam, the taste of death in the new geology of Chambers and Lyell. Unable either to believe or disbelieve, many Victorians inhabit a privileged 'middle world' where decisions are deferred and 'great refusals' made, where commitment is seldom more than an unsatisfied thirst.

But the scruples of reserve that undo or destroy many of the most gifted and imaginative Victorians as persons of practical capacity also allow them to write superb dramatic monologues. 'The war of God and creation, of classicist and romantic,' Robert Lowell says, 'goes on forever.'[37] Browning is both Satan and Christ, both overreacher and deliverer. His great criminals have the double nature of Milton's arch-enemy and Shelley's Prometheus. Since every speech, including Guido's in *The Ring and the Book*, is part of God's 'everlasting soliloquy,' Browning can show why even 'The death of Satan was a tragedy for the imagination' (Wallace Stevens, 'Esthétique du Mal,' 8.1–2). The self-lacerating Andrea anatomizes his sexual bondage to Lucrezia while still in its grip, and the seducer in 'Two in the Campagna' lies freely about his need to be promiscuous while acknowledging 'the core' of his 'wound.' To turn each poem into a new species that represents casuistry and bad faith in all their paradoxical capacity and incapacity is the special achievement of the best dramatic monologues. They possess 'the reckless profundity and balance' that Lowell praises in T.S. Eliot's poetry. Their 'moments of grandeur never roar on into boredom; no caution checks [them] from discovery.'[38]

Like Sir William Hamilton's unknowable deity or masked God, the conflicts of selves and shadow-selves in such poems stretch the heart and mind wide enough to embrace the truth of opposites: the truths of both modern relativism, which allows for only equivocal understanding, and Victorian perspectivism, which concedes that analogical understanding is in theory possible. Perhaps this is just another way of saying that in releasing the poet from accident and incoherence, the wearing of masks far removed from the natural self allows the poet to become 'the mysterious one' invoked by Yeats as his secret double.

> I call to the mysterious one who yet
> Shall walk the wet sands by the edge of the stream
> And look most like me, being indeed my double,
> And prove of all imaginable things
> The most unlike, being my anti-self,
> And standing by these characters disclose
> All that I seek ...
>
> 'Ego Dominus Tuus,' 70–6

Through that 'mysterious' but enabling 'anti-self' the poet of monologues claims his rightful place as the hidden author or masked God of a world he alone has power to make intelligible.

Repairing our blunted powers of empathy, entry into alien lives makes us less blind to our neighbours' secret joys and more tolerant of the hidden gods they worship. But because not even the long-sustained inside view of Guido's two monologues in *The Ring and the Book* brings either Browning or Guido the knowledge each desires, the ultimate mystery of human motives confronts us in the end with what one commentator calls the most distressing category of 'forbidden knowledge': 'the closer one approaches to an event or to a person, the less securely one seems to know it. The trees obscure the forest.'[39] Like Socrates, who anticipates Nicholas of Cusa by claiming that knowledge of our ignorance is the greatest learning, Browning knows that empathy hides more than it reveals. As a master of monologues, he realizes that the more he knows about the mystery of the Roman murder the less he knows. Like

Guido in his final speech, the poet may even have a lingering dread that he has not 'spoken one word all this while / Out of the world of words [he] had to say' (*The Ring and the Book*, 11.2409–10).

As if to compensate for this sense of being denied forbidden knowledge, monologues often delight in and expose the folly of illusion. To understand Fra Lippo we must think of his double the Prior; to understand Arthur we must imagine Galahad; to see Ulysses clearly we must see him as the mirror image of Telemachus. The ironist's art is similar to that of the fool or the clown. In one critic's words, 'he takes the events not as fixed but as subject to inversion, to having another nature than they seem to have.'[40] Behind limited inversions and ironies there is always the metaphysical possibility of an inverted world in which things could be exactly the opposite of what they are.

Single vision scans only the horizon of knowledge. Wisdom requires the double vision of a Socrates, who intimates that mysteries of identity can be studied only in a mirror of reversed images that allow us to see behind any single pair of opposites. Despite T.H. Huxley's high-spirited banter against the 'monopolists of liberal education,' most Victorian humanists refuse to see themselves as high priests or 'Levites in charge of the ark of culture.'[41] They prefer to don the mask of an ironic Socrates, like J.H. Newman, who admits he is 'not unwilling to play with' an opponent by drawing him on 'step by step, by virtue of his own opinions, to the brink of some intellectual absurdity.'[42] For direct glimpses of the pure white light, prisoners in Plato's cave must turn to spiritual testaments like *Four Quartets* and visionary masks like 'Saul.' But even in confining us to shadows on the wall, monologues free us from cultural idolatry by inverting and reversing the images we see. Readers and authors of monologues renew self-knowledge by recovering in their Pluto or Persephone, in their masked god or bride of darkness, some incommunicable wisdom or secret power that transforms them from within.

Notes

Introduction: The Hidden God

1 Fox, review of Tennyson's *Poems, Chiefly Lyrical*, 77.
2 Eliot, 'In Memoriam,' 337.
3 Carlyle, *The Works of Thomas Carlyle*, 1:2072.
4 Eliot, 'In Memoriam,' 337.
5 Pater, *The Renaissance*, 43.
6 Roberts, 'The Ring and the Book,' 39.
7 Keats, 'Lines Written in the MS. of The Cap and Bells':

> This living hand, now warm and capable
> Of earnest grasping, would, if it were cold
> And in the icy silence of the tomb,
> So haunt thy days and chill thy dreaming nights
> That thou wouldst wish thine own heart dry of blood
> So in my veins red life might stream again,
> And thou be conscience-calmed – see here it is –
> I hold it towards you.

8 Miller, *Versions of Pygmalion*, 221. On the relation of personification to death see Miller, p. 48: 'The figure is, in spite of its positive and productive side, haunted by death. It is an obscure "foretaste of the experience of death."'
   A closely related paradox is the power of ghostly invocations to freeze the living as well as animate the dead. According to Paul de Man, 'the latent threat that inhabits *prosopopoeia*' is that 'by making the dead speak, the symmetrical structure of the trope implies, by the same token, that the living are struck dumb, frozen in their own death.' See 'Autobiography as De-facement,' 928.

9 Rader, 'The Dramatic Monologue and Related Lyric Forms.'
10 Scheinberg, 'Recasting "sympathy and judgment,"' 180.
11 Maynard, 'Reading the Reader in Robert Browning's Monologues,' 75.
12 Mermin, *The Audience in the Poem*, 8.
13 Wagner-Lawlor, 'The Pragmatics of Silence, and the Figuration of the Reader in Browning's Dramatic Monologues,' 288.

Works cited in this section include Abrams, *A Glossary of Literary Terms*, 45–6; Armstrong, *Victorian Poetry*, 326; Eliot, 'The Three Voices of Poetry,' 96; Faas, *Retreat into the Mind*; Griffiths, *The Printed Voice of Victorian Poetry*, 74–5; Howe, *The Dramatic Monologue*; Langbaum, *The Poetry of Experience*, especially 83; Martin, *Browning's Dramatic Monologues and the Post-Romantic Subject*, 24; Maynard, 'Reading the Reader in Robert Browning's Monologues,' 75; Mermin, *The Audience in the Poem*; Rosmarin, *The Power of Genre*, 46; Scheinberg, 'Recasting "sympathy and judgment"'; Sinfield, *Dramatic Monologue*, 25; Wagner-Lawlor, 'The Pragmatics of Silence, and the Figuration of the Reader in Browning's Dramatic Monologues'; and Woolford, *Browning the Revisionary*.

Though Joss Marsh does not discuss dramatic monologues, her book *Word Crimes: Blasphemy, Culture, and Literature in Nineteenth-Century England* should be consulted for its searching discussion of the culture of subversion in which the best monologues seem to flourish. She examines the career of the imprisoned William Hone, whose *Every-Day Book* is the source of Tennyson's monologue 'St. Simeon Stylites.'

14 Kneale, 'Romantic Aversions,' 142.
15 Letter of D.G. Rossetti to Robert Browning, dated 13 March 1869. Princeton University Rare Book Library, J.C. Troxell Collection, MS CO1890, box 8, folder 4.

1: Disturbing and Subverting the Stage Play

1 Griffiths, *The Printed Voice of Victorian Poetry*, 132.
2 Dickinson's letter to Higginson is quoted by Shattuck in *Forbidden Knowledge*, 130.
3 Quoted by Chesterton in *Robert Browning*, 69.
4 The phrase is used by Elizabeth Barrett Browning in her letter of 3 February 1845: 'this talking upon paper being as good a social pleasure as another, when our means are somewhat straightened' (*Letters*, 1:12–13).
5 Ibid., 1:3.
6 Ibid.
7 Ibid., 1:271.

8 Ibid., 1:272.
9 Frost, 'Education by Poetry,' 41: 'All metaphor breaks down somewhere.
   That is the beauty of it. It is touch and go with the metaphor, and until you
   have lived with it long enough you don't know when it is going.'
10 *Letters*, 1:364. In his letter of 6 January 1846 Robert tells Elizabeth that 'there
   is safer going in letters than in visits ... In the letter, one may go to the
   utmost limit of one's supposed tether without danger – there is the distance
   so palpably between the most audacious step there, and the next ... which is
   no where, seeing it is not in the letter.'
11 Ibid., 1:450.
12 Letter of 20 December 1845, in ibid., 1:331.
13 Sinfield, *Dramatic Monologue*, 25.
14 Wollheim, *The Thread of Life*, 154–9.
15 All quotations from Tennyson's plays are taken from *The Works of Tennyson*,
   vols. 8 and 9, ed. Hallam Lord Tennyson. Since Hallam's Eversley edition
   does not number the lines of the play, to make the quotations easier to locate
   I have provided the page number in each volume after the act and scene
   number.
16 Wollheim, *The Thread of Life*, 191.
17 Ricks, *Tennyson*, 275.
18 Griffiths, *The Printed Voice of Victorian Poetry*, 209.
19 Matthew Arnold, Preface to First Edition of *Poems* (1853), *Poetry and
   Criticism of Matthew Arnold*, 204, 206.
20 George Eliot, *Middlemarch*, ch. 27, p. 195.
21 Newman, *Apologia Pro Vita Sua*, ch. 5, p. 187. 'Did I see a boy of good make
   and mind, with the tokens on him of a refined nature, cast upon the world
   without provision, unable to say whence he came, his birth-place or his
   family connexions, I should conclude that there was some mystery connected with his history, and that he was one, of whom, from one cause or
   another, his parents were ashamed. Thus only should I be able to account
   for the contrast between the promise and the condition of his being. And so I
   argue about the world; – if there be a God, since there is a God, the human
   race is implicated in some terrible aborignal calamity.'
22 Newman, *Sermons Preached Before the University of Oxford Between 1826 and
   1843*, 201.
23 Rader, 'The Dramatic Monologue and Related Lyric Forms,' 143.
24 Butler, *The Way of All Flesh*, ch. 69, p. 311.
25 The phrase 'self-divided mind' expresses a state of uncertainty and self-
   division more concretely than such synonyms as 'doubt' or 'schism.'
   Because the self is divided from itself by the insertion of 'divided' between

the cognate forms, 'self' and 'mind,' the adjective can use (as well as mention) the idea of division. The hint of hesitancy and of the need for choice is also sustained by the two-way syntax. Is the genitive subjective or objective? Is the self the mere object of division, the divided element, or (as in any insurrection of the self) is it also the agent or instrument of schism?

26 Cameron, *Choosing Not Choosing*.

2: Socrates' Subversive Legacy

1 Browning, *Letters*, 1:519–21. See also 2:954–5.
2 Turner, *The Greek Heritage in Victorian Britain*, 389. I borrow the concept of single and double irony from Empson, who defines the two terms in his essay on *Tom Jones* in *Using Biography*, 132. 'Single irony presumes a censor; the ironist (A) is fooling a tyrant (B) while appealing to the judgment of a person addressed (C). For double irony A shows both B and C that he understands their positions ... Presumably A hopes that each of B and C will think "He is secretly on my side, and only pretends to sympathize with the other"; but A may hold some wise balanced position between them, or contrariwise may be feeling "a plague on both your houses."'
3 Armstrong, *Victorian Poetry*, 13. Armstrong observes that 'the double poem is a deeply sceptical form. It draws attention to the epistemology which governs the construction of the self and its relationships and to the cultural conditions in which those relationships are made. It is an expressive model and an epistemological model simultaneously.' The second quotation is from George Grote, *Plato, and the Other Companions of Sokrates*, 1:387–8.
4 Schleiermacher, *Schleiermacher's Introductions to the Dialogues of Plato*, trans. Dobson (1836), 44, 46. On Browning's ownership of the volume, see Kelley and Colley, *The Browning Collections*. Listed as item A2020, the copy that Browning and his wife owned is inscribed by Browning on the title page. The volume I am quoting from is the reprint edition by Arno Press (New York, 1973).

  Also included in *The Browning Collections* are Benjamin Jowett's translation of *The Dialogues of Plato* (Oxford, 1875), item A1859, Elizabeth Barrett Browning's translation of the dialogue between Criton and Socrates, item D1359, and John Stuart Blackie's *Greek and English Dialogues for Uses in Schools and Colleges* (London, 1871), item A248.
5 Schleiermacher, *Introductions*, 356.
6 Jowett, *The Dialogues of Plato*, 1:125–6.
7 Kierkegaard, *The Concept of Irony*, 240.
8 Ibid., 77. As the translator notes, the 'infinite absolute negativity, as the way

of modernity, was read back into antiquity by Kierkegaard and identified with Socratic irony: the method of questioning in order to humiliate, and answering in order to infuriate, ... the movement of inward transformation which Kierkegaard ultimately calls mastered irony' (33).

9 Kierkegaard, *Repetition*, 38.
10 Jowett, *The Dialogues of Plato*, 2:643–4.
11 Ricœur, 'What Ontology in View,' *Oneself as Another*, 355.
12 Jowett, *The Dialogues of Plato*, 2:639.
13 Segal, *The Dialogues of Plato*, 12–13. Since Jowett's edition of Plato's dialogues is usually available only in academic libraries, I have quoted from Erich Segal's authoritative and far more accessible modern edition when not citing Jowett's own comments directly. The translation of the *Apology* that Segal uses is Jowett's own (1:359).
14 Segal, *The Dialogues of Plato*, 12; Jowett, 1:359.
15 Bradley, *Ethical Studies*, 223.
16 Chesterton, *Robert Browning*, 108–9.
17 Kierkegaard, *The Concept of Irony*, 274.

Among the Victorians, the Socrates expounded by Pater in *Plato and Platonism* most closely resembles the paradoxical Socrates of Kierkegaard. According to Pater, Socrates was 'by natural constitution a twofold power, an embodied paradox. The infinitely significant Socrates of Plato, and the quite simple Socrates of Xenephon,' were 'the not incompatible oppositions of a [single] nature' (87).

Like Kierkegaard and Pater, Nietzsche is also intrigued by Socrates' amalgam of contradictory qualities: 'Everything about him is exaggerated, *buffo*, caricature, everything is at the same time hidden, reserved, subterranean.' Because of his genius for being reserved as well as open, profound as well as frivolous, Nietzsche's 'Socrates was the buffoon who *got himself taken seriously*' (*Twilight of the Idols*, 31).

Whereas Hegel and Grote champion Socrates as the voice of a radical new morality, however, Nietzsche sees Socrates only as an ugly rabble-rouser, a kind of buffoon, for whom dialectic was 'a *last-ditch weapon* in the hands of those who have no other weapon left' (31–2).

18 Kierkegaard, *The Concept of Irony*, 242.
19 Frye, *The Great Code*, 100.
20 Verene, *Philosophy and the Return to Self-Knowledge*, 143.

3: Coleridge's Legacy

1 Kneale, 'Romantic Aversions'; Jonathan Culler, 'Apostrophe.' Kneale argues

that Culler fails 'to distinguish, on either historical or theoretical grounds, between apostrophe and address' (142).

On the function of 'O' as an exclamatatory interjection, readers should also consult Prynne's wide-ranging and erudite essay, 'English Poetry and Emphatical Language.' Drawing on examples from 'The Death of Christ' in the fifteenth-century cycle of York Corpus Christi plays to Samuel Beckett's 'Old Earth' (1974), Prynne asks whether the use of the lyrical 'O' is 'part of the rhetorical apparatus for elevating the tone towards sublimity' or whether it is 'simply language breaking away into some prelinguistic expressivity' (166).

2 Keble, review of Lockhart's *Memoirs of the Life of Sir Walter Scott*, 440, 436.

3 Jonathan Culler, 'Apostrophe,' 135.

4 For a more detailed study of this rhetorical theory of the monologue, see my chapter on 'Browning's Unheard Words' in *Victorians and Mystery*, especially 208.

5 Jonathan Culler, 'Apostrophe,' 139.

6 On the distinction between performative and descriptive utterance, see Austin, *How to Do Things with Words*, 25. 'Doing-by-saying' is a phrase I borrow from Hill, *The Lords of Limit*, 119.

7 In '*Middlemarch* and the Idea of the Classic Realist Text,' in his *After Bakhtin*, Lodge writes: 'If we are looking for a single formal feature which characterizes the realist novel of the nineteenth century, it is surely not the domination of the characters' discourse by the narrator's discourse (something in fact more characteristic of earlier narrative literature) but the extensive use of free indirect speech, which obscures and complicates the distinction between the two types of discourse' (49).

8 Kneale, 'Romantic Aversions,' 147.

9 A closely related paradox is identified in Introduction, note 8.

10 Jonathan Culler, 'Apostrophe,' 153.

11 Bloom, *Poetry and Repression*, 20: 'Metalepsis or transumption thus becomes a total, final act of taking up a poetic stance in relation to anteriority, particularly to the anteriority of poetic language, which means primarily the loved-and-feared poems of the precursors.'

12 Bloom, 'Browning: Good Moments and Ruined Quests,' *Poetry and Repression*, 186.

13 Jonathan Culler, 'Apostrophe,' 154.

14 Chesterton, *Robert Browning*, 21.

15 Houghton Library MS bMS Am 1905 (2053), notebook 7. In this notebook, which contains most of 'Colloquy in Black Rock''s early revisions, including the search for an appropriate auditor to address, Lowell defines material

causes as merely 'passive' and 'potential.' In plotting the elusive relation of final to material causes and of grace to nature in Keats's 'Ode to Autumn,' Lowell is clearly working out an important pattern in 'Colloquy in Black Rock,' the poem he is laboriously composing in the same notebook.

In the margin of a later, more fully revised version of the poem, Houghton Library MS bMS Am 1905 (2065), Randall Jarrell writes, 'I'd use a dash here instead of a comma. It makes the last line have more force as a separate conclusive statement.'

16 Todorov, 'The Origin of Genres,' 162, 164.
17 Miller, *Versions of Pygmalion*, 201.
18 Borg, *Jesus*, 185.
19 Miller, *Versions of Pygmalion*, 221.
20 Sell, *Philosophical Idealism and Christian Belief*, 201. The anecdote about Sir Henry, the author of *Browning as a Philosophical and Religious Teacher* (London: Nelson, 1891), is taken from Hetherington's volume, *The Life and Letters of Sir Henry Jones*, 43.
21 Feuerbach, *The Essence of Christianity*, trans. George Eliot (originally published 1841), and Strauss, *The Life of Jesus, Critically Examined*, trans. George Eliot (1845).
22 Sinfield, *Dramatic Monologue*, 25.

4: The Dangerous Legacy of Keats and Fox

1 See Keats's letter to George and Thomas Keats, December 1817: 'At once it struck me, what quality went to form a Man of Achievement especially in Literature & which Shakespeare possessed so enormously – I mean Negative Capability, that is when man is capable of being in uncertainties, Mysteries, doubts, without any irritable reaching after fact & reason.' On the shocking implications of negative capability, see Keats's letter to Richard Woodhouse, 27 October 1818: 'As to the poetical Character itself, ... it is not itself – it has no self – it is every thing and nothing – It has no character, it enjoys light and shade; it lives in gusto, be it foul or fair, high or low, rich or poor, mean or elevated – It has as much delight in conceiving a Iago as an Imogen.' Reprinted in *Selected Poems and Letters of John Keats*, 261, 279.
2 Fox, review of Tennyson's *Poems, Chiefly Lyrical*, 77.
3 The most original discussion of sympathy in the dramatic monologue occurs in chapter 2 of Robert Langbaum's seminal study of the genre, *The Poetry of Experience: The Dramatic Monologue in Modern Literary Tradition*, 75–108. Langbaum argues that in our sympathy for Browning's Duke of Ferrara 'we suspend moral judgment because we prefer to participate in the

duke's power and freedom, in his hard core of character fiercely loyal to itself' (83).

4 Bishop, *Something Else*, 147.

5 Sartre, *The Words*, 112. T.S. Eliot, *The Varieties of Metaphysical Poetry*, 151: 'I have always been impressed ... by the sense of a "double world" in the tragedies of Chapman, and which made me compare him to Dostoevski.'

The kind of 'doubleness' that T.S. Eliot associates with the tragedies of Chapman, in which an actor may momentarily act 'out another scene than that visible upon the stage' (152), is well illustrated in Elizabeth Barrett Browning's monologue 'Confessions.' Like Lucy Snowe in *Villette*, the woman uses the sacrament of confession to her own ends. Though she had come to the priest for absolution, she is soon able to dispense with the priest and confer her own benediction. 'If I angered some,' she reasons, 'I atoned through my suffering. I loved those who were indifferent or who hated me. If I loved my neighbor better than an alien and alienating God, who is to say I am not faithful to my own beliefs?' By the end of her speech, which is half prayer and half forensic rhetoric, the woman seems to be in rapt communion with a second auditor.

Returning from a higher plane of truth to the priest she is ostensibly addressing, the final stanza allows her auditor to hurl forth his theological countercharge: 'Go, I cried; thou has chosen the Human, and left the Divine!' (9.1). When her censor asks her if her human betrayers have been as kind to her as God would have been, she springs a trap for him. 'The God you have been preaching to me is a god of wrath and judgment,' she asserts, 'the God who appears in the whirlwind to Job. Such a God is more capricious and vengeful than my worst human friends, and certainly less intelligible.'

In Barrett Browning's 'The Runaway Slave at Pilgrim's Point,' the more unhinged and demented the black woman speaker becomes, the more she grows in stature (like the crazed Rizpah in Tennyson's monologue). Though she commits the heinous crime of child-murder, she is no Hetty Sorrel. Her moral authority depends in part upon her address to a double audience. At first she appeals to an ideal audience of dead Pilgrim Fathers, whose historic defence of freedom ratifies her deeds. Only at the end of the monologue does her ideal audience change into a hostile band of slave-owners, sworn to avenge the wrongs committed against the white man who raped her.

When the woman's imaginary listeners, the ghostly Pilgrim Fathers, dissipate in the night air, she is ringed round with the slave-owners who have come to torture her. Turning malediction into a heroic enterprise by prophesying civil war, the slave begins to grow in stature, like a black

Cassandra. In the closing stanza, where the *b c c b c* rhyme scheme turns into triplets (*b c c c b*), the repeated *c* rhymes help her soar morally above her destroyers.

> I fall, I swoon! I look at the sky:
> > The clouds are breaking on my brain;
> I am floating along, as if I should die
> > Of liberty's exquisite pain –
> In the name of the white child, waiting for me
> In the death-dark where we may kiss and agree,
> White men, I leave you all curse-free
> > In my broken heart's disdain!
> > > 'The Runaway Slave at Pilgrim's Point,' 36.1–8

Even as one ripple of tremulous emotion succeeds another, the runaway slave suddenly withdraws her curse, showing that like the black eagle she can be victorious in defeat and more magnanimous than her destroyers.

6 Fox, review of Tennyson's *Poems, Chiefly Lyrical*, 77.
7 Berger, *Ways of Seeing*, 54.
8 Ibid.
9 Notes Lowell prepared for introducing Randall Jarrell at a poetry reading. Houghton Library MS bMS Am 1905 (2842).
10 Ibid.
11 The phrase is used by Robert Browning in his letter of 11 February 1845, *The Letters*, 1:17.
12 Letter of Jane Morris to Ford Madox Ford, July 1872. Princeton Rare Book Library MS, CO1890, box 27, folder 49.
13 Chesterton, *St. Thomas Aquinas*, 154.
14 Fox, review of Tennyson's *Poems, Chiefly Lyrical*, 77.
15 Ibid.
16 The best theorists of the monologue have always sought theological models to account for the poet's curious ability to be simultaneously masked and luminous: both immanent in his impersonations and oddly removed from them. It is surely no accident that Tennyson and T.S. Eliot, two of the most resourceful writers of dramatic monologues, should both have been zealous students of Hindu, Buddhist, and Taoist thought.

Because a poet who invents himself by writing monologues stands in the same relation to his masks as God stands to his creation, it is useful to ask which theological model – the shadowy transmigrations of the Buddha or the more substantial Incarnation of the Christian God – best describes the poet's individuation in a dramatic speaker. Admittedly, the Christian metaphor of Incarnation is always an elusive concept for Eliot, even in his most orthodox formulation of it in 'The Dry Salvages' (5.32): 'The hint half guessed, the gift half understood, is Incarnation.' But in seeking a theological analogy for the masked poet of the dramatic monologues, Eliot needs a more protean model than even a 'hint half guessed, a gift half understood.'

One model that Eliot considers in his lecture notes on Eastern philosophy, Houghton Library MS Am 1691. 14 (12), is the Gnostic model of emanation, according to which the defects of individual speakers are merely imperfect 'reflections of the universal mind.' Eliot's instructor, M. Anesaki, agrees with Schopenhauer that in the end no reason can be given for the ghostly emanations of the god, just as no reason can be given for the appearance of *avidya* (ignorance) 'out of the *Tathata* (thatness, viz. the tranquil neuter substance of all that exists).' Though Anesaki believes that the closest analogy to Buddha's emanations is 'Schelling's theory of a jump (*Absprung*),' he is equally insistent that 'the foundation of Buddhist morality rests on the essential capacity of every human person,' whether male or female, 'for Buddhahood.' See Anesaki, *Buddhist Ethics and Morality*, 8, 10. A student of Anesaki while at Harvard, T.S. Eliot donated his copy of his teacher's monograph to Eliot House. It can now be found in the Houghton Rare Book Library.

17 Frye, *The Great Code*, 100.
18 For a detailed explanation of these theories, see my study *The Lucid Veil: Poetic Truth in the Victorian Age*, especially the sections on 'Conservative Hermeneutics: Keble's Tractarian Typology' (189–98), 'Types and Homotypes: Dobell's New Mythus' (244–6), 'Mansel and Kant: The Limits of Analogy' (123–6), and 'Agnostic Semioticians: Carlyle and Sir William Hamilton' (126–9).
19 Wilde, 'The Truth of Masks,' 158.

5: The Agnostic Legacy

1 See Buchanan, 'The Fleshly School of Poetry,' McGann, '"A Thing to Mind."'
   Other perceptive modern readings of Morris's Arthurian poems include Boos, 'Historicism in William Morris's "The Defence of Guenevere"'; Brantlinger, 'A Reading of Morris' *The Defence of Guenevere and Other Poems*'; Carley, '"Heaven's Colour, the Blue"'; Hale and Stevenson, 'Morris' Medieval Queen'; Hassett, 'The Style of Evasion'; Hollow, 'William Morris

and the Judgment of God'; Post, 'Guinevere's Critical Performance'; Riede, 'Morris, Modernism and Romance'; Silver, '"The Defence of Gueneyere"'; and Staines, 'Morris' Treatment of His Medieval Sources in *The Defence of Guenevere and Other Poems.*'

2 Ricks, 'The Antithetical Sense,' *Beckett's Dying Words*, 128–45.

3 Ibid., 136.

4 Letters are in Princeton Rare Book Library, CO1890, box 8, folder 32.

5 Lang, ed., *The Pre-Raphaelites and Their Circle*, 509.

6 Buckley, *The Victorian Temper*, 176.

7 Morris, 'The Art of the People,' 66.

8 A. Dwight Culler, *The Poetry of Tennyson*, 90–2.

9 Morris, 'Art under Plutocracy,' 139.

10 Santayana, 'Penitent Art,' 274.

11 Huizinga, *The Waning of the Middle Ages*, 292.

12 Ibid., 209.

13 Ibid., 272.

14 Jane Morris's letter to D.G. Rossetti, December 1880. Princeton Rare Book Library, CO1890, box 27, folder 52.

15 Jane Morris's letter to D.G. Rossetti, 1880, no month or day. Princeton Rare Book Library, CO1890, box 27, folder 52.

16 William Morris's letter to William Bell, 27 April 1882. Princeton Rare Book Library, CO1896, box 27, folder 66.

17 For a detailed analysis of this topic see my discussion of 'Presentational Forms: Unconsummated Symbols in Kant, Masson, Mansel,' *The Lucid Veil*, 161–74.

18 Mansel, *Prolegomena Logica*, 14.

19 Langer, *Philosophy in a New Key*, 195.

20 Bradley, *Aphorisms*, aphorism 98.

21 Morris, 'The Prospects of Architecture in Civilization,' 211.

22 Houghton Library MS bMS Am 1905 (2163), undated. Early drafts of 'The Mills of the Kavanaughs' contained in this folder include several passages where shades of the incest story darken the surface narrative.

23 Houghton Library MS bMS Am 1905 (2799), folio 4.

24 In his notes for an essay on the diabolical, Lowell dissects two criminals (Rimbaud and Milton's Satan); two cold men (George Eliot's Grandcourt and Virgil's Aeneas); two comics (Dickens's Sarah Gamp and Faulkner's Popeye); and two manipulators (Goethe's Mephistopheles and Shakespeare's Iago).

25 Persephone's love for Pluto may owe something to the great classical monologue of Tennyson's old age, 'Demeter and Persephone.' In

Tennyson's poem there seems to be something intemperate and perverse about Demeter's resolve to reverse for Persephone alone the doom reserved for all humanity. Who is Demeter to say that her daughter hates being queen of the underworld? Maybe she loves her husband and has no desire to live all year with her mother.

26 Revisions of 'Her Dead Brother' appear in Houghton Library MS bMS Am 1905 (2166).

27 See Keats's letter to George and Thomas Keats, December 1817, quoted in Chapter 4, note 1.

28 Rough notes for these sketches are found in Houghton Library MS bMS Am 1905 (2840).

29 Lowell amplifies this portrait by citing in the same manuscript several quips Santayana is reputed to have made: 'It's a pity the Catholic faith has no bottom. It is too good to be believed'; 'There is no God and Mary is his Mother.' Lowell also reports that when the nuns asked Santayana to attend a papal audience, he answered, 'I never visit celebrities.'

   Lowell sent two of his own monologues for Santayana's perusal. Though Santayana corresponded with Lowell, his letters cannot be quoted.

30 One of the best comments on the structure of Lowell's monologues comes from Randall Jarrell: his poems 'understand the world as a sort of conflict of opposites,' Jarrell contends. 'In this struggle one opposite is that cake of custom in which all of us lie embedded like lungfish ... Struggling within this like leaven, falling to it like light, is everything that is free or open, that grows or is willing to change.' See Jarrell, 'From the Kingdom of Necessity,' *Poetry and the Age*, 208–9. Though the coda of the whirring spheres justifies Jarrell's comment, its other alternatives to the constraining 'cake of custom' are too reminiscent of the ghastly submarine impressions in *In Memoriam* to be consoling.

31 Houghton Library MS bMS Am 1905 (2167).

32 Houghton Library MS bMS Am 1905 (2105). Lines 34–5 originally read, 'until we thought we could not rest / Till we had done as that mad fool had done.' On his copy of the manuscript Jarrell writes, 'the effect seems too obvious.' By contrast, Lowell's revised version may be too obscure: 'until we could not rest / Till we had done with life.' The suicidal impulse is barely intimated now, even though impressions of despair are allowed to deepen.

   Always a critic of contradiction and imprecise diction, Jarrell responds negatively to another phrase: 'quite a noisome stir / Broke in New England.' He complains that 'this sounds too much like Gertrude Stein's remark that something was *rather epoch-making*.' In revising the lines to read 'soon a noisome stir / Palsied our village' (30–1), Lowell allows the metaphoric inventiveness of 'Palsied' to transfer the fanatic's delirium to his fellow villagers. No longer therapeutic but pathological, conversion breeds a distemper that is highly contagious.

I am puzzled by Jarrell's additional comment that, as a 'special case poem,' an epistolary monologue like 'After the Surprising Conversions' cannot be as good as a poem written *sub specie aeternitatem.*' His criticism seems even odder when we read in a letter Jarrell wrote to Lowell – MS bMS Am 1905 (629–75) – that one of the poems' 'biggest limitations' is their lack of people. 'They are more about the actions of you, God, the sea, and cemeteries than about the actions of men.'

33 Lowell, 'An Essay on the Diabolical in Literature,' Houghton Library MS bMS Am 1905 (2799), folio 10. Influenced by Erich Auerbach's interpretation of Dante in *Mimesis,* Lowell speculates that 'Dido does for Aeneas and his epic destiny' what the characters in *The Divine Comedy* do for Dante. Our intimacy with speakers in the best dramatic monologues may imperil our judgments of them in the manner Lowell describes.

34 Lowell is closer in temper to Hopkins, I think, than to Eliot. Though Lowell says he 'wept when Eliot died' and concedes that Eliot's 'influence is everywhere inescapable,' he also insists that it 'is nowhere really usable.' More to the point, Lowell has reservations about Eliot's orthodoxy. 'Christ and the Virgin are present' in Eliot's poems, 'but only as rather icy Congregationalist anatomies. Death and rebirth are at the heart of things, it is true, but in a rather universalist and symbolic guise that perhaps ignores any creed.' Houghton Library MS bMS Am 1905 (2820)

Lowell's affinities with Hopkins, another important precursor, sound more spontaneous. 'Thoreau,' he writes, 'has the shy, sensitive gallantry of Hopkins, Pascal or Herbert. I imagine the gods doomed all four men in adolescence, and then were won over by so much grit and good-nature, and gave each some forty years.' 'Essay on New England,' Houghton Library MS bMS Am 1905 (2840)

35 Jarrell, *Poetry and the Age,* 209.

36 Houghton MS bMS Am 1905 (2105).

37 Houghton MS bMS Am 1905 (2819).

6: The Legacy of the Unconscious

1 Carlyle, 'Characteristics,' *The Works of Thomas Carlyle,* 28:2.

2 Keble, review of Lockhart's *Memoirs of the Life of Sir Walter Scott,* 440, 436.

3 Dallas, *The Gay Science,* 1:195–6.

4 Sartre, 'Bad Faith,' 89.

5 Rosmarin, *The Power of Genre*, 46: 'Let us define dramatic monologues as poems that invite their readers to distinguish the characterized speaker's meaning from the poem's.'

6 Rader, 'The Dramatic Monologue and Related Lyric Forms,' 140.

7 Sartre, 'Concrete Relations with Others,' 538–9.

8 Abrams, *A Glossary of Literary Terms*, 46: In a dramatic monologue, 'the principle controlling the poet's selection and organization of what the lyric speaker says is the speaker's unintentional revelation of his or her temperament and character.'

9 Carlyle, 'Characteristics,' *The Works of Thomas Carlyle*, 28:3.

10 Chesterton, *Robert Browning*, 192–3.

11 Ibid., 202.

12 Beryl Rowland's theory that the Wife of Bath conspired with Jankyn to murder her fourth husband seems to gain in ingenuity what it loses in its awareness of the Wife's touching capacity to achieve a deep and backward-reaching intimacy with Jankyn. Such heartfelt intimacy is seldom possible among criminals (Rowland, 'Chaucer's Idea of the Pardoner'). For other innovative readings see Gottfried, 'Conflict and Relationship, Sovereignty and Survival,' and Donald K. Howard's study of the Pardoner as an anguished clown in *The Idea of the Canterbury Tales*, 339–57.

13 Sartre, 'Bad Faith,' 86–116.

14 Keble, *Lectures on Poetry 1832–1841*, vol. 2. Why, Keble asks, should a poet who 'acknowledges neither Author nor Rule of Nature' be 'lauded as high-priest and interpreter of this very Nature' (333)? He concludes that, despite Lucretius's commitment to atheism, the 'whole tenor and quality' of his frequent digressions appear to 'be on the side of those who love true religion' (336).

15 Dickens, 'George Silverman's Explanation,' *Selected Short Fiction*. For examples of Silverman's addiction to the trick of voice he condemns in Brother Hawkyard, see 388, 394, and 399: 'His manner, too, of confirming himself in a parenthesis, – as if, knowing himself, he doubted his own word, – I found distasteful'; 'Then Brother Gimblet came forward, and took (as I knew he would) the text, My kingdom is not of this world'; 'If I be (as I am) unable to represent to myself any previous period of my life as quite separable from her attracting power, how can I answer for this one detail?'

16 See Landor, 'Dialogues of Literary Men,' *Imaginary Conversations*, 'David Hume and John Home,' 4, 9, p. 16. Each citation lists the numbers of the volume, the conversation, and the pages, in that order.

17 Listed as item A1634 in Kelley and Colley, *The Browning Collections*. The volume contains two pencil notes by Robert Browning and numerous notes in the margins.

18 See Landor, 'Classical Dialogues (Greek),' *Imaginary Conversations*, 'Diogenes and Plato,' 1, 7, pp. 67–122.

   Browning's library contained many volumes of Landor's works, several inscribed to the poet by their author. These include the *Works of Walter Savage Landor* (London, 1853), listed as item A1416 in *The Browning Collections*.

19 See Arnold, *Friendship's Garland*, *The Complete Prose Works of Matthew Arnold*, 5, 6, p. 65. Each citation lists the numbers of the volume, the letter, and the page, in that order.

7: Reading Monologues

 1 Hallam, 'On Some of the Characteristics of Modern Poetry and on the Lyrical Poems of Alfred Tennyson,' 850, 856. Fox, review of Tennyson's *Poems, Chiefly Lyrical*.

 2 Mansel, *The Limits of Religious Thought Examined in Eight Lectures*; Wilde, 'The Truth of Masks,' 157–8; Hamilton, review of M. Cousin's *Course of Philosophy*, 208.

 3 Faas, *Retreat into the Mind*, 24. The quotation from Shaw appears in *Browning Society's Papers*, 1:122.

 4 See Introduction, note 13.

 5 Nietzsche, 'On Truth and Lies in a Nonmoral Sense,' 84.

 6 This treatise, the *Course on Rhetoric*, summarizes the contents of a course Nietzsche taught at Basel during the winter of 1872–3. It is translated by Carole Blair under the title 'Nietzsche's Lecture Notes on Rhetoric.'

 7 Peckham, 'Personality and the Mask of Knowledge,' 87.

 8 Wittgenstein, *Philosophical Investigations*, proposition 109, 47.

 9 Hallam, 'On Some of the Characteristics of Modern Poetry and on the Lyrical Poems of Alfred Tennyson,' 850, 856.

10 Fox, review of Tennyson's *Poems, Chiefly Lyrical*, 76.

11 Armstrong, *Victorian Poetry*. According to Armstrong, the 'poetry of sensation' advocated by Arthur Hallam encouraged political inertia by aestheticizing politics, while the more radical tradition that influenced Browning encouraged a poetry of epistemological scepticism that politicized aesthetics. Armstrong identifies a 'formative moment' (28) in Victorian culture that led to the rise of the 'double poem.'

12 Ibid., 346.

13 Simpson, *Romanticism, Nationalism, and the Revolt against Theory*, 126–7.

14 For a full account of the theory of synchronous association which J.S. Mill develops in his 1833 essay 'What Is Poetry?,' *Monthly Repository* (January– April 1833), readers should consult his editorial remarks in his father James

Mill's *Analysis of the Phenomena of the Human Mind* (1829). The younger Mill speaks of feelings as complex psychological states connected with ideas of aversion or desire that allow the poet to experience pain and pleasure simultaneously. Keats's feminized poet of negative capability shares a comparable experience.

15 Jakobson, 'Two Aspects of Language and Two Types of Linguistic Disturbances.'

16 Sinfield, *Alfred Tennyson*, 53.

17 On the gendering of empathy and projection and on their relation to value and meaning, respectively, see Nozick, *The Examined Life*, 169. 'Value and meaning have, so to speak, a gender. Bringing oneself into an internal unity seems to fit a female way of relating sexually, connecting beyond oneself to a male. Is value to female as meaning is to male? ... In sexual orientation, men go to link outward and women incorporate inward. Yet in the nature of their self-conceptions, women often are described as oriented around notions of relationship and concern, while men view themselves as more autonomously contained within boundaries.' Such reflections are highly speculative, as Nozick himself acknowledges.

18 A reversal of Eucharistic typology in the last stanza of Rossetti's lyric 'A Better Resurrection' turns Christ into a kind of vampire who drinks her blood:

> My life is like a broken bowl,
>   A broken bowl that cannot hold
> One drop of water for my soul
>   Or cordial in the searching cold:
> Cast in the fire the perished thing;
>   Melt and remould it, till it be
> A royal cup for Him, my King:
> O Jesus, drink of me.   17–24

19 Armstrong, *Victorian Poetry*, 325–6.

For the half-comic shrew of Greek legend, Amy Levy's monologue 'Xantippe' substitutes the portrait of a passionate advocate of women's rights. Unlike most Victorian monologues, this Greek feminist's call to battle is not 'dialogical' in Bakhtin's sense. It reads instead as a series of 'set pieces' on the subject of women's education, in which we overhear the overt feminist protest of the first Jewish undergraduate admitted to Newnham College, Cambridge. When Xantippe tries to join the philosophers' conversation, Socrates is contemptuously dismissive: 'I thank thee for the wisdom which thy lips / Have thus let fall among us' (206–7). But after Alkibiades patronizes Aspasia, whose intellectual curiosity is satirized as a wide throat gaping at 'life's ... banquet,' Xantippe settles the score by launching an energetic defence of women.

The closing appeal for light (275–9) works at two levels: as her eyes grow dark with the approach of death, Xantippe longs in vain for the coming dawn. But she also wants 'light' in Matthew Arnold's sense: she yearns for the power of knowledge that an academy of male philosophers has wrongfully denied her. Excluded from the charmed circle of Plato's academy, Xantippe has no chance to take part in Socratic dialogue. Monological discourse is the price she pays for being a scholar in an intellectual community dominated by men.

Charlotte Brontë's monologue 'Pilate's Wife's Dream' replaces Xantippe's Hellenic light with the light of Hebraic revelation: as the shadow of 'unfolding gloom' grows into the substance of faith, her vision 'makes Olympian glory dim' (117, 121, 125–6). A marvelling use of anaphora helps the religious convert ponder the theological paradox that Eliot explores in his monologue 'Journey of the Magi': the paradox that as we contemplate the Nativity or Crucifixion death and birth become hard to tell apart: 'This day, Time travails with a mighty birth; / This day, Truth stoops from heaven and visits earth' (151–2). To grow in stature, Pilate's wife must first oppose her husband's proud contempt for women by ratifying the 'dreadful doom' of Pilate's being devoured by wolves in a mountain solitude of 'trackless snows' (105–6). As a kind of Roman Oenone, Brontë's embattled feminist finds that she has to be despoiled and defiled like the rites of pagan religion (132) before she can be renewed by faith and strengthened by her visions.

Even in 'The Iniquity of the Fathers upon the Children,' an internalized monologue by Christina Rossetti (an exceptionally passive and submissive poet), the illegitimate daughter aligns herself with two other women, the wronged mother and her nurse, to oppose the cruelty of their common male enemy, the unknown father who 'wrought [her] Mother's shame' (5). Most affecting are the reticences of mood and temper which set the complaints of Rossetti's wronged woman apart from the shrill laments of Tennyson's Oenone and Demeter. Instead of openly denouncing her father for deceiving her mother, the speaker twice mutes her curse by preceding it with 'almost.'

But I could almost curse
My Father for his pains;
And sometimes at my prayer
Kneeling in sight of Heaven
I almost curse him still:
'The Inquity of the Fathers upon the Children,' 509–13

Clues about her secret identity as the great lady's illegitimate daughter have to be pieced together like parts of a puzzle. The inference that Rossetti is writing a version of *Bleak House*, and that the high-born woman is a Lady Dedlock, lingers on as the monologue's disturbing afterthought.

20 Mermin, '"The fruitful feud of hers and his,"' 154.

21 Moore, *Care of the Soul*, 85.

22 Perkins, *Is Literary History Possible?*, 17, 175–86.

23 Donoghue, *Walter Pater*, 136, 328.

Though Donoghue takes T.S. Eliot to task for 'thinking in categories and despising those people – Pater among them – who hold themselves apart or aloof from them' (316), Eliot himself is an intellectual heir of Pater, especially in his defence of suspended judgment and scepticism. In *Notes towards the Definition of Culture*, for example, Eliot eloquently defends the sceptic's 'habit of examining evidence and [his] capacity for delayed decision. Scepticism is a highly civilised trait, though, when it declines into pyrrhonism is weakness: for we need not only the strength to defer a decision, but the strength to make one' (29).

24 Carlyle, *The Works of Thomas Carlyle*, 1:212.

25 Anesaki, *Buddhist Ethics and Morality*, 7.

26 The quoted phrases are taken from folder 1 of T.S. Eliot's notes for Professor M. Anesaki's course, Philosophy 24a, MS Am 1691.14 (12). Quotation is by permission of Mrs Valerie Eliot.

27 Hamilton, review of M. Cousin's *Course of Philosophy*; Mansel, *The Limits of Religious Thought*.

For the distinction between 'two mutually exclusive realms of being' I am indebted to Edward Harrison's discussion in *Masks of the Universe*, 264–6. Building on the arguments of St Anselm and Sir William Hamilton, Harrison maintains that 'the universes are the masks of the Universe, and the gods are "the masks of God" (to borrow a phrase used by Joseph Campbell). Even a personal and loving supreme being is a mask, a god, conceived and figured by the human mind. The gods and universes are grand unifying ideas, great schemes of organizing thought, occupying the realm of the conceivable. When God and Universe both occupy the realm of the inconceivable, we know nothing more than our ignorance' (266).

28 James, *The Selected Letters*, xx.

29 Pascal, *Pensées and Other Writings*, fragment 31, p. 9.

30 Jowett, *The Dialogues of Plato*, 2:666–7.

31 Nicolas Cusanus, *Of Learned Ignorance*. According to D.J.B. Hawkins's introduction, 'the mystery' that Nicholas acknowledges 'always remained for him both *mysterium tremendum* and *mysterium fascinans*, and there is

implicit in his work the conviction that the end of enlightened ignorance would be more enlightenment rather than irremediable ignorance' (xxviii).

32 On the theory of 'agnoiology' or ignorance see Ferrier's *The Institutes of Metaphysics*, especially 438. For a detailed study of Ferrier's influence on Tennyson and Victorian culture in general see my discussion of 'Ferrier's Philosophy of Consciousness: The Framing of the Object' in *The Lucid Veil*, 48–53.

33 Harrison, *Masks of the Universe*, 275.

34 Thomas, 'On Matters of Doubt,' 157.

35 William Hamilton, review of M. Cousin's *Course of Philosophy*, 208; and Wilde, 'The Truth of Masks,' 157–8. On Sir William Hamilton's philosophy of the unconditioned and its impact on Victorian culture see my discussions of 'Mansel and Kant: The Limits of Analogy' and of 'Agnostic Semioticians: Carlyle and Sir William Hamilton' in *The Lucid Veil*, 123–9, 30.

36 Arnold, *The Complete Prose Works of Matthew Arnold*, 3:157. Arnold quotes *Aeneid*, 6.314.

37 Robert Lowell's notes for an essay on the diabolical in literature. Houghton Library MS bMS Am 1905 (2799).

38 Robert Lowell's notes for an introduction to a poetry reading by T.S. Eliot. Houghton Library MS bMS Am 1905 (2804).

39 Shattuck, *Forbidden Knowledge*, 162.

40 Verene, *Philosophy and the Return to Self-Knowledge*, 130–1.

41 Huxley, 'Science and Culture,' *Collected Essays of T.H. Huxley*, 3:136.

42 Newman, *Apologia Pro Vita Sua*, 48.

Works Cited

Abrams, M.H. *A Glossary of Literary Terms*. 5th ed. Chicago: Holt, Rinehart and Winston, 1985, 45–6.

Anesaki, M. *Buddhist Ethics and Morality*, n.p., 1912. The copy I consulted was donated by T.S. Eliot to the Eliot House Library, Harvard University. It is now in the possession of the Houghton Rare Book Library.

Armstrong, Isobel. *Victorian Poetry: Poetry, Poetics and Politics*. London: Routledge, 1993.

Arnold, Matthew. *The Complete Prose Works of Matthew Arnold*. Edited by R.H. Super. 11 vols. Ann Arbor: University of Michigan Press, 1960–77.

– *Poetry and Criticism of Matthew Arnold*. Edited by A. Dwight Culler. Boston: Houghton Mifflin, 1961. An accessible selection of representative poetry and prose, with a useful introduction.

Austin, J.L. *How to Do Things with Words*. Cambridge: Harvard University Press, 1962.

Berger, John. *Ways of Seeing*. London: Penguin, 1972.

Bishop, Jonathan. *Something Else*. New York: George Braziller, 1972.

Bloom, Harold. *Poetry and Repression: Revisionism From Blake to Stevens*. New Haven and London: Yale University Press, 1976.

Boos, Florence S. 'Historicism in William Morris's "The Defence of Guenevere."' *King Arthur through the Ages*, vol. 2. Edited by Valerie M. Lagorio and Mildred Leake Day. New York: Garland, 1990.

Borg, Marcus J. *Jesus: A New Vision*. San Francisco: Harper, 1991.

Bradley, F.H. *Ethical Studies*. Oxford: Clarendon Press, 1876. Reprinted London: Oxford University Press, 1970. Edited by Richard Wollheim.

– *Aphorisms*. Oxford: Clarendon Press, 1930.

Brantlinger, Patrick. 'A Reading of Morris' *The Defence of Guenevere and Other Poems*.' *Victorian Newsletter* 44 (1973), 18–24.

Browning, Robert, and Elizabeth Barrett. *The Letters of Robert Browning and Elizabeth Barrett Barrett* [sic] *1845–1846*. Edited by Elvan Kintner. 2 vols. Cambridge, Mass.: Harvard University Press, 1969.

The Browning Society's Papers. 3 vols. London: Trubner, 1881–91.

Buchanan, Robert. 'The Fleshly School of Poetry.' *Contemporary Review* 28 (1871), 334–50.

Buckley, J.H. *The Victorian Temper: A Study in Literary Culture*. Cambridge, Mass.: Harvard University Press, 1951.

Butler, Samuel. *The Way of All Flesh*. Edited by F.W. Dupee. New York: Fawcett World Library, 1967.

Cameron, Sharon. *Choosing Not Choosing: Dickinson's Fascicles*. Chicago and London: University of Chicago, 1992.

Carley, James P. '"Heaven's Colour, the Blue": Morris's Guenevere and the Choosing Cloths Reread.' *Journal of the William Morris Society* 9:1 (1990), 20–2.

Carlyle, Thomas. *The Works of Thomas Carlyle*. New York: Scribner's Sons, 1898–1901.

Chesterton. G.K. *Robert Browning*. London: Macmillan, 1903.

– *St. Thomas Aquinas*. New York; Sheed and Ward, 1933.

Culler, A. Dwight. *The Poetry of Tennyson:* New Haven: Yale University Press, 1977.

Culler, Jonathan. 'Apostrophe.' *The Pursuit of Signs*. Ithaca: Cornell University Press, 1981.

Dallas, E.S. *The Gay Science*. 2 vols. London: Chapman and Hall, 1866.

de Man, Paul. 'Autobiography as De-facement.' *Modern Language Notes* 94 (1979), 919–30.

Dickens, Charles. *Selected Short Fiction*. New York: Penguin, 1976.

Donoghue, Denis. *Walter Pater: Lover of Strange Souls*. New York: Alfred A. Knopf, 1995.

Eliot, George. *Middlemarch*. Edited by Gordon S. Haight. Boston: Riverside, 1956.

Eliot, T.S. '*In Memoriam,*' *Selected Essays*. London, Faber and Faber, 1932.

– *Notes towards the Definition of Culture*. London: Faber and Faber, 1948.

– 'The Three Voices of Poetry.' *On Poetry and Poets*. New York: Farrar, Straus and Giroux, 1961.

– *The Varieties of Metaphysical Poetry*. Edited by Ronald Schuchard. New York: Harcourt Brace and Co., 1993.

Empson, W.H. *Using Biography*. Cambridge, Mass.: Harvard University Press, 1984.

Faas, Ekbert. *Retreat into the Mind: Victorian Poetry and the Rise of Psychiatry*. Princeton: Princeton University Press, 1988.

Ferrier, J.F. *The Institutes of Metaphysics: Theory of Knowing and Being*. Edinburgh and London: Blackwood, 1854.

Feuerbach, Ludwig. *The Essence of Christianity*. Translated by George Eliot. New York: Harper and Row, 1957. Originally published 1841.

Fox, W.J. Review of Tennyson's *Poems, Chiefly Lyrical*. *Westminster Review* 14 (1831). Reprinted in *Victorian Scrutinies*. Edited by Isobel Armstrong. London: Athlone Press, 1972.

Frost, Robert. 'Education by Poetry.' *Selected Prose of Robert Frost*. Edited by Hyde Cox and E.C. Lathem. New York: Collier, 1968.

Frye, Northrop. *The Great Code: The Bible and Literature*. Toronto: Academic Press, 1982.

Gottfried, Barbara. 'Conflict and Relationship, Sovereignty and Survival: Parables of Power in the Wife of Bath's Prologue.' *Chaucer Review* 19:3 (1985), 202–24.

Griffiths, Eric. *The Printed Voice of Victorian Poetry*. Oxford: Clarendon Press, 1989.

Grote, George. *Plato, and the Other Companions of Sokrates*. 4 vols. London, John Murray, 1865.

Hale, Virgina S., and Catherine Barnes Stevenson. 'Morris' Medieval Queen: A Paradox Resolved.' *Victorian Poetry* 30 (1992), 171–8.

Hallam, Arthur. 'On Some of the Characteristics of Modern Poetry and on the Lyrical Poems of Alfred Tennyson.' *The Englishman's Magazine* (August 1831). Reprinted in *Victorian Poetry and Poetics*. Edited by Walter E. Houghton and G. Robert Stange. Boston: Houghton Mifflin, 1968.

Hamilton, Sir William. 'Review of M. Cousin's *Course of Philosophy*. *Edinburgh Review* 50 (1829), 196–221.

Harrison, Edward. *Masks of the Universe*. New York: Macmillan, 1985.

Hassett, Constance W. 'The Style of Evasion: William Morris' *The Defence of Guenevere and Other Poems*.' *Victorian Poetry* 29 (1991), 99–114.

Hetherington, H.J.W. *The Life and Letters of Sir Henry Jones*. London: Hodder and Stoughton, 1924.

Hill, Geoffrey. *The Lords of Limit: Essays on Literature and Ideas*. London: André Deutsch, 1984.

Hollow, John. 'William Morris and the Judgment of God.' *PMLA* 86 (1971), 446–51.

Honan, Park. *Browning's Characters*. New Haven: Yale University Press, 1961.

Howard, Donald K. *The Idea of the Canterbury Tales*. Berkeley: University of California Press, 1976.

Howe, Elisabeth A. *The Dramatic Monologue*. New York: Simon and Schuster Macmillan, 1996.

Huizinga, Johan. *The Waning of the Middle Ages*. New York: St Martin's Press, 1949.

Huxley, T.H. *Collected Essays of T.H. Huxley*. 9 vols. London: Macmillan and Co., 1904–25.

Jakobson, Roman. 'Two Aspects of Language and Two Types of Linguistic Disturbances.' *Fundamentals of Language*. Edited by Roman Jakobson and Morris Halle. The Hague: Mouton, 1956.

James, William. *The Selected Letters*. Edited by Elizabeth Hardwick. New York and London: Doubleday, 1993.

Jarrell, Randall. *Poetry and the Age*. New York: Knopf, 1953.

Jowett, Benjamin. *The Dialogues of Plato*. Translated with analyses and introduction by Benjamin Jowett. Oxford: Oxford University Press, 1871.

Keble, John. Review of Lockhart's *Memoirs of the Life of Sir Walter Scott*. *British Critic and Quarterly Theological Review* 24 (1838), 423–83.

– *Lectures on Poetry 1832–1841*. Translated by E.K. Francis. 2 vols. Oxford: Oxford University Press, 1912. Originally published 1832–41.

Keats, John. *Selected Poems and Letters of John Keats*. Edited by Douglas Bush. Boston: Houghton Mifflin, 1959.

Kelley, Phillip, and Betty A. Colley, editors. *The Browning Collections: A Reconstruction*. Winfield, Kansas: Wedgestone Press, 1984.

Kierkegaard, Søren. *Repetition: An Essay in Experimental Psychology*. Translated by Walter Lowrie. New York: Harper and Row, 1964.

– *The Concept of Irony*. Translated by Lee M. Capel. Bloomington and London: Indiana University Press, 1965.

Kneale, J. Douglas. 'Romantic Aversions: Apostrophe Reconsidered.' *ELH* 58 (1991), 141–65.

Landor, Walter Savage. *Imaginary Conversations*. 6 vols. London: J.M. Dent, 1891.

Lang, Cecil Y., editor. *The Pre-Raphaelites and Their Circle*. Boston: Houghton Mifflin, 1968.

Langbaum, Robert. *The Poetry of Experience: The Dramatic Monologue in Modern Literary Tradition*. New York: Norton, 1957.

Langer, Susanne. *Philosophy in a New Key*. New York: Mentor, 1948.

Lévinas, Emmanuel. *The Lévinas Reader*. Edited by Sean Hand. Oxford: Blackwell, 1989.

Lodge, David. *After Bakhtin: Essays on Fiction and Criticism*. New York and London: Routledge, 1990.

Mansel, H.L. *Prolegomena Logica: An Inquiry into the Psychological Character of Logical Processes*. Oxford: Oxford University Press, 1851.

– *The Limits of Religious Thought Examined in Eight Lectures*. London: J. Murray, 1867.

Marsh, Joss. *Word Crimes: Blasphemy, Culture, and Literature in Nineteenth-Century England.* Chicago and London: University of Chicago Press, 1998.

Martin, Loy D. *Browning's Dramatic Monologues and the Post-Romantic Subject.* Baltimore: Johns Hopkins University Press, 1985.

Maynard, John. 'Reading the Reader in Robert Browning's Monologues.' *Critical Essays on Robert Browning.* Edited by Mary Ellen Gibson. New York: G.K. Hall, 1992.

McGann, Jerome. '"A Thing to Mind": The Materialist Aesthetic of William Morris.' *Huntingdon Library Quarterly* 55 (1992), 55–74.

Mermin, Dorothy. *The Audience in the Poem.* New Brunswick: Rutgers University Press, 1983.

– '"The fruitful feud of hers and his": Sameness, Difference, and Gender in Victorian Poetry.' *Victorian Poetry* 33 (Spring 1995), 149–68.

Mill, J.S. 'What Is Poetry?' *Monthly Repository* (January–April 1833), 60–70.

Miller, J. Hillis. *Versions of Pygmalion.* Cambridge, Mass.: Harvard University Press, 1989.

Moore, Thomas. *Care of the Soul: A Guide for Cultivating Depth and Sacredness in Everyday Life.* New York: Harper Collins, 1992.

Morris, William. 'The Art of the People' and 'The Prospects of Architecture in Civilization.' *Hopes and Fears for Art: Five Lectures by William Morris.* New York: Longmans, 1903.

– 'Art under Plutocracy.' *On Art and Socialism: Essays and Lectures.* Edited by Holbrook Jackson. London: Longmans, 1947.

Newman. J.H. *Sermons Preached Before the University of Oxford Between 1826 and 1843.* London: Rivingtons, 1887.

– *Apologia Pro Vita Sua.* Edited by David J. De Laura. New York: Norton, 1968. Originally published in 1864.

Nicolas Cusanus. *Of Learned Ignorance.* Translated by Germaine Heron, introduction by D.J.B. Hawkins. London: Methuen, 1954.

Nietzsche, Friedrich. *Twilight of the Idols: The Anti- Christ.* Translated by R.J. Hollingdale. Harmondsworth: Penguin, 1968.

– 'On Truth and Lies in a Nonmoral Sense.' *Philosophy and Truth: Selections from Nietzsche's Notebooks of the Early 1870s.* Translated by Daniel Brezeale. Atlantic Highlands, NJ: Humanities Press, 1979.

– *Course on Rhetoric.* Translated by Carole Blair under the title 'Nietzsche's Lecture Notes on Rhetoric.' *Philosophy and Rhetoric* 16 (1983), 94–129.

Nozick, Robert. *The Examined Life: Philosophical Meditations.* New York: Simon and Schuster, 1989.

Pascal, Blaise. *Pensées and Other Writings.* Translated by Honor Levi. Oxford: Oxford University Press, 1995.

Pater, Walter. *Plato and Platonism.* London: Macmillan and Co., 1910.

– *The Renaissance: Studies in Art and Poetry: The 1893 Text.* Edited by Donald J. Hill. Berkeley: University of California Press, 1980.

Peckham, Morse. 'Personality and the Mask of Knowledge.' *Victorian Revolutionaries.* New York: George Braziller, 1970.

Perkins, David. *Is Literary History Possible?* Baltimore: Johns Hopkins University Press, 1992.

Post, Jonathan. 'Guinevere's Critical Performance.' *Victorian Poetry* 17 (1979), 317–27.

Prynne, J.H. 'English Poetry and Emphatical Language.' *Proceedings of the British Academy* 74 (1988), 135–69.

Rader, Ralph. 'The Dramatic Monologue and Related Lyric Forms.' *Critical Inquiry* 3:1 (1976) 131–51.

Ricks, Christopher. *Tennyson.* Macmillan: New York, 1972.

– *Beckett's Dying Words.* Oxford: Oxford University Press, 1993.

Ricoeur, Paul. *Oneself as Another.* Translated by Kathleen Blamey. Chicago and London: University of Chicago Press, 1992.

Riede, David G. 'Morris, Modernism and Romance.' *ELH* 51 (1984), 85–106.

Roberts, Adam. '*The Ring and the Book*: The Mage, the Alchemist, and the Poet.' *Victorian Poetry* 36 (1998), 37–46.

Rosmarin, Adena. *The Power of Genre.* Minneapolis: University of Minnesota Press, 1985.

Rowland, Beryl. 'Chaucer's Idea of the Pardoner.' *Chaucer Review* 14:2 (1979–80), 141–54.

Santayana, George. 'Penitent Art.' *Selected Critical Writings*, vol. 1. Edited by Norman Henfrey. Cambridge: Cambridge University Press, 1968.

Sartre, Jean-Paul. *The Words.* Translated by Bernard Frechtman. Greenwich, Conn.: Fawcett, 1964.

– 'Bad Faith' and 'Concrete Relations with Others.' *Being and Nothingness.* Translated by Hazel E. Barnes. New York: Washington Square Press, 1966.

Scheinberg, Cynthia. 'Recasting "sympathy and judgment": Amy Levy, Women Poets, and the Victorian Dramatic Monologue.' *Victorian Poetry* 35 (Summer 1997), 173–91.

Schleiermacher, Friedrich Daniel Ernst. *Schleiermacher's Introductions to the Dialogues of Plato.* Translated by W. Dobson. Trinity Street, Cambridge: J.J. Deighton, 1836.

Segal, Erich, ed. *The Dialogues of Plato.* New York: Bantam, 1986. An authoritative and accessible modern edition to supplement Jowett's edition.

Sell, Alan P.F. *Philosophical Idealism and Christian Belief.* New York: St Martin's Press, 1995.

Shattuck, Roger. *Forbidden Knowledge: From Prometheus to Pornography.* New York and London: Harcourt Brace, 1996.

Shaw, W. David. *The Lucid Veil: Poetic Truth in the Victorian Age*. London and Madison: Athlone Press and University of Wisconsin Press, 1987.
– *Victorians and Mystery: Crises of Representation*. Ithaca and London: Cornell University Press, 1990.
Silver, Carole G. '"The Defence of Guenevere": A Further Interpretation.' *SEL* 9 (1969), 695–702.
Simpson, David. *Romanticism, Nationalism, and the Revolt against Theory*. Chicago and London: University of Chicago Press, 1993.
Sinfield, Alan. *Dramatic Monologue*. London: Methuen, 1977.
– *Alfred Tennyson*. Oxford: Blackwell, 1986.
Staines, David. 'Morris' Treatment of His Medieval Sources in *The Defence of Guenevere and Other Poems*.' *Studies in Philology* 70 (1973), 439–64.
Strauss, David Friedrich. *The Life of Jesus, Critically Examined*. Translated by George Eliot. 3 vols. London: Chapman, 1845.
Thomas, Lewis. 'On Matters of Doubt.' *Late Night Thoughts on Listening to Mahler's Ninth Symphony*. New York: Bantam, 1984.
Todorov, Tzetvan. 'The Origin of Genres.' *New Literary History* 8 (1976), 159–70.
Turner, Frank M. *The Greek Heritage in Victorian Britain*. New Haven and London: Yale University Press, 1981.
Verene, Donald Phillip. *Philosophy and the Return to Self- Knowledge*. New Haven and London: Yale University Press, 1997.
Wagner-Lawlor, Jennifer A. 'The Pragmatics of Silence, and the Figuration of the Reader in Browning's Dramatic Monologues.' *Victorian Poetry* 35 (1997), 287–302.
Wilde, Oscar. 'The Truth of Masks.' *Literary Criticism of Oscar Wilde*. Edited by Stanley Weintraub. Lincoln: University of Nebraska Press, 1968.
Wittgenstein, Ludwig. *Philosophical Investigations*. Translated by G.E.M. Anscombe. Oxford: Basil Blackwell, 1972.
Wollheim, Richard. *The Thread of Life*. Cambridge, Mass.: Harvard University Press, 1984.
Woolford, John. *Browning the Revisionary*. London: Macmillan, 1988.

Poetry Editions Used

Arnold, Matthew. *The Poems of Matthew Arnold*. Edited by Kenneth Allott. London: Longmans, Green, 1965.

Browning, Elizabeth Barrett. *The Poems of Elizabeth Barrett Browning*. London and New York: Frederick Warne, 1896.

Browning, Robert. *The Complete Works of Robert Browning*. Edited by Roma A. King, Jr, et al. 13 vols. Waco, Texas: Baylor University, and Athens: Ohio University Press, 1969–96.

Chaucer, Geoffrey. *The Complete Poetical Works of Geoffrey Chaucer*. Edited by Walter W. Skeat. 2nd ed. Oxford: Clarendon Press, 1963.

Clough, A.H. *The Poems of Arthur Hugh Clough*. Edited by F.L. Mulhauser. 2nd ed. Oxford: Clarendon Press, 1974.

Coleridge, S.T. *Samuel Taylor Coleridge*. Edited by H.J. Jackson. New York: Oxford University Press, 1985.

Donne, John. *The Complete Poetry of John Donne*. Edited by John T. Shawcross. Garden City, New York: Doubleday and Co., 1967.

Eliot, T.S. *Collected Poems 1909–1935*. New York: Harcourt Brace, 1936.

– *Four Quartets*. New York: Harcourt Brace, 1943.

Hardy, Thomas. *The Complete Poetical Works of Thomas Hardy*. Edited by Samuel Hynes. 5 vols. Oxford: Clarendon Press, 1985.

Hecht, Anthony. *Collected Earlier Poems*. New York: Knopf, 1990.

Hopkins, G.M. *Poems*. Edited by W.H. Gardner and N.H. Mackenzie. 4th ed. London: Oxford University Press, 1967.

Howard, Richard. *Untitled Subjects: Poems by Richard Howard*. New York: Atheneum, 1969.

– 'Nikolaus Mardruz to His Master Ferdinand, Count of Tyrol, 1565.' *Yale Review* 83:3 (July 1995), 20–7.

Jarrell, Randall. *The Complete Poems*. New York: Farrar, Straus and Giroux, 1969.

Keats, John. *The Poems of John Keats*. Edited by Jack Stillinger. Cambridge, Mass.: Belknap Press of Harvard University, 1978.

Leighton, Angela, and Margaret Reynolds, eds. *Victorian Women Poets: An Anthology*. Oxford: Blackwell, 1995. Useful selection of poems by Charlotte Brontë and Amy Levy.

Lowell, Robert. *The Mills of the Kavanaughs*. New York: Harcourt Brace, 1946.

– *Lord Weary's Castle*. New York: Harcourt, Brace and Company, 1946.

– *Life Studies*. New York: Farrar, Straus and Giroux, 1958.

Morris, William. *The Defence of Guenevere, The Life and Death of Jason, and Other Poems by William Morris*. London: Oxford University Press, 1914.

Pound, Ezra. *Personae, The Shorter Poems of Ezra Pound*. New York: New Directions, 1990.

Rochester, John Wilmot, Earl of. *The Complete Poems*. Edited by David M. Vieth. New Haven: Yale University Press, 1969.

Rossetti, Christina. *The Complete Poems of Christina Rossetti*. Edited by Rebecca W. Crump. 3 vols. Baton Rouge: Louisiana State University Press, 1979–90.

Stevens, Wallace. *The Collected Poems of Wallace Stevens*. New York: Knopf, 1954.

Swinburne, A.C. *The Complete Works of Algernon Charles Swinburne*. Bonchurch edition. Edited by Edmund Gosse and Thomas James Wise. 20 vols. London: Heinemann, 1925–7.

Tennyson, Alfred Lord. *The Works of Tennyson*, vols. 8 and 9. Edited by Hallam Lord Tennyson. London: Macmillan, 1908. All quotations from Tennyson's plays are taken from these volumes. Since Hallam's Eversley edition does not number the lines of the plays, to make the quotations easier to locate I have provided the page number in each volume after the act and scene number.

– *The Poems of Tennyson*. Edited by Christopher Ricks. 3 vols. London and Harlow: Longmans, Green, 1987. Except for the plays, all Tennyson quotations are taken from this edition.

Thomas, Edward. *The Collected Poems of Edward Thomas*. Edited by R. George Thomas. Oxford: Clarendon Press, 1978.

Whitman, Walt. *Complete Poetry and Selected Prose*. Edited by J.E. Miller. Boston: Houghton Mifflin, 1959.

Wordsworth, William. *The Poetical Works of William Wordsworth*. Edited by Ernest de Selincourt and Helen Darbishire. 5 vols. Oxford: Clarendon Press, 1940–9.

Index

Numerals in italic type indicate the locations of the main discussions.

248   Index

Plato 6, 11, 50–1, 227; *Apology* 51, 56,
59; *Charmides* 44; *Criton* 44; dialogues of search (aporetic) 42, 44,
45–52, 59, 198; *Euthyphro* 6; *Gorgias*
44, 55; *Hippias* 44; *Laches* 6, 44;
Lysis 6, 44; magisterial dialogues
42, 44–5, 52–6; *Parmenides* 49, 55,
204; *Phaedo* 55; Platonic love 168;
Protagoras 44–5; *The Republic* 42,
44–5, 209; *Symposium* 6; *Timaeus*
54, 199, 201
Pope, Alexander 119; *The Dunciad*
175; *Essay on Man* 118
Pound, Ezra 86; 'Dompna Pois de
me No'us Cal' *96–7*; 'The Flame'
123; 'The Garden' *130*; 'Marvoil'
64, *80–1*; 'Portrait d'une Femme'
121–2; 'The Temperaments' *122–3*;
'Tenzone' 122
Priestley, Joseph 192
prosody 146; anapests 100–1; blank
verse 119; caesural breaks 50, 168,
171; early-breaking caesura 171;
late-breaking caesura 137;
seventh-syllable caesura 136–7;
dactyls 96; distance between
rhyme words 77, 149–50; end–
rhymes 50; end-stopped lines 123;
enjambment 76–7, 115, 142, 150–1,
158, 170; feminine rhymes 119–20;
half-rhymes 159; heroic couplets
26, 142, 153, 158–60, 173; hexameters 46; hypermetric lines 50,
109, 113, 133; iambics 134; imperfect rhymes 136–7; internal
rhymes 104, 140, 142; musical or
vocal 'falls' 139, 148; muted
couplets 22, 176; muted rhymes
116; rhymes for eye versus rhymes
for ear 134; spondees 162; tercets

134; *terza rima* 133–4; tetrameter
quatrain 76, 169; vagrant accents
119
Prynne, J.H. 216

Rader, Ralph 12–13, 165, 212–13, 224
Renan, Ernest 170
rhetoric (*see also* grammar): alliteration 49, 153, 162; anaphora 89,
103, 227; anti-pun 136; antonyms
104; aphorism 108, 195; assonance
162; apostrophe (*aversio*) 5, 9,
15–17, 62–85; apostrophic swerve
13, *15–17, 62–85*; archaism 131,
136; chiasmus *55–6*, 66, 80, 84,
89–90, 198; digression 24; double
audience 13, 16–17, 63, 67, 90–1,
93, 178–9, *218–19*; double poem 16,
18, 191; ecphonesis 62; euphemism
23; *exclamatio* 16, 62, 74–5; forensic
rhetoric 144; free indirect discourse 20, 70, 128; hendiadys 128;
hyperbole 171; indirect discourse
20; *metalepsis* 74, 77, 90, 190; metaphor 154, 189, 194; metaphoric
seduction 168; metonymy 135,
189; Miltonic placement of a noun
between framing adjectives 129,
133; *occupatio* 101; oxymoron 27,
101, 131, 135, 156; paradox 17, 82,
106–7, 139–40, 156, 187–8, 207,
227; paradox of history 207;
paradoxes of the mask 123; *paralipsis* 21, 113, 171, 179; parenthesis
20, 176, 181; pathetic fallacy 75;
periphrasis 157; persuasive redefinition 38, 132, 172–3; prosopopoeia (personification) 16, 62,
77–8, 81–2; pun (word-play) 21,
122, 137, 142–3, 174, 176, 178;

By W. David Shaw

Alfred Lord Tennyson: The Poet in an Age of Theory

Elegy and Paradox: Testing the Conventions

Victorians and Mystery: Crises of Representation

The Lucid Veil: Poetic Truth in the Victorian Age

Tennyson's Style

The Dialectical Temper: The Rhetorical Art of Robert Browning